ABOUT THE AUTHORS

SCOTT BITTLE is executive editor of PublicAgenda.org, where he has prepared citizen guides on more than twenty major issues, including the deficit, Social Security, and the economy. For eight years, he was a reporter, copy editor, bureau chief, and political coordinator for *The Press* of Atlantic City. He has also won two Golden Quill Awards for feature articles and was honored by the Philadelphia Press Association for daily newspaper writing.

As executive vice president of Public Agenda, **JEAN JOHNSON** has more than twenty years of experience understanding public attitudes on a broad range of issues, such as public education, parenting and families, race relations, retirement, and health care. Jean has also written for publications such as *USA TODAY, Education Week, School Board News, National Institute of Justice Journal,* and *Education Leadership,* and has given major speeches for national organizations including the Urban Institute, National Institute of Justice, and National Education Summit of the National Governors' Association.

WHERE DOES THE MONEY GO?

YOUR GUIDED TOUR TO THE FEDERAL BUDGET CRISIS

SCOTT BITTLE & JEAN JOHNSON

Revised Edition

HARPER

NEW YORK · LONDON · TORONTO · SYDNEY

HARPER

WHERE DOES THE MONEY GO? (REVISED EDITION). Copyright © 2008, 2011 by Scott
Bittle and Jean Johnson. All rights reserved. Printed in the United States
of America. No part of this book may be used or reproduced in any manner
whatsoever without written permission except in the case of brief quotations embodied in critical articles and reviews. For information address
HarperCollins Publishers, 10 East 53rd Street, New York, NY 10022.

HarperCollins books may be purchased for educational, business, or
sales promotional use. For information please write: Special Markets
Department, HarperCollins Publishers, 10 East 53rd Street, New York,
NY 10022.

Designed by Nancy Singer Olaguera

First Collins paperback edition published 2008.

FIRST HARPER PAPERBACK REVISED EDITION PUBLISHED 2011.

The Library of Congress has catalogued the original paperback edition
as follows:

Bittle, Scott.
    Where does the money go? : your guided tour to the federal budget
crisis / Scott Bittle and Jean Johnson.—1st ed.
        p. cm.
    ISBN 978-0-06-124187-1
1. Budget deficits—United States. 2. United States—Appropriations and expenditures. 3. Public welfare—United States—Finance. 4. Budget—United
States. I. Johnson, Jean. II. Title.

HJ2052.B58 2008
336.73—dc22   2007026403

ISBN 978-0-06-202347-6

11 12 13 14 15 ID/RRD 10 9 8 7 6 5 4 3 2 1

For our dads,
Mulford W. Bittle Jr. (1934–2000) and John J. Johnson (1917–2005)–
men who would never have left debts for their children to pay

CONTENTS

PREFACE

Where *Does the Money Go? Your Guided Tour to the Federal Budget Crisis* is exactly what it says it is—a straightforward explanation of what politicians, economists, think tanks, and lobbyists are arguing about when they fight about the federal budget. We published an earlier edition of this book in 2008 when the United States' overall debt was about $9 trillion dollars. Even though that's a breathtaking amount of money, we spent quite a few pages of that first book explaining why people should please, please pay attention to this issue. Just three years later, the federal debt is on track to reach $15 trillion by the end of 2011, and our government's habit of spending more than it collects in taxes has become a political firestorm. If the whole situation weren't so alarming, we might be able to enjoy saying "I told you so." But to be perfectly honest, we never thought things would get so much worse, so quickly.

Unfortunately, there is just no more time to savor the moment. What we need to do now is take a sensible, reality-based look at our choices, and, as a country, come to some agreement on what to do.

IT'S GREEK TO US

Not only is the budget a hotter political topic than it was in 2008, recent developments have made the country's predicament even more treacherous. Little did we know when we wrapped up that last edition that in just a few years:

★ The economy would go into a terrifying tailspin, cutting tax revenues, forcing huge government spending in an attempt to stave off disaster, and putting us in a worse budget situation than nearly anyone predicted. This is something we'll be talking about throughout the book.

★ Congress would pass and the president would sign major health care reform legislation that could have good, bad, and unforeseen fallout for the budget—and it may well have all three.

★ Greece would become "exhibit A" for what happens when countries live beyond their means. The United States is not Greece, and if we make some reasonable decisions soon, we'll never have to go there, but the irony of watching Athenians riot in the streets as their country goes bankrupt—well, it does make you think, and it should.

There are a lot of moving parts to the country's budget problem so solving it is not going to be easy, but at its base, the issue is pretty straightforward.

The United States is seemingly addicted to spending more than it takes in. We've already piled up an unbelievable national debt. Even worse, we face truly gigantic expenses as the baby boomers begin to retire and need more health care. Today's problems will seem like a fender bender compared to the economic train wreck the country will face if we don't get the nation's finances under control.

We've written this book because we believe that there

are millions of Americans who are uneasy about where the country is headed and want to understand what the budget situation really is and what the options are. We are also convinced that there are millions of Americans who are tired of political leaders—Republicans and Democrats, liberals and conservatives—who bob and weave around this issue. We think there are plenty of citizens across the country who want to begin to figure this thing out for themselves. As authors, our job is to explain the problem and the options as clearly and fairly as we can.

A WORD ABOUT WHERE WE'RE COMING FROM

Where Does the Money Go? is not a book for policy makers and economists. It's a guide for people who care about where the country is going, but don't have the time or inclination to become budget experts. And for readers who do get a bit hooked on the topic—sometimes people do—we've provided lists of publications, organizations, and Web sites specializing in things budgetary in the appendix, so you can go forth and multiply. The country definitely needs more of you. For most of us, however, the first order of business is to grasp the essentials so your votes and your contributions can go to candidates who truly represent your interests.

Since we're presuming to explain this topic, and since it is complicated and controversial, we believe readers have a right to know where we're coming from. We both work for a nonprofit, nonpartisan research organization called Public Agenda where we write about public policy issues and conduct public opinion research (you can check out the organization at www.publicagenda.org). Consequently, both of us have spent a lot of time listening to very knowledgeable people talk about the federal budget, the deficit, the debt, and the aging of the baby boomers. We also have a

lot of experience translating expert information into terms
and concepts nonexperts can understand. It's been part of
our jobs. Here's the approach we've taken in *Where Does the
Money Go?*

★ First, we consider ourselves translators, not budget experts. We have done our homework on the issue (our
   reading list is in the appendix), and we've asked for and
   gotten advice from some of the most informed and in-
   tellectually honest people in the country. We've pulled
   that "best advice" together in one volume. We hope we've
   done it in an understandable and readable way.

★ Second, we're explainers, not advocates. You want to find
   "the man with the plan"? There are books, articles, and
   op-eds in the thousands pushing for specific solutions to
   the country's financial problems. That's not our purpose
   here. Instead, we've tried to lay out the information and
   the choices so you can come to your own conclusions
   about what should be done. Our last chapters contain
   tools enabling you to do just that—decide the matter for
   yourself. Naturally, there are areas where the facts and
   figures are in dispute and where experts disagree (it's
   just part of their job description to disagree). When this
   happens, we try to help you understand the nature of the
   disagreement. When there seems to be a pretty strong
   consensus of expert opinion one way or the other, we tell
   you that, too.

★ Third, we're optimists, not pessimists. As you will read
   in the following pages, the federal government has been
   spending more money than it takes in for some time now,
   and we have some huge financial commitments coming
   due. A lot of experts believe the country is taking grave
   risks with the economy and our future standard of living
   by not addressing the problem. Some of the predictions

for what could happen ten or twenty years down the road are frightening. But there are steps the country can take to reduce these risks, and we believe there are solutions and compromises that would be acceptable to millions of Americans. We're also convinced that most people, once they understand what's at stake, will want to act and elect leaders committed to tackling this problem. As we said, we're optimists.

★ Fourth, we believe that decisions about the country's budget problems can't be postponed any longer. You can certainly find experts who argue that creating jobs is a higher priority than tackling the deficit or fixing the problems facing Social Security and Medicare. Some economists say that raising taxes now will endanger the economy. Some believe that now is the time for government to spend more—to make investments that will spur economic growth and create jobs in the future. Given what the U.S. economy has been through recently, there are certainly fair arguments about how fast to move on the budget issue and exactly where to start. But what we can't do any longer is to continue to sweep this problem under the rug. We can't keep pretending that sometime in the future, there is going to be a better time to take it up. Many solutions need to be phased in gradually, and many will take years to make a real impact. The country as a whole faces a major learning curve. So it is time— right now, this year—to start grappling with our choices. We need to take an honest, clear-eyed look at where this country stands financially. We need to put everything on the table and start talking about real solutions. And then, we need to agree on a plan and stick to it.

★ Fifth, we believe voters need to know what we've learned writing this book. We don't have a recommended candidate, and we're not about to tell you that one party will handle the country's finances better than the other. So far, neither party has really stepped up to the plate with practical ideas for solving the country's long-term budget mess. But it's worse than that. Some elected officials, candidates, and commentators—and they come from across the political spectrum—are gliding over the facts, ignoring the dangers of delay, and vastly oversimplifying the choices before us. That means it's time for voters to start asking tough questions and stop accepting slogans and sound bites as answers. But to do that, we have to be realistic ourselves. There will always be politicians who promise to lower taxes without saying what they'll cut or promise new and better services without saying how they'll pay for them. There will always be politicians who just keeping blasting the other side hoping no one will notice the cock-and-bull in their own proposals. For a long time, too many of us have bought their lines and given them our votes. The bottom line is that we simply can't afford to do that anymore. Frankly, from where we stand, we don't expect much to happen unless and until voters begin to take the problem seriously—or until the country faces a financial crisis that would be extremely unpleasant for all of us. So it's time for voters to demand that candidates talk about this issue and spell out their approaches to it. It's time for voters to demand more candor and leadership from elected officials once they're in office. But to do this, voters need to be realistic themselves. There will always be politicians who promise more services and lower taxes—don't worry, be happy—but we don't have to buy their line.

★ Sixth, this issue changes all the time. *Where Does the Money Go?* includes a lot of information about what the government spends on this and that, which taxes collect how much money, and what experts predict for the bud-

get if X or Y happens. Most of these numbers change
every year depending on what Congress and the president do, the health of the economy, and other factors. As
we take this book to press, there are a couple of important moving targets you need to keep an eye on. What
Congress does or does not do about extending the tax
cuts passed in the Bush administration and how long we
keep large numbers of troops in Afghanistan are key factors. If there are major changes to the 2010 health care
legislation—either to repeal it or reduce its cost or improve its coverage—that would of course affect the budget. Finally, a lot of people in Washington are placing
their hopes in the recommendations of the bipartisan
fiscal commission set up by President Obama. Changes
like these are obviously important, and you do need to
keep up with the news. But rest assured (if that's the
right phrase in this instance), no matter what happens
in Washington in the next couple of years, the big picture
is the same. This country has a huge budget challenge
coming up, and a couple of nips and tucks on taxes or
spending will not make it disappear.

★ Seventh, it's taken us years to get ourselves in this mess,
and no doubt it's going to take us years to get out of it.
There's just not a quick, simple way to turn this thing
around. What's more, probably every single one of us will
have to accept some changes we don't like. But keeping
on the way we're going would be inexcusable. This problem can be solved. Let's get on with it.

CHAPTER 1

The Six Points
You Need to Know
to Understand the
Federal Budget Crisis

Finance Minister:	Here is the Treasury Department's report, sir. I hope you'll find it clear.
Groucho Marx:	Clear? Huh. Why, a four-year-old child could understand this report . . . Run out and find me a four-year-old child—I can't make head or tail of it.

—Duck Soup, *1933*

Open any newspaper, tune in to any newscast, and someone will be tossing around billion- and trillion-dollar estimates about government spending and squabbling about the nation's finances. It certainly sounds important, but they don't make it easy for people who aren't policy wonks to understand. The numbers are mind-boggling, and the jargon is even worse. Unfunded liabilities, revenue neutral tax reform, entitlement spending, discretionary domestic programs, baseline assumptions, percentage of GDP. Faced with phrases like these, most of us reach for the remote to see what's going on in TVLand. But this debate is crucial to our future. Deep inside, you know it matters; otherwise, you wouldn't have opened this book.

For years, the budget issue was a sneaky, slow-boil kind of a problem, one that was easy for most of us to avoid. After all, politicians don't like to talk about cutting programs or raising taxes—which we'll no doubt need to do in some form or another in order to fix this budgetary mess. And yes, fellow Americans, we've earned our share of the blame, too.

Let's be frank. When was the last time you cast your vote for a candidate who campaigned on getting the country's finances back on the right track? What about one who wanted to cut government programs you like and raise taxes (which no one likes)? What do we talk about instead? Who had the most glittering celebrities at their fund-raiser. Who had the best zinger in the debate. Which candidate is making the cleverest use of YouTube. What a candidate did or did not do when he or she was twenty-something. No wonder so few people want to run for office these days—how would you like to have to defend everything you did and said in your twenties, or your thirties for that matter? And what about that pet question from the pre-pre-election polls: Which candidate would be more fun to have dinner with? How many Americans actually have dinner with presidential candidates, anyway? Go ahead, ask John McCain or Barack Obama to meet you at Chili's sometime. See what happens. Is this what we really want from these people? Why do we spend time on this?

The truth is that those of us who aren't in government or politics—those of us who generally watch from the sidelines trying to make sense of it all—had better start paying much more attention to the debate about the federal budget and the huge expenses we face in the coming decades. What's decided (or not decided) over the next few years will spell big changes for the way we live our daily lives. How the country solves or doesn't solve this problem will affect our paychecks, our investments, our mortgages, our kids' prospects in life, what kind of health care we'll get, our chances of ever getting to retire—even whether we live in a country that's fair, stable, and prosperous. And let's not kid ourselves. Right now, the savvy and well connected are already strolling the halls of Congress pushing for solutions that benefit them. So ignoring this debate is really not a very good option.

Fortunately, once you strip away all the confusing terms and unnecessary shouting, the budget problem isn't as hard to understand as the people in charge would like you to think.

THE BUDGET DEBATE, PARKING LOT VERSION

If you missed this on *Entertainment Tonight* or *Entourage*, a "parking lot version" is what Hollywood producer types call the shortest, simplest description of a movie or TV idea. Basically, it's what you can say to a studio exec if you're lucky enough to meet one in the parking lot, and you have to pitch your idea in the time it takes to walk to your cars. In Manhattan, which is short on parking lots, it's called the "elevator version."

We've reduced the budget issue to six essential points. Get these, and you're a long way to understanding what all the hoopla is about.

1. For thirty-one out of the last thirty-five years, the country has spent more on government programs and services than it has collected in taxes.
2. Every year the government comes up short, it borrows money to cover the difference. We've now built up a very

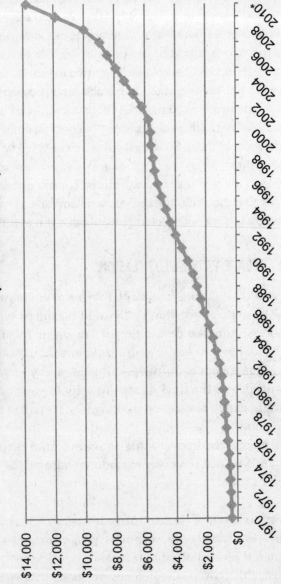

Gross National Debt (in billions of dollars)

*The national debt always tends to increase, but as you can see, over the past few years the debt has leaped up, to the point where the U.S. government is now roughly $14 trillion in debt. *Source: Budget of the United States Government, FY 2011*

big debt—approaching $15 trillion by the end of 2011, and yes, that is *trillion* with a *t*.

3. The country will have humongous additional expenses over the next couple of decades as the baby boomers begin to retire and health care costs rise.

4. There is no realistic way government can lower taxes (or even keep them at current levels), spend money on everything people want the government to do (at least according to the polls), and still end up with a balanced budget.

5. If we keep on going the way we're going, the debt will get bigger and begin to endanger the U.S. economy and our own personal finances and plans. And the government won't have enough money to pay for Social Security and Medicare for the boomers and still do what most of us expect government to do.

6. A substantial portion of the country's debt is held in foreign countries. Right now, these foreign investors consider U.S. government bonds one of the safest places in the world to put their money, but they could decide at some point that China or some other place is a better bet. This would be the global equivalent of a store clerk seizing your credit card and cutting it up.

If the country's state of financial affairs reminds you of people who spend more money than they make nearly every month, while cheerfully adding on to their credit card debt hoping that nothing will go wrong, you're not that far wrong. Obviously, government finances and family finances are different. For one thing, the government can probably raise taxes a lot more easily than most of us could just suddenly raise our own salaries substantially. The worst-case scenario is also much different. The president isn't going to walk out of the White House one morning and find out someone's repossessed the armor-plated limousine. But the concept is pretty similar. You can live beyond your means for quite a while without too much fuss (as long as nothing goes wrong). But at some point, the amount you owe begins to take its toll on the way you live.

SO WHY DO THEY KEEP DOING IT?

Given the dangers and the fact that everyone knows that the huge baby-boom generation is coming up for retirement now, *why* does the government keep on spending more than it takes in, you may ask in your best Cindy Lou Who voice. After all, politicians talk about balancing the budget and cutting the deficit all the time. The simple answer is there's always something people want more, whether it's tax cuts or better benefits or a stronger military. In some cases, that can be a perfectly reasonable choice. The country ran large deficits during World War II, for example.

DEFICITS BEGIN TO FEEL NORMAL

There are good reasons for the country to run a deficit every so often, but if you do it long enough (thirty-one out of thirty-five years, for example), it starts to feel normal. It's nearly always easier for politicians to add to the debt than raise taxes or cut popular programs. In fact, in Washington these days, they don't even seem able to cut *unpopular* programs—if some politically connected someone somewhere likes it, it stays in the budget. And like a slow-growing tumor in the national economy, the debt just keeps on growing until it becomes really dangerous—dangerous enough to affect the livelihood and lifestyle of nearly every single American.

What would actually happen if the country keeps on

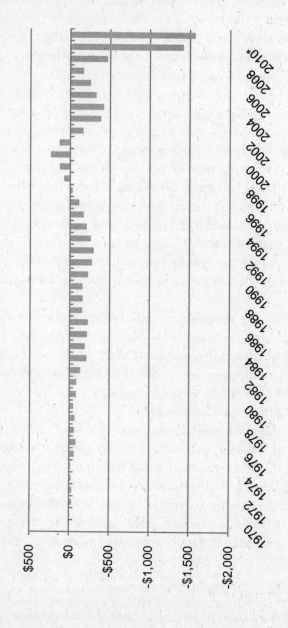

Federal Budget Deficits/Surpluses

*Deficit spending has become routine for the U.S. government, with the government running in the red for thirty-one of the last thirty-five years. *Source: Budget of the United States Government, FY 2011*

spending more than it takes in, and the debt continues to mount?

When we wrote about the country's budget problems a couple of years ago, there were some optimistic experts who didn't think much would happen at all. They just didn't think the country's debt was so serious given how large our economy is. Many believed that in the new global economy, there would always be people in other countries with money to lend to the U.S. government (by buying government bonds). To them, that meant that the United States could carry a fairly hefty amount of debt without much fuss.

Not much good came out of the global economic meltdown of 2008 and 2009, but it did give us a really unpleasant preview of what it's like to be carrying a huge debt and suddenly hit economic bad times. That was true for a lot of us personally, and it was certainly true for the country as a whole.

When the recession hit, the U.S government was suddenly getting much less money coming in from taxes. Fewer people were working, and many of those who were working weren't making as much money. Businesses weren't making much money either, so tax revenues plummeted more than $400 billion from 2008 to 2009.[1]

At the same time, there was a very long line of people wanting the U.S. government's help getting through the tough times. Maybe your mind has immediately flown to the gigantic banks that were deemed "too big to fail" despite their risky bets on subprime mortgages, or AIG, the high-flying insurance company that underwrote those crazy risks and had to be bailed out by the government. Yes, they

---

[1] Congressional Budget Office, The Budget and Economic Outlook: Fiscal Years 2010 to 2020, January 2010, Executive Summary, A Review of 2009. www.cbo.gov/ftpdocs/108xx/doc10871/Chapter1.shtml.

were there with their hands out, complete with pinstripes, tasseled loafers, and limo driver waiting outside. No, we don't feel sorry for them either. But there were plenty of other people who needed and got government help: people collecting unemployment insurance who needed extended benefits because the job market was so terrible; states and cities who wanted the federal government's help so they wouldn't have to lay off teachers and police officers during the downturn.

And finally, there was the very grim possibility that the world economy would tip into a second Great Depression. The credit markets were "frozen," which simply means that the world's banks were so overstretched and so scared that they effectively stopped lending—and without credit, not much happens in the economy. Bailing out Wall Street, the outgoing President Bush and incoming President Obama said, was the only way to get money flowing again. And if the private sector wasn't putting people to work, the Obama administration argued, then spending money on "economic stimulus" like public works was the only way to create jobs. All in all, the difference between what the government took in and paid out in 2009 alone was $1.4 trillion dollars.[2]

There is a huge dispute about whether the Obama administration has done the right or wrong things to help the country survive and pull out of the recession (and we'll explain more about what their decisions have meant for the debt in the coming pages). Given the scale of the financial crisis, there's probably no way the government could or should have avoided running deficits for at least a few years.

---

[2] Budget of the United States Government: Historical Tables, Fiscal Year 2011. Table 1.1—Summary of Receipts, Outlays, and Surpluses or Deficits (-): 1789–2015, www.gpoaccess.gov/usbudget/fy11/hist.html.

What's not in dispute is that the country's budget situation has gone from bad back before the recession to genuinely appalling now.

It's harder to find people now who truly think the country can sustain the fiscal path we're on. In fact, a growing number of sober organizations keep using the same word to describe the projections on the national debt: "unsustainable." That includes the White House budget office, the government's own auditors (the Government Accountability Office), the Congressional Budget Office, and several independent blue-ribbon panels, like the Committee on the Fiscal Future of the United States and the Peterson-Pew Commission on Budget Reform.

Regrettably, that doesn't mean we're actually facing up to the problem. As a nation, we still seem to be pushing the tough choices down the road. Some people don't want to make any hard decisions until the economy gets back to where it was before the recession. Some seem to think we can grow our way out of the problem (which we can't, and we'll explain more about that later). Our elected officials seem to be spending more time arguing and speechifying and getting ready for the next election than getting down to work solving our problems.

Herb Stein, an economist who advised President Nixon and is the father of the economist (and *Ferris Bueller* star) Ben Stein, proposed his own law of economics back in the 1980s: "If something cannot go on forever, it will stop."[3] That's about where we are with the country's budget problem. We can't go on like this, and we are getting very close to the time when some very bad things will start to happen unless we get a move on.

---

[3] "Herb Stein's Unfamiliar Quotations On Money, Madness, and Making Mistakes," Salon.com, May 16, 1997, www.slate.com/id/2561/.

THREE REALLY BIG RISKS

So here's a sampling of what keeps a lot of economists and policymakers awake at night.

No. 1: Monster expenses (that we know are coming) will wipe us out. Unless there's some sort of "Hot Zone" plague that wipes out a substantial portion of the baby boomers before they reach retirement (since your authors are boomers themselves, we're not recommending that), the government is facing gigantic increases in Social Security and Medicare expenses over the next couple of decades. This is the one big threat to the budget and the economy that nearly every reasonably sane expert we can find agrees on. Yes, there is a Social Security trust fund, and yes, it does have enough money to pay benefits as promised for another couple of decades. But the trust fund consists of bonds that are essentially, IOUs from the government. We don't believe that the government would default on its obligations, but the money has to come from somewhere. In 2010, the Government Accountability Office (an agency that does exactly what it sounds like it would do) warned that unless policymakers take action to address the country's budget problems, spending for entitlement programs like Social Security and Medicare combined with interest on the debt "could absorb 92 cents of every dollar of federal revenue in 2019."[4] There would be almost no money for anything else, except maybe a basic national defense, unless, of course, we keep borrowing. You can read the grisly details in the coming pages.

---

[4] Government Accountability Office, Statement of the Comptroller General of the United States, February 26, 2010, www.gao.gov/financial/fy2009financialreport.html.

No. 2: The economy goes down, down, down. When the government borrows more and more money, it makes it harder for the rest of us to borrow because it drives up interest rates. This risk is widely accepted among mainstream economists,[5] and it's pretty clear to anyone who has ever shopped for a mortgage why high interest rates are a bad thing. But mortgages are just the tip of the iceberg. High interest rates jeopardize nearly every part of the economy. Businesses can't get loans. Their costs go up. When they get in a pinch, they start cutting jobs. When the economy goes into a tailspin, there are more layoffs, fewer raises, more cuts in benefits, more businesses failing, bigger consumer debt, people's investments getting savaged, and more. Think "very, very bad recession, something as bad or even worse than what we've seen over the past few years."

No. 3: We'll come to regret relying on the kindness of strangers. More than a quarter of U.S. government debt is held by foreign governments, banks, and investors, and right now, they seem reasonably happy to keep sending their extra money here. But the truth is that international politics and economics sometimes change in what seems to be the blink of an eye (remember back when you had never heard of Osama bin Laden?). What would happen if some big debt holders abroad suddenly wanted their money back right away? Would there be a mad scramble to raise taxes? Would Congress suddenly slash spending with no time for

---

[5] It's basically supply and demand. The risk is that all this government borrowing will crowd out other lending. There's only so much money out there to borrow, and every dollar investors put into Treasury bonds is a dollar that isn't available for stocks, corporate bonds, real estate, venture capital, or anything else in the private sector. So the rest of us have to jump higher hurdles and pay higher interest to borrow money.

the country to think about how to do it fairly? Would the stock market hurtle downward? Would everyone else holding U.S. Treasury bonds suddenly start dumping them—including Americans themselves? No one really knows. Something like the big, fat Greek debt crisis—which threatened to bring down the economy of nearly every nice vacation spot in Europe—is one possibility. But Greece is tiny compared to the United States, which is still the world's economic superpower. If a collapse in the U.S. mortgage market can set off a worldwide recession, what would happen if the U.S. government really couldn't come up with the money to pay its bills? The fact that no one can really know exactly what would happen makes the prospect even more alarming.

Some of these dangers could rise up suddenly—like the iceberg that appears dead ahead in that *Titanic* movie. Or the changes could be gradual. We might face a slow decline in our standard of living, an economy that just never recovers, a government that is less and less able to provide services that people value. But note the recurring theme here: if things go badly, it nearly always comes out of *your* hide, as the taxpayer and citizen. Either life gets a lot more expensive, or you have to make do with less help from the government, or most likely both at once.

The bad news is that politics as usual—the gridlock, the polarization, the sloganeering, the inability to compromise or move ahead on much of anything—could be setting the country up for a real smashup.

THE GREAT BUDGET DEBATE POP QUIZ

In this book, we'll try to avoid the wonk words and pie charts (well, we do have a pie chart or two). Even so, it's helpful to have a few facts in hand. So we'll start off with a pop quiz. If you've been watching C-SPAN and all those Sunday morning news shows, you'll probably ace this. However, if you're not as well informed, try the quiz anyway. You'll pick up a few things, proving once again that sleeping late on Sunday doesn't automatically keep you from getting ahead in life.

2. True or False? If the government hadn't spent so much money bailing out Wall Street and Detroit, we wouldn't have this huge problem with the budget and the rising debt.

ANSWER: *If only this were true. The roughly $700 billion appropriated for the bailouts is a lot of money, but the government has actually gotten most of that money back now that these bailed-out companies are doing better. We'll leave it to you to decide whether using taxpayer money to rescue failing companies like Bank of America, Citicorp, General Motors, and AIG was the right decision or not, and we talk more about this in chapter 5. But just looking at the budget (which is what we're focused on here), the bailouts aren't going to be our biggest financial problem—not by any stretch of the imagination. In the bailouts, Congress made the $700 billion available so the U.S. government could buy stock in these huge, teetering businesses— to keep them from biting the dust. The companies could buy* the stock back when they got back on their feet, which is what has been happening. As we go to press, the "bailout" is projected to cost U.S. taxpayers about $66 billion,[6] but in 2009, the country spent $1.4 trillion more than it collected in taxes. You can swear at the big banks all you want (or cuss if you're a southerner). We're not saying they don't deserve it. But you can't really blame the bailouts for America's red ink. We were in big budget trouble before the bailouts, and we'll still be in big budget trouble afterward, even if the government gets back every red cent.

2. True or false? If it weren't for the war in Iraq, the federal budget would have been balanced.

ANSWER: *Not quite.* The Iraq war has cost a lot of money, but the country wouldn't have balanced its budgets over the last few years even without the war (as amazing as that may seem). Between 2001 and 2010, the country spent about $706 billion on the Iraq war and close to $1.1 trillion if you add in Afghanistan and other parts of the "war on terror."[7] That's not pocket change to be sure, but during the same period, the country ran deficits totaling nearly $5 trillion (that's trillion with a "T").[8] So it's not just the war—not by a long shot. You can say that the Iraq war made the already-hefty budget deficits for recent years

---

[6] Congressional Budget Office Director's Blog, "CBO's Latest Projections for the TARP," August, 10, 2010, http://cboblog.cbo.gov/?p=1322.

[7] Congressional Budget Office, "Funding for Operations in Iraq and Afghanistan and for Related Activities," The Budget and Economic Outlook: Fiscal Years 2010 to 2020, January 2010, www.cbo.gov/ftpdocs/108xx/doc10871/Chapter1.shtml#1099353.

[8] Congressional Budget Office, Historical Budget Data,"Revenues, Outlays, Deficits, Surpluses and Debt Held by the Public, 1970 to 2009, in Billions of Dollars," Table F-1, January 2010, www.cbo.gov/ftpdocs/108xx/doc10871/historicaltables.pdf.

bigger. But you can't say that without the war, the country would have been in the black. And remember, just balancing the budget isn't enough to solve the long-term problems with Social Security and Medicare. It's a good thing to do, no doubt, but it's only the beginning.

3. True or false? If we just rolled back the Bush tax cuts, we could solve all our problems with the federal budget.

ANSWER: *Nope, that's not true, either. President Bush and Congress enacted a series of different tax cuts—for families, investors, businesses—and most were set to expire at the end of 2010. Congress has been debating whether to make these cuts permanent, extend them for a few years, let them go back to what they were under President Clinton, or come up with some other combination or plan. Much of this is still up in the air as we go to press. Since the U.S. economy has been rocky of late, and since in a democracy, it is much easier to give tax cuts than take them away, hardly anyone thinks Congress will roll all of these taxes back to their Clinton-era rates. But even if that happened, it still wouldn't get us out of our financial jam. With the boomers beginning to retire, Social Security and Medicare costs are going to mushroom, and repealing the Bush tax cuts doesn't provide nearly enough money to cover the gap. All the major numbers crunchers agree on this one.[9] In fact, the nonpartisan Congressional Budget Office projects that we'll see deficits of more than $6 trillion through 2020 even if we let all of these tax cuts expire. So you can be for 'em or agin 'em (much more on this in chapter 13), but you can't say that rolling back the Bush tax cuts will by itself solve the problem.*

---

[9] Congressional Budget Office, The Budget and Economic Outlook: Fiscal Years 2010 to 2020, January 2010, www.cbo.gov/ftpdocs/108xx/doc10871/Chapter1 .shtml#1096758, accessed May 15, 2010.

★★★★★★★★★★★★★★★★★★★★★★★★★★★★★★★

4. Which of the following areas do budget experts worry about most—because its costs are so hard to control and could rise out of sight? A. The defense budget. B. The budget for FEMA, the agency that is supposed to help people when there are floods, hurricanes, and other big disasters. C. Social Security. D. Medicare, which pays for health care for older people.

ANSWER: *D for Medicare. Its costs are skyrocketing out of sight. Right now, Medicare is a little over 12 percent of the federal budget, and its costs are rising much faster than the rate of inflation. Since Medicare's costs are joined at the hip with the country's health care costs overall—that's what Medicare pays for, after all—predicting what will happen down the line is all the more complicated. The health care bill passed in 2010 includes measures designed to rein in Medicare costs, and bought us more time to work on this problem. But even if those changes work like a charm (and there is plenty of debate about whether they will or won't), the country still faces massive expenses for Medicare as the boomers age. Or as Federal Reserve chairman Ben Bernanke puts it, with the deadpan economist phrasing you have to have to run the Fed: "Projections of future medical costs are fraught with uncertainty."* [10]

5. True or false? Foreign aid is one of the top ten expenses in the federal budget.

ANSWER: *Not even close. Foreign aid is about 1 percent of federal spending each year.*

---

[10] Testimony of Ben S. Bernanke, chairman of the Federal Reserve Board of Governors before the House Committee on the Budget, February 28, 2007, www.access.gpo.gov/congress/house/house04ch110.html.

★★★★★★★★★★★★★★★★★★★★★★★★★★★★★★

6. True or false? Money in the Social Security trust fund is only spent on Social Security.

ANSWER: *Nope. Money raised through Social Security taxes that is not immediately needed to pay Social Security benefits to elderly Americans can be lent (and has been lent) to the federal government to cover other programs and tax cuts. Sometimes people are distressed, even infuriated, when they learn about this, but the "borrowing" isn't illegal or even secret. In recent years, the huge baby-boom generation has been working and paying Social Security taxes, so there has been quite a bit of "extra money" in the trust fund. The rest of government has depended on the Social Security piggy bank to avoid having to raise taxes or cut other kinds of government spending. Social Security does have IOUs for money that's been spent elsewhere (actually, Treasury bonds), but it will need to start redeeming them in massive quantities when the boomers start retiring in larger numbers. The government is legally obligated to back the trust fund, but since it routinely operates in the red and is now approaching $15 trillion in debt, coming up with the money to cover those IOUs is not going to be easy. See chapters 6 through 9 for the particulars.*

Got all five right? Congratulations! You're ready to start your own "let's balance the budget" blog. If you missed something, read on. There's a lot to learn and think about in this strange little corner of public policy.

If you enjoyed this little exercise, you can throw yourself into the nitty-gritty details of balancing the nation's budget in chapter 15. Why not make it a party—just ask a few friends over, pull out the calculator, set out the beer and chips, and let the games begin.

So Whose Fault Is It, Anyway?

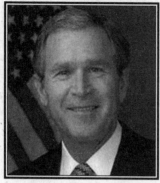
President George W. Bush

President Barack Obama

When President Clinton handed the presidency over to President Bush on January 20, 2001, the United States had a budget surplus, and the total debt was about $5.7 trillion. When President Obama came into office in January 2009, the debt had grown to about $10.6 trillion,[11] and during his first year, we added about $1.4 trillion of red ink to the books.

It's easy to find Americans who believe that the country's exploding debt is mainly President Bush's fault, and just as easy to find people who put the blame on President Obama. Let's take a look at some of the key decisions each of these men made. How much did their policies contribute to the huge financial burdens we face now? Why did they do it? How guilty are they? And how guilty are we? How many of us actually cheered them on when they were cutting taxes and increasing spending?

---

[11] You can check on how much the debt is today, yesterday, or any day since 1993 by going to the U.S Treasury's "Debt to the Penny" Web site at www .treasury direct.gov/NP/BPDLogin?application=np.

Let Them Eat Tax Cuts
Both presidents have cut taxes. It's a very popular thing to do.

What He Did

President Bush signed tax cuts with something for nearly everyone. He lowered income taxes, taxes for married people filing jointly, and taxes on dividends and capital gains, and he doubled the child credit.[12]

What He Did

Hoping to pull the economy out of its doldrums, President Obama signed the American Recovery and Reinvestment Act (ARRA) in early 2009. It included tax cuts that, according to the administration, benefited "95 percent of working families."

Why He Did It

Cutting taxes was one of his major campaign promises. He believed it would stimulate investment, entrepreneurship, and economic growth. The economy did grow rapidly during most of his presidency, but it took a nosedive in 2008.

Why He Did It

In his campaign, he promised to keep the Bush tax cuts for families earning less than $250,000 a year. Since the country was in a massive recession when he came into office, he also included tax cuts as part of his "stimulus" plan in 2009.

What It Cost

About $2 trillion so far.[13] Most of these cuts are set to expire at the end of 2010. It would cost even more—about $3.7 trillion—to continue them to

What It Cost

The whole "stimulus" package was projected to cost $862 billion, including money for state governments (think then Florida governor Charlie Crist hugging the

---

[12] Tax Policy Center, The Bush Tax Cuts: How did the 2001 tax cuts change the tax code? www.taxpolicycenter.org/briefing-book/background/bush-tax-cuts/2001.cfm and The Bush Tax Cuts: How did the 2003 tax cuts change the tax code? www.taxpolicycenter.org/briefing-book/background/bush-tax-cuts/2003.cfm, accessed May 8, 2010.

[13] Tax Policy Center, The 2001–2006 Income Tax Cuts With and Without Conforming AMT Rate Cuts, Static Impact on Individual Income Tax Liability and Revenue ($ billions), 2001-10. August 10, 2007, www.taxpolicycenter.org/numbers/displayatab.cfm?DocID=1651&topic2ID=40&topic3ID=57&DocTypeID=5, accessed May 8, 2010.

2020.[14] There's much more on this in Chapter 13.

president) and spending to create jobs (all those highway projects). But it also included $288 billion in tax cuts.[15]

Hey, Big Spender
Both presidents supported major new spending programs—both in health care, as it happens.

What He Did

President Bush added prescription drug coverage to Medicare.

What He Did

President Obama signed legislation designed to extend health insurance coverage to 32 million Americans. If the law is successful, about 94 percent of Americans will have insurance.[16]

Why He Did It

Seniors were facing higher and higher drug costs. Republicans and Democrats, including President Clinton and Vice President Gore, all thought this was a good idea.

Why He Did It

In 2008, there were some 46 million Americans without insurance,[17] and medical bills are a leading cause of personal bankruptcy. President Obama promised to close this gap in his campaign, and Democrats have wanted to solve this for years.

---

[14] Tax Policy Center, "Department of the Treasury Revenue Estimates for Extension of 2001 and 2003 Tax Cuts and the Administration's High-Income Tax Proposals Impact on Tax Revenue ($ billions), 2010-20," July 29, 2010, www.taxpolicycenter.org/numbers/displayatab.cfm?DocID=2785.

[15] Recovery.gov. www.recovery.gov/Pages/home.aspx. Accessed May 8, 2010. 16 Centers for Medicare and Medicaid Services, "The 2010 Annual Report of the Boards of Trustees of the Federal Hospital Insurance and Federal Supplementary Medical Insurance Trust Funds," Table V.E8.—Operations of the Part D Account in the SMI Trust Fund (Cash Basis) during Fiscal Years 2004–2019, www.cms.gov/ReportsTrustFunds/downloads/tr2010.pdf.

[16] See www.healthcare.gov for more details about the law.

[17] Kaiser Family Foundation, The Uninsured: A Primer, October, 2009, www.kff.org/uninsured/upload/7451-05.pdf.

What It Cost

The cost is projected to be about $445 billion between 2004 and 2014.[18]

What It Cost

In theory, the law will pay for itself. To get more people covered, spending will go up over $800 billion between 2010 and 2019. But the bill also cuts over $500 billion from Medicare and contains other measures to cover the cost. Unfortunately, many experts are very, very nervous about whether these estimates will hold. For more on this, see chapter 7.[19]

It's What You Don't Expect That Can Get You

Both presidents faced historic national crises that seemed to come right out of the blue. For President Bush, it was the 9/11 terror attack. For President Obama, it was the worst economic downturn since the Great Depression.

What He Did

After the terror attack, the president upgraded homeland security and took the nation to war in Afghanistan and Iraq—the "global war on terror."

What He Did

He offered billions of dollars to major banks and auto companies—the infamous "bailouts." But he wasn't alone in this. The bank bailout was actually enacted while President Bush was still in office, although the Obama administration has made most of the decisions.

---

[18] Centers for Medicare and Medicaid Services, "The 2010 Annual Report of the Boards of Trustees of the Federal Hospital Insurance and Federal Supplementary Medical Insurance Trust Funds," Table V.E8.—Operations of the Part D Account in the SMI Trust Fund (Cash Basis) during Fiscal Years 2004–2009, www.cms.gov/ReportsTrustFunds/downloads/tr2010.pdf.

[19] Richard S. Foster, Chief Actuary, Centers for Medicare and Medicaid Services, Department of Health and Human Services, "Estimated Financial Effects of the "Patient Protection and Affordable Care Act," as Amended," April 22, 2010, page 4, http://graphics8.nytimes.com/packages/pdf/health/oactmemo1.pdf.

Why He Did It

The 9/11 attacks were the first attack on U. S. soil since Pearl Harbor, and the decision to go to war in Afghanistan had worldwide backing. Most Americans supported invading Iraq at the time, and you probably cheered when they got Saddam Hussein no matter which side of the debate you were on.

What It Cost

Between 2001 and 2010, the combined cost of the "war on terror" comes in at about $1.1 trillion with most of the total spent in Iraq.[21]

Why He Did It

The whole world was in full economic panic mode. Financial giants like Lehman Brothers and Washington Mutual had collapsed. General Motors and Chrysler were on the verge. The Dow Jones Industrial Average had its worst year since 1931, with stocks losing over a third of their value.[20]

What It Cost

The number that sticks in everyone's mind is the dreaded $700 billion, but remember, the idea was for these companies to return the money once things returned to normal, and amazingly, this has been happening. The Congressional Budget Office has estimated that the actual toll will be more like $66 billion—not peanuts for sure, but not $700 billion either.[22]

---

[20] BBC News.com, "Record Stock Market Falls in 2008," December 31, 2008, http://news.bbc.co.uk/2/hi/business/7805644.stm, accessed May 8, 2010.

[21] Congressional Budget Office, "Funding for Operations in Iraq and Afghanistan and for Related Activities," The Budget and Economic Outlook: Fiscal Years 2010 to 2020, January 2010, www.cbo.gov/ftpdocs/108xx/doc10871/Chapter1.shtml #1099353.

[22] Congressional Budget Office Director's Blog, "CBO's Latest Projections for the TARP," August 10, 2010, http://cboblog.cbo.gov/?p=1322.

The Bottom Line?

President Bush both lowered taxes and increased spending, and the country's debt rose about $4.9 trillion while he was in office—and that was in pretty good economic times.

Like President Bush, President Obama has both lowered taxes and increased spending, but he's faced an abysmal economic climate. When people aren't working and companies aren't earning money, they don't pay taxes, so the country's tax revenue plummeted over $400 billion just between 2008 and 2009. No one really expects revenues to return to normal until 2011 at best. The Obama administration itself has projected that the country could add more than $5 trillion in debt between 2009 and 2012, and, like many others, calls the country's financial path "unsustainable." [23]

[23] Office of Management and Budget, "Mid-Session Review: Budget of the United States Government, FY2011" Table 1, "Change in Deficits From the February Budget," July 23, 2010, www.whitehouse.gov/omb/budget/MSR/.

★★★★★★★★★★★★★★★★★★★★★★★★★★★★★★

CHAPTER 2

So What's the Worst That Could Happen?

We gotta get out of this place!
If it's the last thing we ever do . . .

The Animals[1]

Experts can't predict exactly what will happen if the country keeps on adding debt and doesn't make changes in light of the upcoming retirement and health care costs of the boomers, but it isn't going to be good.

NOT ENOUGH NUMBERS ON THE DEBT CLOCK

Until fairly recently, the country's debt was ominously climbing skyward, and most of us barely noticed. It's true, we've had other issues to worry about, and some have been pretty serious. Then there's that segment of the public that's

---

[1] Barry Mann and Cynthia Weil, songwriters.

The late Seymour Durst spent his own money to put up the debt clock in the 1980s to call attention to the nation's debt problems. If you aren't coming to New York soon, you can download your own debt clock widget from Public Agenda.[2] Be forewarned though; watching the numbers spin by can be a little like watching *Avatar* in 3-D. It gives some people motion sickness. *Credit: Susan Wolfe Bittle*

been so mesmerized by *Dancing with the Stars* and the Tiger Woods drama that the prospect of the country going broke can't begin to compete for their attention. Most Americans didn't even bat an eye a couple of years ago when the country's debt hit the $10 trillion mark, and the national debt clock—located in the heart of New York City—didn't have enough space to record the number. It's a discouraging reminder of how long we've let this problem build up and how little we've done to address it. Here's the story.

Back in 1989, a real estate developer named Seymour Durst (he was worried about the nation's spending habits even then) paid to have a big sign put up in Midtown Manhattan that tallied the national debt pretty much like the mileage odometer in a car. It was an imaginative idea, but Durst's imagination failed in one respect. Since the debt was less than $3 trillion back then—and given how unimaginably huge a trillion dollars is—the clock was only

[2] It's at www.publicagenda.org/pages/get-widgets.

designed to go up to $9,999,999,999,999.[3] Unfortunately, along about October 2008, the debt climbed to $10 trillion.[4] The debt clock people decided to move the dollar sign out of its box and paint it on the side in order to have room for the extra digit. It's not quite as elegant, but as far as the debt clock is concerned, we're good to go for another $90 trillion or so. Too bad the country can't solve its budget problems quite so easily.

In chapter 1, we pointed out three big risks. Here's a quick recap just in case you didn't take notes. Risk numero uno is that Social Security and Medicare for boomers will bust the federal budget wide open. To be precise about it, this one is not a "risk." It's a certainty unless we make some adjustments in the way these programs work and are paid for. Risk number two is that the country's colossal debt and all the borrowing needed to handle it begin to drag the economy down. We could have the lovely symptoms of an economic recession around for a very long time. And risk number three is that people holding billions of dollars in U.S. debt—say, in China—will suddenly decide to put their money elsewhere, unleashing a financial crisis and probably sending the stock market into the basement.

HITTING THE WALL

A financial crisis is a lot like dying. For some people it happens slowly, like cancer. For others it's fast, like a car crash. The debt could hit us either way.

Let's say we (meaning the United States) keep going as

---

[3] U.S. Debt Clock Running Out of Time, Space, Yahoo News, AFP, March 27, 2006.

[4] M. J. Stephey, "A Brief History of the Times Square Debt Clock," Time.com, October 14, 2008, www.time.com/time/business/article/0,8599,1850269,00.html.

we are. We don't rein in spending. We don't raise taxes. We keep Social Security and Medicare just the way they are now (and fail to effectively control health care costs in general). Remember that handy little GAO (Government Accountability Office) calculation? Unless we make some changes, nearly every dollar the government collects in taxes will be needed for Social Security, Medicare, and Medicaid and paying interest on the debt, and it could happen sooner than we think.[5] Obviously, the government wouldn't be able to do a lot of things we normally expect—invest in research, offer college loans, enforce health and safety laws, take care of the national parks, and so on. And let's say that the government, lacking the guts to do anything that might upset voters, keeps borrowing money to pay the bills. And the rest of the world keeps buying our Treasury bills because we're still the safest place for foreigners to park their money.

Until something happens.

The "something" could be a lot of different things. Something could seriously disrupt the world's oil supply, for example—a war in the Mideast or a wave of Islamist revolution that brings hostile new regimes to power. Or something could undermine the U.S. economy dramatically, such as the collapse of a major industry or the failure of an overstrained power grid. That's not so hard to imagine. After all, the government had to spend billions bailing out the U.S. auto and banking industries in 2009. You can sit around all day and easily come up with your own list of possible disasters if you enjoy doing that sort of thing.

It could be something slower, too. Perhaps the U.S. economy just starts looking a little less competitive compared

---

[5] Government Accountability Office, Statement of the Comptroller General of the United States, February 26, 2010, www.gao.gov/financial/fy2009financialreport.html.

with markets overseas, a little sluggish, not quite keeping up with other nations on the science-and-technology front. Not a crisis, but something bankers and bond traders talk about until they reach one of Malcolm Gladwell's famous "tipping points."

SOME BANKER IN BEIJING

But either way, it starts like this: a banker in one of those glass-walled office buildings that look the same whether they're in Beijing, London, or Singapore rubs his eyes, walks over to the vending machine, thinks a bit, sits back down, and says to his colleagues, "You know, I think we're holding too many U.S. Treasuries."

After years of having U.S. government bonds be the money market fund to the world, it's the awful moment. The idea spreads. Washington can't sell the bonds anymore. The Treasury Department jacks up the interest rates to make them more attractive. When the Treasury rate goes up, all the commercial banks raise their rates, too. Everything from your credit card bill to your mortgage gets more expensive overnight. And the foreign banks still aren't lending us enough money to cover the government's costs.

Now Washington doesn't just have a deficit problem, it's got a cash flow problem. And it's got to be solved now. Elected officials start raising taxes and cutting government programs in an attempt to come up with the cash and convince foreign investors that the country means business about getting its economic house in order. The economy starts to slump because of the high interest rates and the sudden shock of huge tax hikes. The stock market plummets as people lose confidence and draw on their stocks to try to maintain their lifestyle. Even American investors start moving money overseas. How many people are really patriotic enough to stand by and watch the savings of a life-time lose value?

Still hard to visualize? It's time to bring all this a little closer to home. What would all this mean for a typical American family, people who work for a living, have kids, try to save for the future, hope to be able to retire at some point? Now we could make up an imaginary family, but why should we when Frank Capra has already done most of the work? We're going to borrow a very-well-known family living in that classic all-American hometown, Bedford Falls.

BEDFORD FALLS IN A DOWN-AND-OUT AMERICA

If you're reading this in December, we probably don't have to refresh your memory about Bedford Falls. It's Jimmy Stewart's hometown in the 1946 Christmas movie *It's a Wonderful Life*. If you're one of those people who absolutely refuse to watch it, Jimmy Stewart is good-guy George Bailey, whose family runs the local savings and loan while the villainous Mr. Potter runs the local bank. Thanks to Mr. Potter's nefarious dealing, Bailey gets into financial trouble, and thinks about killing himself. He wishes aloud that he had never been born.

In what's often viewed as the movie's signature sequence, guardian angel Clarence escorts a "nonexistent" George Bailey around Bedford Falls so he can see what the town would have been like if he had in fact never been born. Instead of being a Norman Rockwell vision of comfortable American middle-class life, Bedford Falls is now Pottersville. The wicked Mr. Potter has been given free rein, and Bailey's family, friends, and his hometown generally have hit upon hard times and various misfortunes.

In the movie, Bedford Falls becomes Pottersville because

Things always turn out all right in the end for George Bailey and family in the Christmas reruns. But Clarence the angel is no financial planner, and we may all be living in Pottersville unless we put the nation's fiscal house in order. *Credit:* It's a Wonderful LIfe, *1946*

one man (Mr. Potter) is greedy and awful. But Bedford Falls could also become Debtville (sorry, it was irresistible) because millions of Americans aren't paying attention to the country's budget problems and because too many of their leaders apparently lack the courage, candor, and integrity needed to tackle them before there's real trouble.

Let's take a look at what happened in Pottersville without George Bailey and what might happen in Debtville if the country's addiction to spending beyond its means keeps on going.

POTTERSVILLE

Mr. Potter takes over the Bailey Building & Loan, and people end up living in Potter's own run-down development with the somewhat alarming name of Potter's Field.[6] George Bailey wasn't there to help people of middle-class means buy nicer, but affordable homes.

Mrs. Bailey, George's mother, has become a bitter old woman forced to take lodgers into the family home to make ends meet. George wasn't there to make sure she lived in reasonable comfort.

Uncle Billy, George's bungling but lovable uncle, is in an insane asylum and, Mrs. Bailey reports, no one has seen him for years. George wasn't there to protect and guard over him.

Mary, George's wife, is a spinster working at the local library. She and George never fell in love and never married.

Zuzu, Bailey's daughter, doesn't exist because her dad wasn't around to marry Mary and start a family.

Harry, George's war hero brother, also doesn't exist. He drowned as a child because George wasn't there to save him.

Bert and Ernie, George's old buddies, the local cop and taxi driver, are gruff, rough, and sour men, not the generous, funny, friendly characters who inspired the *Sesame Street* Muppet names.

DEBTVILLE

In Debtville, **Mr. Potter** doesn't have to do the dastardly deeds himself. Massive federal debt drives up interest rates pushing the country into recession. Chinese investors decide they want their money back (and other investors around the world follow suit), setting off an economic crisis. The

---

[6] That man needed a good publicist more than anyone in movie history.

stock market loses almost half of its value in less than a month. In a last-ditch attempt to pay the Chinese and cover basic expenses, Congress raises taxes and slashes support for education, small businesses, local police, housing, and other services. Even Social Security benefits take a hit. The financial situation is so grave that Congress even ends the politically popular home mortgage deduction. With high interest rates and no deduction to ease the pain, owning a home becomes a dream for most middle-class Americans.

Still, characters like Mr. Potter thrive even in the worst economic times. At the first hint of trouble in the U.S. economy, he moved his money to the Cayman Islands. His run-down Potter's Field rental complex is bursting at the seams.

Mrs. Bailey, George's mother, is still bitter and taking in lodgers. When the debt crisis hit the government, her Social Security benefits were cut, and the little nest egg she had in the stock market nearly evaporated. Mrs. Bailey is barely making ends meet, and she's worried about getting sick. Medicare, too, has been slashed.

Uncle Billy used to get supplemental Social Security payments because of his disabilities, which enabled him to live decently and independently. But these funds were gutted in the budget emergency. Like many of the country's most vulnerable people, Uncle Billy has joined the ranks of the homeless and the hungry (food stamps were cut back, too; they're just for families now—not enough money to help singles).

Mary still works at the library, but since it's only open a few hours a day, she's having a tough time, too. The library was funded by the state and the town of Pottersville, but with all the federal cutbacks, local governments have had to scramble to make up the difference. Keeping the library open on a full schedule is too much of a luxury.

We've let **Zuzu** live (maybe she's someone else's daughter), but she isn't going to college. With the government spending nearly everything it takes in to cover even pared-down Social Security and Medicare benefits, college loans are a thing of the past. She's living at home with her mom—jobs are few and far between for people just coming into the workforce.

We've let **Harry** survive, too, and he's a war hero like he was when George Bailey lived his normal life. But despite Harry's service to the country in time of war, his veterans' benefits were cut. Normally, this is one of the last places the American public wants to scrimp, but the government's financial crisis was so sudden and so dire, even the most broadly supported government programs have been lacerated.

Bert and Ernie? Well, Bert the police officer is working overtime and without much backup. The poor economy and high rates of unemployment have caused crime rates to soar. And the Pottersville Police Department has had to take its share of cutbacks, just like the library did. As for Ernie the taxi driver, the government's double-digit increases in the gas tax, and the fact that hardly anyone can afford to take a cab these days, have devastated his livelihood as well.

That's the thing about a government in crisis and an economy in a deep recession. Nearly everyone suffers, except for the very rich.

When Good Economies Go Bad, or, Don't Cry for Me, Argentina

What happens when a government hits the wall and can't pay its creditors? Greece is the most recent example of a country in financial crisis, but when it comes to financial crises, it's still tough to beat Argentina. In December 2001, there were riots in the streets over Argentina's financial problems, riots so bad that martial law was declared and two presidents were forced from office. Argentina's situation is very different from our own, but what occurred there should get our attention about what happens when a country can't pay its bills.

Like the United States, Argentina is rich in natural and human resources, but economically speaking, the country has had its ups and downs. In the late 1980s, Argentina was facing "hyperinfla-tion" of 200 percent *a month*—the kind of inflation where it pays to go grocery shopping in the morning because by nightfall things will cost more. To fight this, Argentina made several policy changes encouraged by the International Monetary Fund, including pegging the peso to the U.S. dollar and liberalizing trade rules. Argentina also started borrowing heavily from the IMF and other international banks, hoping to keep its budget going until the reforms took hold.

For a while in the 1990s, that plan worked—in fact, it worked re-ally well. Argentina saw strong economic growth and started getting cited as an economic model for others. But when the world market for farm products softened and currencies in other Latin American countries fell, Argentine products had trouble finding a market. That led to a recession, which cut tax revenues to the government.

The IMF and international banks told Argentine officials to go on a strict government austerity plan, but with unemployment at 18 percent they (not surprisingly) resisted that until 2001. Then the government devalued the peso and slashed its budget dramatically, including a move to cut old-age pensions and use the money to pay international debts.

The country's credit rating sank and there was a national run on banks, with Argentines pulling $1.3 billion out of their accounts in a single day. Dozens were killed in street protests so serious that the government imposed martial law, froze bank deposits to stop the run, then defaulted on more than $141 billion in foreign debt—the biggest loan default in history. The recession that followed was brutal. More than half of the population was in poverty between 2001 and 2002.[7] Unemployment hit nearly 21 percent and the economy contracted by 11 percent.[8] By contrast, during the "Great Recession" in 2009, the U.S. economy shrank 2.6 percent and unemployment reached 10 percent.[9]

Nearly a decade later, Argentina is still working its way out of this corner. The government has paid off its IMF debt early, after an elaborate debt-swap deal that left most of its international creditors getting 35 cents on the dollar. [10] Unemployment has fallen, and until the global financial crisis hit the economy was growing at a healthy 7 or 8 percent annually. But there are still creditors dogging Argentina, and as of 2010, the country still can't borrow on international credit markets. The burden to average Argentines has been immense (tens of thousands have reportedly left the country to find work and more than a quarter are

[7] International Monetary Fund Country Report 05/236, July 18, 2005.

[8] "IMF Executive Board Concludes 2006 Article IV Consultation with Argentina," International Monetary Fund Public Information Notice No. 06/93, August 9, 2006 (www.imf.org/external/np/sec/pn/2006/pn0693.htm).

[9] Bureau of Labor Statistics, "Labor Force Statistics from the Current Population Survey," www.bls.gov/cps/, accessed Sept. 6, 2010, and Bureau of Economic Analysis, National Economic Accounts, "Table 1.1.1. Percent Change From Preceding Period in Real Gross Domestic Product," www.bea.gov/national/nipaweb/SelectTable.asp, accessed Sept. 6, 2010.

[10] BBC News, "Argentine Restructuring Success," March 4, 2005.

below the poverty line).[11] Overall, Argentina still counts as the biggest national debt default in history.

And Greece? As we write this in mid-2010, the Greek debt crisis is still breaking news. European nations arranged a bailout of Greece in return for austerity measures that caused riots in Athens. But many other European nations were considering tightening their own belts, worried that their own national debts will come back to bite them. Remember, most of the other industrial nations did the same thing the United States did in response to the global financial crisis: bailed out shaky banks and launched new spending to stimulate the economy. Most of the world saw its public debt skyrocket in the past couple of years, to the point where the IMF warns properly managing these debt levels are important to maintaining the global recovery.[12]

The United States isn't Greece, or Argentina for that matter.

Even if the worst happens here, it probably won't happen in the same way. The U.S. economy is much bigger and more diverse than Argentina's, plus we have the advantage that the U.S. dollar is the standard currency for international banking. Argentina had to borrow (and repay) its debt in U.S. dollars, which was pretty tough when the value of their own currency, the peso, was in free fall. You can also have a really passionate argument on whether the IMF's advice led Argentina into a blind alley. That probably won't be a factor for the United States.

We're better off than Greece as well. The Greek government was seriously overextended, with promises made (like retirement as early as age 50) that it couldn't afford to pay. But the Greek

---

[11] Congressional Research Service, Argentina's Defaulted Sovereign Debt: Dealing with the "Holdouts", April 28, 2010, http://opencrs.com/document/R41029/2010-07-02.

[12] International Monetary Fund Fiscal Monitor, "Navigating the Fiscal Challenges Ahead," May 13, 2010, www.imf.org/external/pubs/cat/longres.cfm?sk=23814.0.

economy is much weaker than ours, their debt is much larger (bigger than their entire economy, in fact), and they have had rampant, almost routine tax evasion. Plus, because they'd adopted the euro, Greece doesn't control its own currency, and that limits their financial options severely.[13]

But the point to remember is that the national debt—that abstraction that lives on the computers of big banks—became very real to the Argentine people. The debt cost them real cash and real jobs because their government mishandled it. And that absolutely could happen to us.

---

[13] Atlantic Wire, "Could Debt Drive the U.S. to Collapse Like Greece?" May 12, 2010, www.theatlanticwire.com/opinions/view/opinion/Could-Debt-Drive-the-US-to-Collapse-Like-Greece-3578.

So Where in the World Is the Debt?

At the close of 2009, the debt owed by the United States was about $12 trillion, and a little over $3.5 trillion of that amount was owed to foreign banks and other international investors. This is a nice vote of confidence in the U.S. economy in some respects. People around the world think their money will be safe invested in U.S. Treasury bonds. In fact, during the world financial crisis of 2008–09, you couldn't keep investors away from Treasuries, because they seemed like the *only* safe place to park your money. Still, there's a risk that at some point, international investors might decide to put some of their money elsewhere, and that could drive up interest rates and cause turmoil in the stock and currency markets—not such a pretty picture.

The Top Ten Foreign Holders of U.S. Debt in November 2009:

Country	Amount
China, Mainland	$789.6 billion
Japan	$757.3 billion
United Kingdom	$277.5 billion
Oil Exporters (including Ecuador, Venezuela, Indonesia, Bahrain, Iran, Iraq, Kuwait, Oman, Qatar, Saudi Arabia, the United Arab Emirates, Algeria, Gabon, Libya, and Nigeria)	$187.7 billion
Caribbean Banking Centers (includes the Bahamas, Bermuda, Cayman Islands, Netherlands Antilles, Panama, and British Virgin Islands)	$179.8 billion
Brazil	$157.1 billion
Hong Kong	$146.2 billion
Russia	$128.1 billion
Luxembourg	$91.7 billion
Taiwan	$78.4 billion

Source: Department of the Treasury/Federal Reserve Board as reported in CRS report "The Federal Government Debt: Its Size and Economic Significance," Feb. 3, 2010, http://assets.opencrs.com/rpts/RL31590_20100203.pdf

The China Syndrome, or, How Bankers in Beijing Affect Your Mortgage

So when the U.S government borrows money, who does it borrow from? Well, anyone who's willing to buy Treasury bonds, for a start. Lots of Americans—individuals and institutions—own U.S. Treasuries. So do lots of foreigners. And in the last few years, few nations have had a bigger appetite for U.S. Treasury bonds than the People's Bank of China, Beijing's central bank.

Right now, China's economy is growing fast, and it's a country that exports a lot more than it imports (mainly because low-wage labor makes Chinese goods cheap to produce, but doesn't give Chinese workers enough spending money to acquire a taste for imported products). That means China is taking in a lot more money than it can spend, and it needs to stash it somewhere. China's central bankers, being cautious as bankers usually are, put that extra cash into safe investments. And Treasury bonds have always been among the safest investments going.

As of 2009, China owned $790 billion in Treasury bonds and is steadily buying more. That provides a lot of benefits to the United States—and poses a lot of risk.

In addition to allowing the U.S. government to go on spending money it doesn't have, the fact that we can always count on China to buy T-bills helps keep U.S. interest rates down. When somebody's always willing to lend you money on good terms, nobody has to haggle and rates stay low for everybody. That means your mortgage payments, car payments, and credit card bills are lower than they might be if the U.S. government had to struggle to get anyone to take its bonds.

The risk is pretty simple: Maybe someday the People's Bank of China will decide it doesn't want Treasury bonds anymore.

Maybe it will decide something else is a better investment. Or maybe we'll get into an argument with the Chinese over the future of Taiwan or human rights and China will get ticked off enough to start unloading its bonds on the world market. That could drop the dollar through the floor in international markets, not to mention jacking up every adjustable rate mortgage in the United States overnight. All of a sudden, you could find yourself with a lot less spending money every month.

The Chinese don't even have to stop buying bonds completely to cause us a lot of trouble. All China needs to do is slow down to set off alarms among currency traders around the world. Everybody in the financial world is watching for a sign that China has changed its mind, so they'll know when to dump their Treasury bonds, too.

Ironically, this is what makes U.S. debt a mixed blessing from the Chinese perspective. China needs stable world financial markets, and it needs Americans to keep buying Chinese products. All of which means the Chinese don't want to shake up the U.S. economy too badly. So they can't stop buying bonds, even if they could make more money elsewhere. It's another version of the old adage that "if you borrow $100,000 the bank owns you, but if you borrow $100 million you own the bank."

So does that mean there's no real risk? We're happily co-dependent forever? Well, maybe—or maybe not.

In the short term, what this most likely means is that China doesn't really have to listen to the United States on issues like human rights. Ever borrow money from someone and then try to give them advice or, worse, lecture them on morality? No, neither have we, but we don't think it would work. Do we really want to be in that position with the Chinese government? One in which American diplomats are trying to push an issue and the Chinese officials are sitting there thinking, "Yadda yadda yadda, wonder how many T-bills we bought today?"

In the long run, it's also dangerous to assume China will need our gizmo-hungry consumers forever. Someday Chinese consumers will take up some of the slack, or people in new emerging markets will get rich enough to start buying their own gizmos, and then maybe China won't need the United States so much anymore. Plus, there may be flashpoint situations (like Taiwanese independence) in which Beijing might be willing to sacrifice its own prosperity to get what it wants.

Look, the Japanese and the British hold a lot of Treasury bonds, too, but nobody makes a big deal about it. The Bank of England has no political reason to stick it to us. (Although it's worth remembering that if U.S. finances get screwed up badly enough, even our close allies might find other places to park their money. As the Corleones like to say in *The Godfather* movies, "It's not personal. It's strictly business.")

How you feel about this depends on what you think about the Chinese government and what it's after. China has a powerful weapon it could use against us, which it would rather not use. But because China is a rival instead of an ally, we can't assume it never will.

CHAPTER 3

A Little Clarification
Is in Order

There are a lot of things people don't understand. Take the
Einstein theory. Take taxes. Take love. Do you understand
them? Neither do I. But they exist. They happen.

—*Screenwriter Dalton Trumbo in*
The Remarkable Andrew, *1941*

Most books that try to explain complicated topics—topics
most of us don't chat about daily with friends and family—include a glossary of the hard words to make things
clearer. You've lucked out here because we've decided to spare
you that. After all, it's the key facts—and the decisions the
country needs to make—that we want you to think about,
not the specialized words economists and politicians use.

THE D-WORDS

Even so, there are two words we do need to spend some time
on. Reporters and politicians tend to fling them around like

crazy, and unfortunately, they both start with *d*, just to add to the potential confusion. They are, however, very different things, and making sure that you don't mistake the deficit for the debt is important to understanding this issue. (OK, you're thinking, "Oh come on, everyone knows that." Excellent; you've been paying attention while some of us were a little distracted. You move on to chapter 4.) For the rest of us, let's just get this little mix-up out of the way.

First, there's **the deficit.** When the government spends more money in a year than it collects in taxes and fees, it has a deficit for that year. In 2008, the U.S. government took in about $459 billion less than it spent, so it had a $459 billion deficit for that year. In 2009, the government took in about $1.4 trillion less than it spent. So for that year, the deficit was _____? Yes, you've got it—$1.4 trillion.[1] And yes, we did go from the billions into the trillions.

Then there's **the debt,** which is what the government owes when deficits add up over time. You can see that the deficits for 2008 and 2009 alone add up to really big bucks (2008's $459 billion + 2009's $1.4 trillion = nearly $1.9 trillion). And that's just two years' worth, although they were admittedly two truly awful years. So after spending more money than it collects for 31 out of the last 35 years, the U.S. had built up a debt of over $12 trillion by the end of 2009. And of course, we've just been adding to the debt since then.

The dilemma for those of us with things to do and people to meet is that deficits go up and down all the time. Unless the country actually has a surplus, the debt is really

---

[1] Budget of the United States Government: Historical Tables, Fiscal Year 2011. Table 1.1—Summary of Receipts, Outlays, and Surpluses or Deficits (-): 1789–2015, www.gpoaccess.gov/usbudget/fy11/hist.html.

just getting bigger. For example, let's start with that whopper deficit of $1.4 trillion in 2009. By the close of 2011, the federal deficit is expected to fall to about $1.3 trillion, and break out the champagne for 2012 when it's projected to drop to a mere $828 billion.[2] Out with the trillions; back to the billions—happy days are here again. The problem is that you may well see headlines that say "U.S. Deficit Down Nearly Half a Trillion." Sounds terrific, and it would even be true. But it will also be true that government just added billions of dollars to the debt. It's red ink on top of red ink, and that's not the direction we want to go in.

HERMIONE'S DEFICIT SPENDING FALLS IN JANUARY

Dealing with numbers in the billions and trillions and using words like deficit and debt can make the whole thing confusing, but the basic financial dilemma is common enough. Plenty of American households are in the same situation. Let's take our friend Hermione. She has a pretty good job, but month after month, she uses her credit cards to live beyond her means—a new leather sofa here, that new designer coat there. Now she owes more than $22,000 on her credit cards. Some months are a little better than others, of course. In December (we all know how this goes), Hermione added $1,000 to her credit card debt. In January (after making some New Year's resolutions in this area), she added only $100 to the overall total. You could write an entirely truthful headline about Hermione's little step in the right direction: "Hermione's

---

[2] Office of Management and Budget, "Mid-Session Review: Budget of the United States Government, FY2011," Table 1, "Change in Deficits from the February Budget," July 23, 2010, www.whitehouse.gov/omb/budget/MSR/.

January Deficit Spending Falls by $900." But Hermione is still in big financial trouble. She overspends. She underpays. And despite her New Year's resolutions, she's still courting financial trouble.

So the next time you see a news report about the federal deficit dropping by billions of dollars, don't get too excited. It's certainly better than the deficit growing, but it hardly means that the country is home free. For one thing, the federal deficit tends to be bigger or smaller depending on the state of the economy, regardless of whether the government has done anything to get its spending in line with its income or not. When the economy is good, people and companies make more money, and they pay more in taxes. During the economic boom between 1998 and 2001, the government actually ran a surplus for a few years. The opposite is also true. When the country is in a recession, people and companies earn less and pay less in taxes, and the deficits tend to be bigger.

What's more, virtually all economists believe there are times when the government should run a deficit. Sometimes it is just sensible and necessary. For example, the U.S. government ran large deficits during the Great Depression and throughout World War II. After the war, the government's record on deficits was mixed. Starting in 2008, with the United States undergoing the most serious economic recession since the Great Depression, we've had deficits on steroids.[3]

HEADING IN THE WRONG DIRECTION

In the last year or two, the gargantuan size of our debt and

---

[3] Budget of the United States Government: Historical Tables, Fiscal Year 2011. Table 1.1—Summary of Receipts, Outlays, and Surpluses or Deficits (-): 1789–2015, www.gpoaccess.gov/usbudget/fy11/hist.html.

our supersized annual deficits have been hot topics in politics, but the U.S. government has been indulging in a steady diet of deficits since the 1970s. We did have those nice four years of surplus between 1998 and 2001, but the overall picture has not been pretty for quite some time. By 2009, the accumulated debt was over $12 trillion, and in 2011, we'll be zooming past $14 trillion and headed for the $15 trillion mark. Yes, we are 14 going on 15. Let's hope we don't get to the actual *Sound of Music* version—"16 going on 17"—too soon.

It's probably fair to say that most economists, politicians, and business leaders are beginning to worry about that number, but there are some who believe it's not especially terrible in an economy as large and powerful as ours. After all, our friend Hermione's $22,000 credit card debt may be excessive for her, but Bill Gates or Oprah Winfrey wouldn't even blink if they had to send in a check for the entire amount.

MORTGAGING THE FUTURE?

So maybe the country's having a big debt is just like a family having a big mortgage? Well, yes and no. The country's debt (about $13.7 trillion at the close of 2010) is about six and a half times the federal government's annual income from taxes and fees (about $2.1 trillion for 2010). That's along the lines of a person making $50,000 a year carrying a $300,000 mortgage. Like those of us with mortgages, the government also pays some hefty interest on its debt. It shocks a lot of Americans to learn that for the last several years, the government has actually spent more money on interest payments than it has spent on education or veterans' benefits or science. The sad fact is that the United States spent more on interest last year than it spent on all three of those areas combined.

But there are some major differences. People with mortgages follow a very specific plan to pay off what they owe. The U.S. government has no such plan. Relatively few members of Congress are even talking about developing one. Other countries have set budget targets their government has to meet, but not us. Most people with mortgages don't routinely add more and more to their debt every year—and those who do take on second mortgages, big home equity loans, and lots of credit card bills typically end up in trouble. In contrast, the government routinely adds to the debt.

Theoretically, the U.S. government could sell off everything it owns (condominiums in Yellowstone, anyone?). State governments do that pretty regularly—selling off some piece of infrastructure to raise cash, say, an office building or a turnpike, and then leasing it back. Homeowners can sometimes do something along these lines—sell the house and use the proceeds to pay down what they owe, although if you owe more on your mortgage than you can get for your home, even that doesn't work. On paper, the U.S. government's total assets, including facilities and inventory, total nearly $2.7 trillion.[4] But in the real world, that's just not a plan most Americans will tolerate. Even state governments that do this frequently end up getting criticized for phony accounting. Ever hear those news reports about a state or city with a miserable bond rating?

THE REAL KICKER

But the most nerve-racking thing about the government's "let's add to the debt and worry about it tomorrow" mental-

---

[4] Government Accountability Office, Fiscal Year 2009 Financial Report of the United States Government, Financial Statements: Balance Sheets as of September 30, 2009 and September 30, 2008, page 49, www.gao.gov/financial/fy2009financialreport.html.

ity is what's to come. The country is quickly approaching a time when it will face some very big new expenses. Leaders in government and business all know this, and you should, too, because, as a country, we need to decide how to handle it. Members of the baby-boom generation are starting to retire. Very soon, they'll begin to have the kind of high health care expenses older people typically have. The government will have to pay for most of these expenses (trust us on this for now; we'll explain in chapters 6 through 9). Unfortunately, the country is doing almost nothing to prepare for this.

This is the big financial crunch to come—the one that could mean serious problems for our economy and our way of life. To tackle that one, federal deficits need to fall and keep on falling for a good number of years. We need to watch our expenses like the perennial hawk. And we're probably going to need to cut some expenses and raise money in ways we would rather not. It's like our friend Hermione, who needs to stop buying things unless she really, really needs them. And she needs to start paying more than the minimum on her credit card bill for many months to come. And she needs to drop that expensive gym membership and start running in the park instead.

The rest of *Where Does the Money Go?* will help you think for yourself about how the country should address this problem. We'll explain how the government gets its money, how much it takes in, what it spends it on, and what kinds of choices there are to address the problem. We aim to give you information that will help you begin to gather your own thoughts about how to put things in balance. And we aim to give you the facts that will help you—good citizen that you are—start holding our elected officials' collective feet to the fire on this.

WHEN A BILLION DOLLARS DOESN'T MEAN MUCH

But before we go there, here's one last friendly reminder about understanding the budget debate. We all know this, but with all the numbers and statistics flying off the shelves these days, we just have to remember to watch those billions and trillions. For you or me, a billion dollars is a ton of money. For the federal government, it's chicken feed. Remember, in its 2009 budget, the government spent $1.4 *trillion* more than it took in.

The point is this: Just don't be too impressed when you hear or read that the government's deficit is down by $30, $40, or even $50 billion. That's not going to do the trick, especially if it's just for one year. As a country, we need to decide whether we want to cut back on government spending, change the way Social Security and Medicare work, raise taxes, or do some of all three. And after that, we're really going to have to stick with the plan.

What's a Billion Worth?

The trouble with big numbers is that they're hard to visualize. The $60 you take out of the ATM on Monday morning is crisp and tangible. You know what it takes to get through the week, and you know whether you're going to have to stop at the bank again before Friday.

A billion is just a number. There's no billion-dollar bill (although it's fun to speculate which president would be on it).[5] A trillion is even worse. These are important ways of keeping score, but really difficult to grasp. And when you start talking about big numbers, you ought to know how much they really mean in practice—as Dr. Evil found out as he tried to look threatening when he made his demand for "one *million* dollars."

But the best way of dealing with intangibles is to make them concrete. There's a Barenaked Ladies song called "If I Had a Million Dollars." Like some other songs, it's (a) been co-opted for a TV commercial and (b) can be difficult to get out of your head if you're not careful. But if you had a billion dollars and an inclination to play Santa, you could:[6]

★ Buy about 250 million bottles of aspirin (or about 126 million bottles, if you go with a name brand. See how it pays to buy generic?)

A billion dollars buys 250 million bottles of aspirin.
Credit: IStockphoto.

---

[5] Ever wonder why certain famous people are on particular bills—for example, why Hamilton's on the $10 and Jackson's on the $20, instead of the other way around? Well, the official answer from the Treasury Department is "We don't remember." The current lineup was set in 1928 and the records don't cover why. See www.ustreas.gov/education/faq/currency/portraits.html.

[6] Our figures are based on retail prices in January 2010—not counting taxes, coupons, or bulk purchase discounts.

★ Give four spiral notebooks to every student in public school in the United States (about 39.2 million children)

★ Get a pair of Gap jeans for everyone in Australia (21 million, not counting shipping). Or, if you'd rather work closer to home, that's enough to give all 5 million people in Minnesota their own iPod Nano.

A billion dollars buys five spiral notebooks for every U.S. public school student. *Credit: Photo by the U.S. Census Bureau, Public Information Office (PIO)*

A billion dollars buys nearly 2 million Manolo Blahniks. *Credit: IStockphoto.com*

★ If you're a shoe-obsessed fashionista like Carrie in *Sex and the City*, you could buy yourself 2 million pairs of Manolo Blahniks. (If you're shoe-obsessed but less self-absorbed, that would allow you to give a pair to everyone in Manhattan and Staten Island. Including the men.)

★ You could also provide all thirty-five thousand students at the University of Houston with their own Toyota Camry. Not the base model, either—

A billion dollars would buy a fairly nice car for each of the University of Houston's thirty-five thousand students. *Credit: Photo by the U.S. Census Bureau, Public Information Office (PIO)*

you could get the optional leather seats and high-end sound system.

★ You could keep about forty-five thousand people in a four-year private college for a year—or, depending on their behavior, in prison. The College Board says private tuition and fees average $23,712 a year; the Bureau of Justice Statistics says the average cost per inmate is $22,650 a year.

★ You could pay the salaries of about eighteen thousand rookie cops to put on the streets of Los Angeles (starting pay: $47,048). There are only about 9000 officers in the LAPD now.

★ You'd have enough money to build a thousand-bed hospital (the rule of thumb is that a hospital costs $1 million per bed). Or, if you already had the hospital, you could conduct cardiac valve replacement surgery on nearly twenty-three thousand patients.

★ Based on the Census Bureau's median prices, you could buy homes for nearly 12,700 families in Mississippi, or nearly 3,158 homes in pricier California.

Big-ticket items, of course, cost more, and you get less for your money. A billion will only get you:

A billion dollars buys 3,158 big, fancy houses in California. *Credit: Photo by the U.S. Census Bureau, Public Information Office (PIO)*

★ Four Boeing 777 airliners.

★ Almost half of a *Trident* nuclear submarine, at $1.9 billion each.

★ One-third of New York's proposed Freedom Tower ($3.1 billion).

But what about trillions? They're really mind-boggling. To figure that out, just add three more zeros to any of the numbers above.

For example, instead of building a thousand hospital beds with $1 billion, $1 trillion would allow you to build a million hospital beds—and in 2005, there were only about 840,000 in the United States.

Or instead of only four Boeing 777s, you could get 4,000, enough to replace the fleets of six or seven major airlines (for example, American Airlines and its American Eagle subsidiary have about 890 planes).

A billion dollars would pay for about half of a nuclear submarine. *Credit: U.S. Navy photo by Gene Royer*

But let's make it as down-to-earth as possible. There are about 300 million people in the United States, more or less. And let's say you wanted to do something for every one of them. With $1 billion, split evenly, you'd have a little more than $3.33 to spend on each one.

With $1 trillion, you could spend $3,333.33 apiece.

A Deficit Here, a Deficit There, Here a Deficit, There a Deficit . . .

You might as well brace yourselves because you're going to read the word *deficit* a few hundred times in this book. Here, we're talking about the federal budget deficit—the gap between what the U.S. government spends on programs and services and what it takes in from taxes and a few other sources. Obviously, it's an important issue because when the government runs a deficit—which it is doing routinely—the country's debt and the interest we pay on it swells. Rather than saving up to cover the big expenses ahead when the baby boomers stop working, the country is actually digging itself into an even deeper financial hole.

DEFICITS TO THE LEFT OF US, DEFICITS TO THE RIGHT

But the budget deficit's not the only deficit in town. There's also the country's trade deficit—the difference between the amount of goods and services Americans buy from abroad and the amount we supply to the rest of the world. According to Federal Reserve Board chairman Ben Bernanke, "the U.S. economy is consuming more than it's producing, and the difference is made up by imports from abroad." At the close of 2008, the country's trade deficit was nearly $700 billion.[7] The country's trade deficit actually fell to $375 billion in 2009, but since the country was in the throes of a major recession, we weren't buying that much from abroad (or from here either, for that matter).[8]

All you champagne and marzipan lovers can hang your heads

---

[7] U.S. Census Bureau, Foreign Trade, U.S Trade in Goods and Services—Balance of Payments, 1960-2009, March 11, 2010, www.census.gov/foreign-trade/statistics/historical/gands.txt, accessed May 15, 2010.

[8] Ibid.

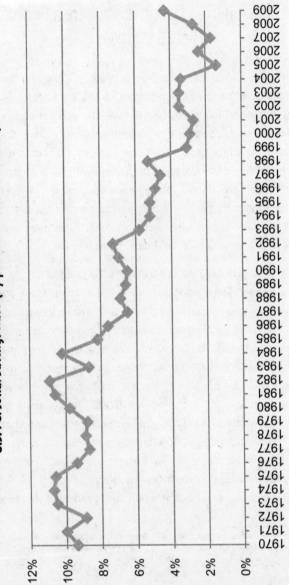

U.S. Personal Savings Rate (by percent of annual income)

Sometime over the last thirty years or so, Americans just stopped saving money, in good times and in bad. The savings rate has plummeted, and that has real implications for the nation's economy and for the federal budget. *Source: U.S. Bureau of Economic Analysis*

in shame, but when it comes to the trade deficit, a taste for European fine food and drink is probably the least of it. The country imported nearly $254 billion worth of oil in 2009.[9] And then there are the cars and consumer electronics. Our 2009 trade deficit with China alone was nearly $227 billion.[10] Like our problem with budget deficits, trade deficits have become routine. The United States has been running one since 1970.

"THE TWIN DEFICITS"

How large can the trade and budget deficits get before the American economy starts to sag?

Debate over how much risk the country faces from what is often referred to as "the twin deficits" is, as the *Washington Times* puts it, "probably the biggest parlor game on Wall Street, at the Federal Reserve and inside think tanks and university economics departments in recent years."[11] It's a complicated question involving the value of the dollar, interest rates, and the degree to which investors around the world see the United States as a good place to stash money. Most economists believe prolonged and expanding trade deficits are signs of a troubled economy, but others say the trade issue isn't dire yet given the wealth of the United States overall. Harvard economist Robert Lawrence is in the latter group. "We are so rich as a country," he told the *Christian Science Monitor*. "We're borrowing, we're running down our assets, but we're very wealthy."[12]

---

[9] U.S. Census Bureau, Foreign Trade Statistics, Annual Trade Highlights, 2009: Imports, www.census.gov/foreign-trade/statistics/highlights/annual.html, accessed May 15, 2010.

[10] U.S. Census Bureau, Foreign Trade Statistics, Annual Trade Highlights, 2009: Country and Other Highlights, www.census.gov/foreign-trade/statistics/highlights/annual.html, accessed May 15, 2010.

[11] "Is the Trade Deficit Sustainable?" *Washington Times,* December 29, 2005.

[12] Mark Trumbull, "Giant Trade Gap; No End in Sight," *Christian Science Monitor,* March 10, 2006.

A SCARY FUTURE?

But that's not all, as they say in all those infomercials selling knives and folding colanders. The United States is also the proud holder of yet a third deficit—the savings deficit. Since average Americans aren't known for socking away a lot of money in the bank, and since we continue to buy all those alluring new products and rack up credit card debt, we're not helping out, either. In 2008, Americans on average saved about 2.7 percent of their disposable income. In the 1970s, we were generally saving 9 or 10 percent.[13] Add the savings deficit to the budget and trade deficits, and you begin to get an unsettling economic picture. Our government spends more than it takes in, so it needs to borrow. Our economy imports more than we export, so we need money to cover that gap. Since Americans don't save and invest all that much (unlike China, where people are savings whizzes), the country needs to borrow money from abroad to keep the whole thing glued together. So far, so good—but can we really keep this up?

Former U.S. comptroller general David Walker has talked forcefully and repeatedly about the risks the country is running with its free-spending, freewheeling financial ways. Walker often refers to four deficits—the budget deficit, the trade deficit, the savings deficit, and the leadership deficit. "We are in much worse financial condition than advertised," he says. "The future is scary."[14]

---

[13] Eugene P. Seskin and Shelly Smith, Improved Estimates of the National Income and Product Accounts, Results of the 2009 Comprehensive Revision, Bureau of Economic Analysis, September, 2009, www.bea.gov/scb/pdf/2009/09%20September/0909_nipa_text.pdf, accessed May 15, 2010.

[14] Rob Christensen, "Doomed by Debt?" *News & Observer* (Raleigh, N.C.), March 19, 2006.

LAYING DOWN THE BASELINE

Here you'll see three different projections about what's likely to happen to the federal budget over the next few years. And as you can see, they're all bad, but some are much worse than others.

How can the numbers be so different? Well, there is a reason.

There are plenty of organizations in the budget-projection business, but for lots of people in Washington, the rule has been "when in doubt, use the CBO figure." The Congressional Budget Office is an independent, nonpartisan agency without a cause to promote. They're all about the numbers. You'll see that the CBO has the most optimistic projection of the three. That's assuming, however, that all of the Bush tax cuts will expire on schedule in 2010, producing a surge of revenue. Yet both Democrats and Republicans have said they want most, if not all, of the Bush cuts extended. So if they're so smart and independent, why did they say it? Because by law, the CBO is required to assume that the law as written will stand, even if everyone knows that won't happen.

The second projection is from the White House Office of Management and Budget, which is also full of very sharp budget experts, just like the CBO. Unlike the CBO, they all work for one human being: the president. That doesn't mean the OMB numbers are wrong, but it does mean that it's committed to the president's agenda. The OMB is assuming that all of President

Projected Federal Budget Deficits/Surpluses
(in billions of dollars)

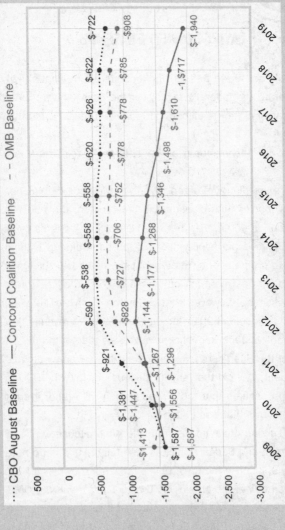

When it comes to projecting the federal budget deficit, it all depends on the assumptions you make. The Congressional Budget Office, the White House Office of Management and Budget, and the Concord Coalition end up with very different estimates about the deficit over the next decade. *Source: Congressional Budget Office, Office of Management and Budget, and the Concord Coalition*

Obama's proposals are enacted, including continuing most of the Bush tax cuts, and its estimates of economic growth and unemployment are different than the CBO's.

The third is from the Concord Coalition, a prominent non-partisan group advocating fiscal responsibility—in other words, "deficit hawks." In Concord's figures, it makes some guesses about political reality, including assuming that the tax cuts will be made permanent, that Congress will limit the unpopular alternative minimum tax, that government spending will exceed the rate of inflation, and that spending on Iraq and Afghanistan will come down. Its projections are a lot grimmer.

Our advice? Whenever you see people or organizations making estimates about the federal deficit going up or down, ask what their assumptions are. Do taxes go up or down? How much will the government spend? Does the economy grow, and if so, how fast? Unless you know these basics, any projection is pretty much meaningless.

Despite all their disagreements about projections in the short term, however, CBO, OMB, and Concord all use the same term when they look at the long-term outlook: "unsustainable." So whatever the budget looks like over the next few years, in the long run none of the projections look good.

CHAPTER 4

The Tax Tour
(or, Money Comes...)

Death and taxes and childbirth! There's never any convenient time for any of them!

—*Scarlett O'Hara in* Gone with the Wind,
Margaret Mitchell, 1936

In some respects, the budget issue is fairly simple. After
all, there are only a couple of ways to look at it. By this
point, we think you'll agree that ignoring the problem and
hoping it will go away is not an option. (If you're still set on
that strategy, there's got to be something worth watching on
ESPN.) Other than that, you're left with raising taxes or cutting spending or putting together a plan where you do some
of both.

There are experts who think the country can make a
good dent in the problem by cutting waste in government
and keeping the economy growing at a healthy pace (when
the economy is good, the government collects more taxes
because people are earning more money). We discuss these

strategies and what they could do for the budget picture in chapters 10 and 13. But almost no one we can find thinks there is enough sheer waste in government to offset the deficits the country is running now—not to mention the red ink we're facing with the big baby-boom expenses coming up. And while it would be great to have an economy that boomed all the time, it now seems pretty clear that no one really knows how to make that happen—especially not in the rapidly changing and confusing world economy we have now.

Sources of Federal Revenue, 2009

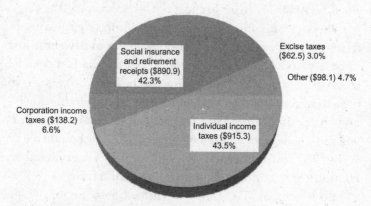

Personal income taxes—the money withheld from your paycheck and the forms you submit every April 15—are the largest single share of federal revenue, bringing in nearly 44 percent of the government's money in 2009. *Source: Budget of the United States Government, FY 2011*

TIME TO GRAB THE ASPIRIN

Given that, we have to think about raising taxes or cutting spending or finding some "not too cold, not too hot" combination platter. So now it's time to take a closer look at the options, starting with the tax tour. You might think of it as

"Taxes 101." It's designed to get you thinking about taxes in general. We return to the tax question and the big choices facing us in the next few years in chapter 13.

Some of you may want to grab the aspirin right now, because for a lot of Americans, the very thought of taxes produces a headache. Partly it's those three-inch-thick books on display in your local bookstore every January—the ones on how to prepare your own tax return. Or the fact that millions of not particularly rich people feel they have to buy software or hire someone to do their taxes for them (nearly everyone agrees the U.S. tax code is insanely complicated). And partly it's that fear of having to make a check out to the "U.S. Treasury" on April 15. Taxes are just not a cheery topic.

Plus, it's only fair to warn you right up front: we're entering territory where experts don't agree and where, just in case you've been asleep at the wheel for the last decade, there's a lot of political fistfighting. In the end, you're going to have to make your own decision based on conflicting "facts" and competing claims. But honestly, that's not a big deal. If you've signed up for cell phone service lately, or bought a flat-screen TV, you're used to that. We make decisions based on contradictory, confusing information all the time.

So here goes. The U.S. government gets money, which totaled $2.1 trillion in 2009, from four main sources.

INCOME TAXES

Almost 44 percent of the money the government spends comes from individual income taxes paid by you and me. For nearly everyone reading this, that includes people who are poorer than you and people who are richer (Mr. Gates, if you're reading this, you're the exception). Income tax rates have fallen fairly dramatically since World War II, when the top tax bracket was 94 percent, meaning that if you earned

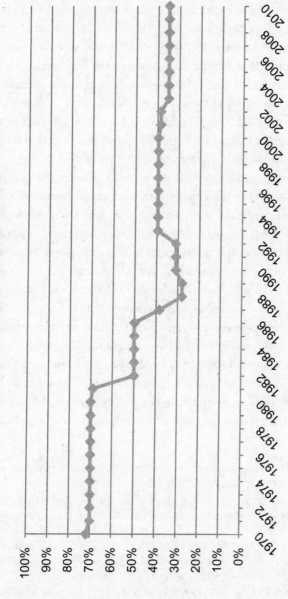

Top Federal Income Tax Rates, 1970–2010

The very top income tax rate—the so-called marginal rate—has fallen dramatically since the early 1970s. *Source: Tax Policy Center*

over $200,000 (which was a lot of money back then), the government took 94 percent of what you received over that.[1] Those rates dipped down over time, but by the time President Reagan came into office in 1981 the top rate was 70 percent. The Reagan tax cuts brought the top bracket down to 50 percent. In the 2000 presidential election, President Bush campaigned vigorously on his plan to cut taxes, and in 2001 and 2003, Congress passed big tax cuts bringing the top tax bracket down to 35 percent.[2] Some 18 million Americans earn so little that they don't even need to file a tax return, while another 34 million end up paying nothing at all.[3] With certain tax credits for children for example, some receive money back even though they are too poor to owe taxes. All told, some 47 percent of American households did not owe any income tax in 2009, mostly the poor, especially the poor who have children, and the elderly. Being poor or elderly, of course, doesn't take you off the hook for payroll taxes, state sales taxes, or local property tax. [4] For a variety of political reasons, nearly all of the tax changes enacted under President Bush are set to expire in 2010, so the battle over whether to keep them is already under way. As most liberals see it, the cuts are a major reason the country has had such big budget deficits the last few years. Most liberals don't want the tax cuts extended—at least those affect-

---

[1] This is what economists and accountants call a "marginal tax rate"— it's the tax rate you pay on the last dollar you earn.

[2] Tax Policy Center, Tax Facts, Historical Top Tax Rate, October 26, 2009, www.taxpolicycenter.org/taxfacts/displayafact.cfm?Docid=213, accessed April 24, 2010.

[3] Tax Policy Center, Tax Facts, Nonfilers and Filers With Modest Tax Liabilities, 2003, www.taxpolicycenter.org/taxfacts/displayafact.cfm?Docid=283, accessed April 24, 2010.

[4] Tax Policy Center, "Who Pays No Income Tax?", July 8, 2009, http://taxvox.taxpolicycenter.org/blog/_archives/2009/7/8/4243062.html.

ing higher-income Americans. As most conservatives see it, the tax cuts have helped the economy and let people keep more of their own money. For conservatives, too much government spending is what's causing the budget problems. You can read a lot more about what's at stake in the big tax battle ahead of us in chapter 13.

Payroll Taxes

A little over 40 percent of the money the government spends comes from Social Security and Medicare taxes, unemployment taxes, and retirement payments made by federal employees. Social Security and Medicare take nice little chunks out of your take-home pay—those dreaded FICA deductions on your pay stub, although Social Security taxes stop for people who earn over a certain amount ($106,800 in 2010). Because of this, Social Security taxes are often considered "regressive," since they tend to hit nearly everyone on the lower end of the income scale while letting the people who earn the big bucks off the hook at a certain point. One consolation is that your employer has to pay, too (the same amount as you), and, in theory at least, you'll get some personal benefit from these taxes down the road when you retire or need health care as an older person. The money from the payroll tax you and your employer pay is used to cover Social Security and Medicare for people who are elderly right now. These programs were designed that way—Social Security back in 1935 and Medicare in 1965—so they could help older people who needed it right away (chapters 6 through 9 have a lot more on this). Because the baby-boom generation is so large, and because most boomers are still working and paying these taxes, there is a surplus in the Social Security program. However, the government "borrows" from this surplus to cover other kinds of expenses, and so it won't have to raise income taxes (more about this in chapters 6 through 9 as well).

Corporate Taxes

About 7 percent of the money the government spends comes from taxes on corporations. Corporation taxes were particularly hard hit by the recession in 2008 and 2009, essentially cut in half. No profits means no taxes, and business wasn't doing well in those years. You're probably thinking ExxonMobil or Time Warner when we say *corporation*, but this category also includes little shops and restaurants, dry cleaners, hair salons, exterminators, and other small businesses owned by families and individuals. If you have any 401(k) money invested in stocks, you can count yourself as something of a business "owner," because whatever happens with corporate taxes affects you, too. Because so many of us picture "big business" when the subject of corporate taxes comes up, we often assume these taxes could easily be raised without much impact on us. After all, these corporate dudes work in awfully nice offices, wear really nice clothes (there's a reason why they're called "suits"), and you always seem to see them flying business or first class. There's no reason why big corporations shouldn't be asked to pay their share of the nation's tax burden, but there are complications to keep in mind. One is that we want corporations to hire people and give them good salaries and benefits, and the more taxes businesses pay the less money they have for their workers. We also want corporations to invest in technology and new products so we don't get eaten alive in the global marketplace by all these up-and-coming foreign economies. And finally, we want these companies to stay here, not to move to some other country where labor is cheap and the government is less ambitious. So when we're looking around for people to pay more taxes, the idea of socking it to business is a little more complicated than it initially might seem.

Alcohol, Tobacco, and Gas–the Excise Taxes

About 3 percent of the money the government spends comes from excise taxes, mainly on alcohol, tobacco, airline tickets, and gas. Three percent might seem skimpy given how steep these taxes are when you have to pay them. Actually, that little 3 percent was about $63 billion in 2009, a huge amount of money even though it's a small piece of the government's overall income. But there's another reason these taxes generate comparatively small amounts for the federal government even though they seem pretty hefty when you fill 'er up or buy a bottle of Johnnie Walker. Some of this money goes to state and local government. This varies by state, of course, and it's one of the reasons why smokers in New York and New Jersey think about stocking up on cigarettes if they visit Mississippi or Missouri.[5]

There are a few other smaller sources for the money the government spends, but we'll leave those for you to check out yourself if you're curious. We've listed several useful Web sites in the appendix.

HOW MUCH BLAME DOES WASHINGTON DESERVE?

This last point about the excise taxes on gas and cigarettes brings up another issue that sometimes gets lost in the hub-bub. The Feds are hardly the only tax collectors around. We pay property taxes to the states and towns where we live (it's included in the rent even if you don't own a home yourself). Most of us also pay state and local sales taxes. Many states have their own income tax. Some states tax new-car sales and real estate transactions. Some interesting calculations by Kevin Hassett, a senior fellow at the American Enterprise Institute, suggest that for those worried about the tax burden

---

[5] "State Excise Tax Rates on Cigarettes," Federation of Tax Administrators, available at www.taxadmin.org/fta/rate/cigarett.html.

on middle- and lower-income families, state and local taxes are the real culprit—not the federal income tax. "That's because the federal income tax, which is steeply progressive— the higher your income, the more you pay in taxes—gets all the media attention. But other taxes that are less visible, such as sales taxes, hit lower-income families with a heavy thud," Hassett writes.[6] So while it's convenient to blame "Washington" when we think about taxes, remember that it's not Washington alone.

But whether it's federal taxes or those collected by states and cities, views on whether to raise taxes to deal with budget problems often depend largely on whether we believe government programs and services are useful and helpful. Essentially, we ask ourselves whether what we're getting is worth paying for. In the next few chapters, we'll try to help you understand where the government spends money now, how much is "wasted," and whether some of what government does now could be done better and less expensively by someone else—maybe even you personally.

But before we close out our tax primer, there are a few other questions to think about. Just looking at the arithmetic, there's little question that raising taxes would help the country's budget's bottom line. If more money comes in, there's less of a hole. But before you leap, spend a moment or two considering these four questions. The experts are all over the map on these, so your own cogitating on these may not be so bad.

DO TAX CUTS PAY FOR THEMSELVES?

Some prominent leaders—actually, very prominent ones like President Bush and Vice President Cheney—point out

---

[6] Kevin Hassett, "Why We Pay without a Whimper," *Washington Post*, April 15, 2007.

that in fact tax cuts can bring money into the U.S. Treasury. In 2007, for example, former vice president Cheney said that lower taxes are "a powerful driver of investment, growth, and new jobs for America's workers. And that increased economic activity, in turn, generates revenue for the federal government."[7] The argument goes like this: When the economy grows, people and businesses make more money. When people and businesses make more money, they pay higher taxes. And when those higher taxes come in, they help cover any shortfall caused by cutting taxes in the first place. Those advancing this line of argument often point to what happened after the Bush administration passed tax cuts in 2001 and 2003: revenues to the U.S. Treasury increased. When the Bush administration issued its budget for 2008, it reported: "We have seen remarkable growth in Federal tax receipts. In 2004, tax receipts rose 5.5 percent. In 2005, tax receipts rose 14.5 percent, the largest one year growth in receipts since 1982. In 2006, tax receipts rose another 11.8 percent."[8] Some people and companies have made a lot more money.

But was it enough money to cover the cost of the tax cuts? Well, unfortunately, no. Not even conservative experts—those who generally want taxes to be low and tend to back President Bush's economic policies—think tax cuts can actually bring in enough extra money to pay for themselves. Economists' estimates vary depending on which taxes you're talking about and what kind of assumptions and economic projections their calculations make. It's not a

[7] Vice President Dick Cheney, speech to the Conservative Political Action Conference, Omni Shoreham Hotel, Washington, D.C., March 1, 2007.

[8] Budget of the United States, Fiscal Year 2008, Building a Strong Economy, www.gpoaccess.gov/usbudget/fy08/browse.html.

simple matter predicting exactly what will happen. But well-respected economists like N. Gregory Mankiw, who chaired President Bush's Council of Economic Advisers, and Douglas Holtz-Eakin, who worked in the Bush White House, for Congress, and in John McCain's presidential campaign both have said that tax cuts don't bring in quite that much money. Mankiw estimated that cuts in capital gains taxes (paid on profits from selling property or stocks) can generate revenue to cover about half their costs; Holtz-Eakin put the "replacement value" for cutting personal taxes up to 22 percent for the first five years and up to 32 percent in the following five.[9] The *Washington Post*'s Sebastian Mallaby, who covered this controversy in his column, concludes that the "free-lunch mantra is just plain wrong."[10]

Of course, the argument doesn't really stop there, and it shouldn't. Most knowledgeable experts agree that specific tax cuts don't generate sufficient revenue to pay for themselves. What's more, as we have seen, low taxes—and income tax rates are low by historic standards—can't *guarantee* a good economy. Real estate bubbles, banking woes, and plain old human greed can do in the economy even if tax rates are relatively low. However, there is an important debate about whether an economy with very low taxes works better over the long term than an economy with higher ones. So that brings us to our next question.

---

[9] Douglas Holtz-Eakin, Congressional Budget Office, "Analyzing the Economic and Budgetary Effects of a 10 Percent Cut in Income Tax Rates," December 1, 2005, and Gregory Mankiw's analysis at http://economics.harvard.edu/faculty/mankiw/files/dynamicscoring_05-1212.pdf.

[10] Sebastian Mallaby, "The Return of Voodoo Economics: Republicans Ignore Their Experts on the Cost of Tax Cuts," *Washington Post,* May 15, 2006, A17. See also editorial, "A Heckuva Claim; Mr. Bush Is Oblivious to the Consequences of His Tax Cuts," *Washington Post,* January 7, 2007.

WILL RAISING TAXES HARM THE ECONOMY?

It would be nice to give you a simple yes-no answer on this one, but we couldn't find it. Most economists are worried about the country's budget problems, especially the gargantuan financial hole we face when the boomers start to retire and need health care in big numbers. And there's no doubt that at some point raising taxes too much can harm the economy. This is because money that could be invested (which is good for the economy) or spent on products and services (also good for the economy) goes instead to the government.

Raising too many taxes too quickly can upset the stock market and lead investors to look for opportunities in other countries instead of here. It can sap the enthusiasm of entrepreneurs, inventors, and others who take risks and put their money into new economic ventures. Offering these risk-taking folk plenty of incentive to do their thing has given the United States a pretty good economic run for a very long time now, so you do have to be careful about killing the goose that lays the golden egg. Raising taxes on very specific parts of the economy can also pack an unexpected wallop. See "Lost at Sea: A Short History of Taxing Yachts," on page 81, to find out what went wrong when Congress decided that taxing very big, expensive boats would affect only the very rich. Nearly all economists have strong reservations about raising taxes when an economy is in a depression or deep recession.

On the other side of it, federal income taxes were significantly higher in the 1950s and 1960s and the U.S. economy had plenty of very good years back then. Robert Rubin, one of President Clinton's economic advisers (and secretary of the treasury from 1998 through 1999) argued that raising taxes to reduce the deficit could help the economy grow. After his recommended policies took hold ("Rubinomics" it was called),

Tax Burden in Selected Countries (by percent of income)

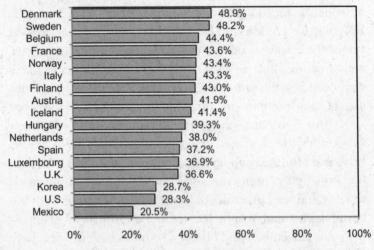

The total tax burden in the United States (including state and local taxes) is considerably lower than in most European countries. *Source: Organization for Economic Cooperation and Development*

the economy perked up very nicely for a number of years.[11] Some economists and policy makers point out that when the government uses tax money to invest in education, research, highways, air traffic control, and other services, this can help the economy. There's also the argument that the government itself buys goods and services, which is also good for the economy. Just ask anyone who lives near a military base.

Others like economist and *New York Times* columnist

---

[11] Robert Rubin was widely admired for his economic acumen until the great economic meltdown of 2008 when his judgments about how sound Wall Street practices were turned out to be just plain wrong. But Rubin is in impressive company. In being absolutely wrong here, he can stand shoulder to shoulder with Alan Greenspan, key players in both the Bush and Clinton administrations, nearly all the big boys in real estate and banking (forgive us, but most of them were guys).

Paul Krugman question whether strong economic growth, spurred by low taxes, really means anything if the benefits aren't shared broadly. An ardent critic of the Bush tax cuts, Krugman acknowledges that the economy grew after the tax cuts were passed, but says that the main result has been a growing gap between the very wealthy and other Americans. "Where did all the economic growth go?" Krugman asks. "It went to a relative handful of people at the top."[12]

Some experts believe that Europe—where taxes are quite a bit higher than here—is at or near the point where high taxes eat away at and weaken the economy, and that high unemployment rates there show this; others point to the Europeans' longer vacations, shorter workweeks, and tough job protections as the factors that hold back growth. And some people say it's both. Of course, you can find plenty of Europeans who pay the higher taxes, get more government services in return, and are happy to tell you how much better their system is than ours—even if their economies are not growing as rapidly as ours and their unemployment rates are generally higher.

Still, get three economists in a room, and you'll probably have four opinions on what's better for the United States—raising taxes to help get the budget in line or keeping taxes low and cutting spending. You can't even find agreement within the same family of politicians. The first President Bush raised taxes to solve budget problems in the early 1990s, and just a few years later the economy was booming. The second President Bush cut taxes substantially, and whether the economy got better or worse seems to depend on which statistic you choose and whom you talk to. One unfortunate fact is that we're just in a different place right

---

[12] Paul Krugman, "The Great Wealth Transfer," *Rolling Stone*, November 30, 2006.

now. Deficits have gotten so large, and the debt has gotten so high, that most experts believe that at some point at least some tax increases are virtually a given.

WILL IT BE FAIR?

Another big wrinkle in the tax issue is whether, if we raise taxes, we can do it in ways that are fair. We all bring our own values to the table on this one. Conservatives typically believe that individuals should be able to keep most of what they earn, and that government's call on our tax dollars should be very, very limited. They don't think government does that many things all that well; they say individuals make better decisions about where money should go. Liberals typically believe that government has done many good things with taxes (Social Security is a favorite example), and that wealthier Americans should help pay for services that help and protect the poor and the middle class. The wealthy, they argue, have benefited from our society, and there's nothing wrong with asking them to pay for things like health care, child care, and college loans—things that give other people a chance. Besides, most liberals say, the wealthy will barely even miss it.

It's just two different points of view. Still, the situation gets confusing when advocates for both sides start throwing in the dueling statistics. Consider the argument over the income tax cuts ushered in by President Bush. As most conservatives tell it, these tax cuts benefited nearly all Americans. As most liberals tell it, most of the cuts benefitted the wealthy. Actually, both of these statements are true. How does it work? We'll use an imaginary illustration because examples from the real-life U.S. tax code with all its brackets and deductions are nearly incomprehensible.

Suppose the government cuts taxes by 10 percent. Someone who owes a million dollars in taxes saves $100,000, enough for a couple of Mercedes, or, if you prefer, Hummers (which could soon become collectors' items). But someone who owes $1,000 saves $100—nice to have, certainly, but more in the Razor Scooter price range. So both the millionaire and the typical Joe benefited. But most of the tax cut went to the millionaire. Is it fair—allowing people to keep more of their own money? They made it, after all. Or is it just a windfall for the rich—one that should be ended so we can get the budget back on track?

There's an old Washington saying (attributed to the late Louisiana Senator Russell Long) that boils tax policy down to three short phrases: "Don't tax you, don't tax me, tax that fellow behind the tree." Hardly anyone wants to pay taxes, and most of us think there's someone else somewhere who should be paying more, so we don't have to pay as much. In the end, it's probably impossible to create a tax system that meets everyone's vision of fairness.

DOES IT HAVE TO BE SO HARD?

And the fourth big complication is the complication itself. If you've ever done your own taxes, you don't need to be told that the federal tax code is fiendishly dense and convoluted. A quick trip to the post office or the IRS Web site for tax forms will confirm that. There's also reason to believe it's getting worse, not better. Federal tax rules and regulations have increased from 40,500 pages in 1995 to more than 67,000 pages in 2007[13]—*War and Peace* is a pamphlet by

---

[13] Cato Institute, "The Simple (Tax) Life," April 17, 2006, available at www.cato.org/pub_display.php?pub_id=6345 and *USA TODAY*, "Our Opinions: 67,204-Page Code Confounds Taxpayers, yet Congress Sits By," April 4, 2007, www.usatoday.com/news/opinion/2007-04-03-edit_N.htm.

comparison. By one analysis, businesses, nonprofits, and individuals spent 6 billion hours calculating their taxes and otherwise complying with federal tax rules, at a total cost of $265.1 billion.[14]

So does anyone have any good ideas for making things simpler? Sure, but it's surprising how complicated simplicity can be. The problem is that if you want to keep the basic structure of the progressive income tax we have now (rather than move to a national sales tax or a flat tax, which would be simpler plans, whatever you might think of them), the job's not as easy as it sounds. A progressive income tax system—where higher-income people pay a higher tax rate—is by its very nature more complicated. After all, you have to keep track of what people are earning, a big challenge in and of itself. That's what led to our existing system, which withholds taxes from your paycheck before you even see it, and in which banks and investment firms have to report your interest and dividends directly to the IRS.

Another hurdle is that most exemptions and exceptions in the tax code—the features that make it so intricate and complex—are there to help and please potential voters. You're probably already grousing about big business and big oil, and if you are, you're not alone. But in all likelihood, you're a big beneficiary, too. Some of the features that make current tax forms so complicated are also very popular and aimed at average people: deductions for home mortgage interest and charitable contributions, getting a tax break to save for college or retirement, or to pay for child care.

And that brings up a related issue. Although the main purpose of the tax system is to raise revenue for the govern-

---

[14] Tax Foundation, "The Rising Cost of Complying with the Federal Income Tax," January 10, 2006, available at www.taxfoundation.org/publications/show/1281.html.

ment, we also use it as a tool for social policy—to encourage people to do good things and discourage others. If we want businesses and individuals to buy more fuel-efficient vehicles and energy-efficient appliances, we give them tax breaks for doing it. If we want people to save more for college or retirement, we add tax breaks for that, too. You're able to deduct your mortgage interest because, as a society, we've decided it's better for everyone if people own their own homes rather than rent. The tax code would be simpler if we didn't do this, but since getting out of paying some tax is such a good motivator, our society has found this strategy very useful. If we give up the idea of using taxes for social change, just how *are* we going to do these things?

Nearly everyone—except maybe tax lawyers and accountants—likes the *idea* of simplifying taxes, and politicians often say that this is what they, too, want. Scott McClellan, President Bush's press secretary between 2003 and 2005, once claimed that the president's effort to repeal the estate tax was making the tax code simpler. The president "is open to ideas that move us in the direction of a simpler and fairer tax code," McClellan said. "And one thing that—one real important step we took to make the tax code simpler was to eliminate the death tax. We need to make that permanent. That is a great way to simplify the tax code; you eliminate 90 pages in the tax code right there."[15] Of course, that still leaves more than 66,000 pages of tax regulations, instructions, and clarifications. And since most Americans never have to worry about the estate tax anyway, this may not be quite what most are hoping for.

In chapter 14, we describe the short, bleak life of the President's Advisory Panel on Federal Tax Reform, a bipar-

---

[15] "Press Gaggle by Scott McClellan, Aboard Air Force One En Route to Albuquerque, New Mexico," August 11, 2004, available at www.white house.gov/news/releases/2004/08/20040811-4.html.

tisan commission put together by President Bush to look at how to simplify taxes. The panel's ideas never got much traction, but you might want to see what the panel suggested to ease what they call the "headache of burdensome record-keeping, lengthy instructions, and complicated schedules, worksheets, and forms—often requiring multiple computations that are neither logical nor intuitive." You can find it at http://govinfo.library.unt.edu/taxreformpanel/.

CLOUDY AND IMPERFECT

So here's our question for you. Given that the current system is cloudy and far from perfect, what should we do? If you look only at the arithmetic, it's certainly possible to solve the country's budget problems without raising taxes at all, but almost no one thinks that will happen. It's just not possible politically. It would mean making deep cuts in government programs that affect real people's lives and jobs. As you'll read in chapter 5, solving the problem just by cutting spending will mean slashing and even eliminating many programs that have the support of millions of Americans. You'd probably even have to cut some things you like yourself. (You can try your hand at this in our "OK, If You're So Smart . . ." chapter starting on page 287). On the other hand, if and when we decide to raise taxes, we'll need to be very careful and thoughtful about how to do it.

Lost at Sea: A Short History of Taxing Yachts

It seemed like such a good idea at the time. It's 1990, and the federal government is running in the red. President Bush (the first one) and Congress need to raise money. Better to tax the wealthy than the millions of voters in the middle class. Rich people buy yachts. Lo and behold. Congress passes a 10 percent luxury tax on yachts selling for more than $100,000. The luxury tax also applied to furs, jewelry, and watches costing over $10,000, planes costing over $250,000, and automobiles costing over $30,000. Just a reminder— back in the early 1990s, a $30,000 car was still pretty swish.

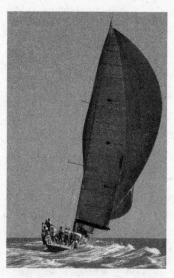

Putting a special tax on yachts seemed like a good idea until yacht builders in New England began to go out of business. *Credit: IStockphoto.com*

But while the plan sounded good to a lot of people in Washington and elsewhere, it went badly wrong. The yacht tax was intended to help the federal government out of a funding crunch, but it ended up devastating the boatbuilding industry. Socked by the double whammy of a recession and a hefty tax on their product, boatbuilders saw sales of bigger yachts drop by 70 percent.[16]

---

[16] Shepard W. McKenney, "Taxing Jobs Away," *Washington Post*, November 24, 1992. McKenny was chairman of a yacht-building company in Southwest Harbor, Maine.

Several prestige yacht manufacturers even filed for bankruptcy during the period.[17]

For conservative columnist George Will, the upshot was obvious: "People bought yachts overseas. Who would have thought it?" he wrote in one of his columns.[18] But even those not ideologically opposed to taxes on wealthy Americans had to admit that this one was backfiring.

One boatbuilder chronicled the cascading impact: "The truth is that while yachts are a luxury for the rich, they are a necessity for American yacht workers. Yachts are in fact great redistributors of wealth. A typical $1 million yacht requires 12,000 labor hours (eight worker years) to build, not counting all the manufactured parts supplied by other domestic industries that provide their own employment, or the considerable labor required to maintain such a yacht. When the buyer pays for the yacht, the money goes to the workers."[19] Not too long after, Republican president Bush joined Democratic Senate majority leader George Mitchell in calling for repeal. In 1993, Congress complied.

This little tale of unintended consequences demonstrates the pitfalls of jumping on easy answers to solve the country's budget problems. It also illustrates some of the subtleties lawmakers (and voters) need to keep in mind when considering raising taxes. Taxes on "luxuries" such as yachts and furs affect more than the buyers. Taxes on "sins" like buying alcohol and cigarettes have advantages of reducing their use (good for people's health), but they, too, affect workers and shareholders in the companies that produce them (not so good for tobacco-raising North Carolina, for example). The effect of raising income taxes is more spread out, but this is definitely not a popular idea. What's more, most economists point out that pushing income taxes up

---

[17] Nick Ravo, "Big Boats Take It on the Chin," *New York Times*, April 14, 1991.

[18] George Will, "Tax Breaks for the Yachting Class," *Washington Post*, October 28, 1999.

[19] McKenney, "Taxing Jobs Away."

too high leaves people with less to spend on products and services, which also jeopardizes the economy. Broad-based (meaning nearly everyone pays them) "consumption" taxes (essentially sales taxes) are the least likely to harm the economy, according to many economists, but sales taxes are some of the most unpopular taxes of all.

Then, of course, if you think you can tackle the country's budget problems without raising taxes at all—well, let's just say that there's a lot of slashing to be done. Think you can cut the fat without hitting any bone? You can have at it in chapter 15, but it's just so much easier said than done.

THE AWOLS (OR, SOME IMPORTANT THINGS WE LEFT OUT OF THIS CHAPTER)

You know those "Great Moments in Music" recordings that serve up snatches of Beethoven and Brahms (rumor has it that there's a "Great Square Inches of Art" parody showing Mona Lisa's smile, but no Mona Lisa). Our Taxes 101 intro left out some important stuff, too. Now that we've covered the basics, there are some other considerations you need to think about. We take up some of these later, but you may want to rev up your search engines and delve into these in more detail yourself.

The alternative minimum tax. This is the tax nearly everyone wants to cut—liberals, conservatives, and even a fair number

★★★★★★★★★★★★★★★★★★★★★★★★★★★★★★★★★★

of budget hawks—and there are some pretty good reasons to change it. It's a weird, complicated hyperspace of the tax system originally aimed at the wealthy. The problem is it's now beginning to affect lots of people who are a long way from rich. But fixing the AMT, as it is affectionately called, will mean a big, big loss to the Treasury. We cover the issue in chapter 13.

The estate tax. There's a lot of agreement that Congress should fix the AMT so it only applies to people who are really wealthy, but bring up the estate tax, and you've got a fight on your hands. In 2001, Congress passed legislation to gradually reduce the estate tax over a decade and repeal it entirely in 2010. However, if the legislation isn't renewed—and as we take this book to press, Congress hasn't acted yet—the tax will go back up to what it was in 2000. We discuss the estate tax in chapter 13, but you can also get a good sense of the pros and cons by visiting www.clubforgrowth.org, an organization that urges repeal, and www.faireconomy.org, an organization that opposes repeal.

More on fairness and simplification. We just scratched the surface on the fairness and simplification issues here. There's talk, for example, of replacing the income tax with a national sales tax (check out www.FairTax.org for some ideas on this) or a value-added tax (see chapter 9). Former Republican presidential candidate Steve Forbes has long been an advocate of a "flat tax," and he's written about his ideas extensively (www.pbs.org/newshour/bb/congress/forbes_flat_tax.html). Oregon senator Ron Wyden also has a proposal that would reduce the tax code to three tax brackets and allow just a few deductions (yes, the home mortgage interest deduction is one of them).[20] You can visit his Web site (www.wyden.senate.gov) to find out more about his approach.

---

[20] Floyd Norris, "Tax Plans of Candidates Are a Mystery," *New York Times,* June 8, 2007.

Showdown at Tax Gap

Every year, lots of Americans don't pay the government everything they owe in taxes. (No, we didn't mean you. And don't look at us, either.) The IRS estimates the "tax gap," the difference between what people should pay and what they actually pay, at between $312 billion and $353 billion. Between late payments and the IRS actually chasing down tax cheats, the agency says it manages to recover about $55 billion of that, leaving at least $250 billion still out there.[21]

You'll hear a lot about this in the coming years. By Washington standards, this is a "fun fact," because it opens the possibility that the government could go a long way toward closing its annual deficit just by chasing down what's already owed. Which would also mean there's no need for a tax increase or program cuts.

So where is this money, anyway? And why doesn't the government get it already?

One key thing to understand about the U.S. tax system is that it runs on "voluntary compliance," the idea that citizens pay their taxes out of their own free will rather than because they're afraid of the IRS. (No, really. Stop laughing.) Think about it. When you figure out your Form 1040 every year, the government is pretty much relying on you to put down honest numbers. And to look at the tax gap another way, Americans pay about 84 percent of the taxes they owe—a pretty high percentage.

Of course, there are a lot of reasons to fill out that tax return accurately. One is that with many common sources of income, the government has adopted Ronald Reagan's old maxim of "trust, but verify." If you get paid a regular salary or wages, the government withholds the taxes before you even see your check and then re-

---

[21] "Understanding the Tax Gap," Internal Revenue Service fact sheet, March 2005 (www.irs.gov/newsroom/article/0,,id=137246,00.html).

quires your employer to report the totals (the near-universal Form W-2). More recently, the government started requiring banks and investment firms to report how much you're earning in interest and dividends. IRS studies show there isn't much cheating in these "third-party reporting" areas, because there are too many people looking over your shoulder.

So where does the gap come from? Underreporting the income that nobody's watching (mostly income from partnerships or other small-business activity) accounts for 80 percent of the gap, according to the IRS.[22] In those cases, the IRS has one other tool to chase down the money: the dreaded tax audit.

The problem is that there are fewer audits than there used to be. And, many experts argue, the main reason for that is that Congress told the IRS to be nicer to people. (Again, stop laughing). In the early 1990s, there were congressional hearings into IRS horror stories—property and businesses confiscated for incorrect back-tax claims, people facing years in court to clear up book-keeping errors, even people driven to suicide. In 1996, Congress passed the Taxpayer Bill of Rights, leading to a major push to help taxpayers avoid mistakes in the first place instead of chasing them down afterward. As a result, audit rates plummeted. In 1984, 1.19 percent of individual returns went through a "face-to-face" audit with an IRS examiner; by 2004, that number dropped to just 0.15 percent. The IRS has been increasing enforcement efforts, but in 2009 only about 1.03 percent of the 138.9 million individual tax filings went through any kind of examination (either by correspondence or in person).

And most definitions of the tax gap don't even cover big cor-

---

[22] "New IRS Study Provides Preliminary Tax Gap Estimate," Internal Revenue Service, March 29, 2005 (www.irs.gov/newsroom/article/0,,id=137247,00.html), and Internal Revenue Service, Fiscal Year 2009 Enforcement Results, Dec. 22, 2009, www.irs.gov/pub/irs-drop/fy_2009_enforcement_results.pdf.

porations, which have huge accounting staffs and legal teams devoted to paying the least possible amount of taxes, within the law. That makes auditing big corporations a time-consuming business, and the IRS seems to be pulling back from it.[23] Despite the fact that Congress has given the IRS more money to pursue audits, and that individual audits are increasing, audits of corporations with more than $250 million in assets have actually declined by one-third since 2005, according to an independent study. The IRS also says more Americans are using abusive off-shore tax shelters to hide their income, but those shelters are also difficult to chase down.

So closing the tax gap isn't exactly found money. It's a lot of hard work and it leads to a fundamental question: How in-your-face do we want the IRS to be? We could audit more people, but who gets audited, like who pays taxes in the first place, has all kinds of political ramifications. We could also expand those third-party reporting requirements to cover more small businesses, but that's going to be a burden to mom-and-pop operations.

Everyone wants to close the tax gap. Everyone thinks cheaters should have to fork over the money they owe. But would you be as enthusiastic about closing the gap if it meant your own chances of being audited went up? (Remember, most audits occur because the IRS suspects something's wrong, but some are triggered by honest mistakes or just as random spot checks.) So, as we said up top, you can talk tax gap all you want, but closing it is another story entirely. Or as the Rolling Stones so nicely put it, "You can't always get what you want."

---

[23] Transactional Records Access Clearinghouse, "IRS Turns Away From Auditing Big Business," April 12, 2010, http://trac.syr.edu/whatsnew/emall.100412.html.

CHAPTER 5

... And Money Goes

No government ever voluntarily reduces itself in size. Government programs, once launched, never disappear. Actually, a government bureau is the nearest thing to eternal life we'll ever see on this earth!

—*President Ronald Reagan, TV address, October 27, 1964*

The federal government is vast. Mind-bogglingly vast. With 2.7 million civilian employees and another 1.4 million active-duty military personnel, it dwarfs anything in the private sector.

By contrast, Walmart, the world's largest private employer, has about 1.8 million employees. If you consider the fact that Walmart has yet to field an armored division, they're not too far behind. (But if you think they're tough on competitors now, consider what they could do with cruise missiles.) Yet Walmart is involved in only one business: retail stores. The federal government has millions of tasks it has to perform every day, in a wide range of fields. And the roster isn't limited to just what federal employees do directly. Even more jobs are handled by federal contractors, or conducted by state or local

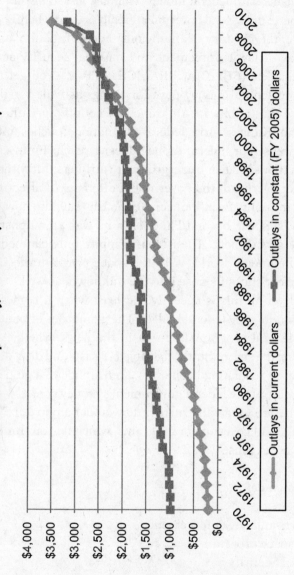

U.S. Government Spending, 1970–2010 (in billions of dollars)

— Outlays in current dollars

— Outlays in constant (FY 2005) dollars

If you think the federal government is spending more than it used to, you're right, even when using "constant dollars" to adjust for inflation. *Source: Budget of the United States Government, FY 2011*

governments with federal money. Walmart just *seems* like it's everywhere; the federal government really *is* everywhere.

Sure, the military is an obvious federal function, as is the array of law-enforcement and national security acronym agencies: (FBI, CIA, DEA, ICE, ATF . . . you get the idea). But federal money pays for things as wide-ranging as research stations in Antarctica to county agricultural agents in Kansas. And federal regulation touches most of the areas that federal money doesn't reach. From coal mines a thousand feet underground to airliners thirty thousand feet overhead, the government attempts to affect the lives of millions. Even Pioneer 10, the tiny satellite now off in the vast space beyond Pluto, is in its way an outpost of the U.S. government. The Roman Empire only claimed to affect the known world. With the space program the U.S. government sticks its nose into the unknown, as well.

And yet all this is deceptive, at least when it comes to understanding the federal budget. The glamorous or controversial federal programs that get in the news, whether it's launching the space shuttle, fighting terrorists and drug dealers, or even regulating businesses, aren't much of a guide to where most of the federal government's money goes.

So before we go any further, how about a pop quiz? Of all the federal government programs, which do you think is the largest expense:

★ National defense
★ Foreign aid
★ Courts and law enforcement
★ The space program
★ Social Security

Yes, it's a trick question (you probably figured that out already). And to really understand the answer, a little tour is in order, a trip through the federal budget and how much is spent on what. If we're going to start cutting and rear-ranging, we all need to know where the money is. You probably opened this book with definite ideas about what federal programs could get chucked. You may close the book with those exact same ideas, and that's fine. But you have to know what those cuts will actually do for the budget.

Because for all its complexity, for all its reach, the fact remains that if you gauge it by the federal budget, the main function of the world's greatest superpower is . . .

. . . writing checks to retired people.

Yeah, we know. Surprised us, too. You'd better sit down and have a look at this pie.

Federal Spending, 2009 (in billions of dollars)

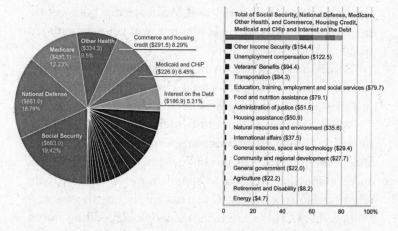

The U.S. government spent more than $3.5 trillion in 2009, and the biggest individual slices were Social Security, defense, and Medicare. *Source: Budget of the United States Government, FY 2010*

Not what you thought, was it? The fact is that the federal government spends about 62 percent of its money on just five things: Social Security, national defense, Medicare, Medicaid, and interest on the money we've already borrowed, thanks to previous deficits. The rest of the budget, from veterans' hospitals to welfare, from small-business loans to office chairs, takes up less than 40 percent.

It gets better (or worse, depending on your point of view). Not all federal government programs are created equal. Some of them are "discretionary," which basically means that what Congress giveth, Congress can also take away. A budget item may be truly vital, like national defense or law enforcement, and still be discretionary. Congress can spend as much or little as it thinks fit.

Other programs are "entitlements," services set up so that as long as you qualify, the government has to pay you the money. Social Security and Medicare are both entitlements. So long as you're old enough, you get payments, no matter what.

Sometimes people say you can't cut entitlements. That's not really true. Congress could change the eligibility requirements or trim the payments if it wanted to.

What is true about entitlements is that they're on autopilot. Unlike other programs, Congress doesn't have to review them as part of the budget process every year and make a specific decision to spend more or less on them. What is also true is that Congress rarely has the nerve to change them. There are a lot of people depending on entitlements, and nobody wants to hurt old people, or even suggest a change that might remotely look like they want to hurt old people. Besides, since the entitlements are on autopilot, Congress doesn't *need* to make any decisions. The spending formulas are set, the taxes are collected, the payments are made. So why go looking for trouble?

And, as you've probably already noticed, of the "big five" budget items, two of them are entitlements. Another slice of the pie, interest on the national debt, isn't an entitlement but is also off-limits. If the government doesn't pay the banks, they won't lend the government any more money.

This pie looks a lot different than it did even a couple of years ago, and that's largely because of the bailouts and stimulus spending. Because of the money that Washington has been attempting to pump into the economy to stem the "Great Recession," a couple of budget slices that were pretty negligible in previous years have suddenly become significant parts of the budget. That isn't expected to last. Some of these slices may shrink back to their previous size once the recession (and the stimulus) goes away. What we can be sure of is that the "big five" items will remain the big five for the foreseeable future, because their spending is on auto-pilot, and projected to keep climbing as the baby boomers age and health care costs continue to climb.

Let's go through the major sections of the budget, slice by slice, and see where we stand.[1]

Social Security: 19.4 percent of the budget, $683 billion

Nearly 59 million Americans were getting Social Security benefits in 2010. And working Americans who aren't getting Social Security now are paying taxes to support those who are.

That's a key fact to understand about Social Security. It's set up as a "pay-as-you-go" program. People in the work-

---

[1] These are all 2009 figures, the most recent available when this book went to press. If you want to check on what happened in 2010 or go into these expenditures in more detail, all the numbers are at www.gpo.gov/usbudget.

Social Security and Medicare Take a Larger Share

1970		2009
$159.1	Other federal spending	$2,404.6
$30.3	Social Security	$683.0
$6.2	Medicare	$430.1

Note: Federal outlays totaled $195.6 billion in 1970.

Note: Federal outlays totaled $3.5 trillion in 2009.

This gives you a real sense of what's going on—Social Security and Medicare are taking up a much larger share of the federal budget than they did a generation ago, and it's only going to continue. *Source: Budget of the United States Government, FY 2011*

force now pay taxes to cover the check your grandma gets every month. And the money Grandma paid in? That went to pay for people who were retired while she was working. Social Security isn't a savings or investment program. There's no account with your name on it where your Social Security taxes are actually set aside. You do, of course, get a "statement" tallying up how much you've paid into the system, but almost all the money has already been used to pay benefits for older people.

But what about this Social Security trust fund politicians talk about? For a number of years Social Security has run a surplus—the taxes we all pay have been in more than enough to cover all the people currently getting checks, and there's some money left over. So the government is supposed to bank that extra money in a trust fund. Ideally, that fund is a hedge against the long-term problem facing Social Security, which is that once the baby boomers start retiring there will be a lot more people drawing checks than paying in taxes. At some point, however, the trust fund will run dry (currently projected to occur in 2037). Lots of people think Social Security will be bankrupt at this point, but that isn't really accurate. The system will still operate, but there will only be enough money coming in to pay for about 75 percent of the benefits needed. Which is not, technically speaking, bankruptcy, but it isn't terribly comforting, either. Just think what would happen if all the older people on Social Security now saw their benefits drop by 25 percent.

There's only one problem with the Social Security trust fund. It mainly exists on paper. Rather than let the surplus Social Security money sit in the bank, the government has been borrowing it for day-to-day operations. The government promises to pay the fund back, and there's no reason to doubt it, given how unpopular it would be to fail to pay benefits. But that still means the government will have to come up with the money at some point.

National Defense: 18.8 percent of the budget, $661 billion

This pretty much means what you'd think it means: the Pentagon and the nation's far-flung national security apparatus, including the intelligence agencies and nuclear weapons programs. It also means the wars in Iraq and Afghanistan, although you won't find a line item marked "Iraq" in there. The war money is spread out among many different accounts, so it's hard to tell how it's actually being spent. The CBO says the U.S. military spent about $146 billion on the wars in 2009, down from $180 billion in 2008 during the "surge" (not counting foreign aid or diplomatic operations). Put another way, the Defense Department says the two wars cost about $11 billion a month.

Big as this slice is, it's been bigger. Back in the 1950s, when the federal government had relatively few social programs and the Cold War was at its height, the military regularly accounted for 60 percent or more of total spending. Even in the 1980s, the defense budget was a quarter or more of the total federal budget. And in the 1990s, when the United States cut back on military spending after the fall of the Soviet Union (sometimes called the "peace dividend"), the defense budget was as little as 16 percent of spending.

Even so, there are two things worth keeping in mind about the defense budget. One is that we have the most powerful military force in the world by far, and yet the armed forces are still overstretched. Numerous experts, in and out of government, worry that we've been asking too many soldiers to do too many tours in Iraq and Afghanistan. That raises critical questions about whether we're spending our money in the right way: are we buying too many ships and high-tech fighter planes, rather than spending on the special forces, intelligence, and infantry we need to fight insurgents in places like Afghanistan?

The second point is that the defense budget is the largest part of federal spending that *isn't* on autopilot. Military spending isn't driven by formulas or demographics in the same way as Social Security or Medicare. Fundamentally, the decisions about the defense budget are about deciding who it is you're going to have to defend against, and how far our military has to reach to do it. Some critics argue that the "military-industrial complex," the web of military officials, politicians, and contractors in involved in developing weapons, keep us maintaining a much larger military than we need. Perhaps so, but that did not keep us from reducing military spending after the Cold War. In this end, this is still about how much military we need to be secure in the world. If we screw up on assessing the threats against us, we'll screw up this budget as well.

Medicare: 12.2 percent of the budget, $430 billion

Medicare is the government's health insurance program for the elderly. Like Social Security, it's an entitlement. If you're over the age of sixty-five, you can get it, and almost everyone does—more than 45 million Americans. Essentially, Medicare has all of the challenges of Social Security, plus some twists of its own.

Medicare has multiple "parts." Part A, financed by a payroll tax paid equally by employees and their employers, is a hospital insurance program that covers most inpatient hospital costs. Older Americans can elect to enroll in Part B supplementary insurance, which covers physician and outpatient services. Recipients pay premiums for this, and the rest comes from the government. Medicare spending that isn't covered by payroll taxes and premiums comes directly from the federal government, up to 45 percent of the total program bill. There's also the newer Medicare Part D, passed in 2003, which helps older Americans buy prescription drugs.[2]

Medicare has two unique problems of its own. One is health care costs. Just as all other health insurance is becoming more expensive, so is Medicare. Scientists keep finding new treatments for older people, who are living longer and longer, which is wonderful—and expensive. And it would be hard to find someone on the political left or the political right who doesn't think that there is some significant amount of waste and duplication in the health care system (they, of course, have very different explanations and cures for it, but more about that in chapter 9). The other is that Medicare's trust fund is being depleted even faster than

---

[2] Wondering where Part C is? Yes, there is one. It's the Medicare Advantage plan, in which seniors can get all their services from a single HMO/PPO.

Social Security. The health care plan passed by Congress in 2010 made a number of cuts and changes in Medicare that are expected to extend the life of the trust fund by 12 years, but that still leaves Medicare's fund running out in 2029.

Health: 9.5 percent of the budget, $334.3 billion

There didn't used to be much going on in this category, and most of it was in the area of public health services, research and disease prevention: organizations like the Surgeon General and the Public Health Service, the Centers for Disease Control and Prevention in Atlanta, the National Institutes of Health. That changed big-time in 2009, jumping up from $280 billion in 2008, partly because of the recession, and partly because of the run-up to the fight over health care reform. For one thing, the federal government gave nearly $34 billion to the states to keep governors from cutting back on Medicaid programs for the poor, thanks to the government's occasional strange accounting that money gets counted here instead of under Medicaid itself. The Obama administration also put significant amounts of money into what it called a "down payment on health care reform." That mostly meant initiatives that the administration hopes will pay off in lower health care costs down the road, such as information technology to enable patient records to be better managed and research into "best practices" for improving the quality of care.[3]

Commerce and housing credit, 8.3 percent of the budget, $291 billion

This is the other category that used to be hardly worth mentioning, only $27.8 billion in 2008, and even smaller in 2007,

---

[3] Stimulus.org, "Health Care Spending," Committee for a Responsible Federal Budget, http://stimulus.org/financialresponse/health-care-spending, accessed April 30, 2010.

at only $487 million. Yes, million, not billion. It's a grab-bag category with a lot of functions, some of which (like the Postal Service) are actually supposed to pay for themselves. And in the world of government accounting, this also includes some tax credits, which count as spending (since a tax credit represents money going out of the government, not coming in).

But the reason this became an enormous slice of the pie is because a lot of the stimulus and bailout spending is happening here. The Troubled Asset Relief Program lives in this category, as do the bailouts to automakers like General Motors and Chrysler and the government-backed mortgage brokers, Fannie Mae and Freddie Mac. In the end, of course, the government is getting a lot of that money back (see the sidebar on page 107). Federal deposit insurance for banks and credit unions is also counted here, and you know how busy they've been over the last couple years. So does the extra federal stimulus aid to homeowners through the mortgage credit.

If all goes well, this category should go more or less back to "normal" over the next couple of years. As of early 2010, the Office of Management and Budget is projecting this category will actually make money in 2010 (about $25 billion) and cost a more modest $22 billion in 2011.

Medicaid and CHIP: 6.45 percent of the budget, $226.9 billion

The health insurance program for the poor is actually a partnership between the federal government and the states. The states run it, and the federal government pays part of the costs. That goes for both Medicaid (for adults) and the Children's Health Insurance Program (designed to cover kids in "working poor" families without insurance). So while people under a certain income level are eligible for it, the program isn't running on autopilot like Social Security and Medicare. The federal government can cut how much it pays if it wants. Of course, that sticks the states with the bill. Your federal taxes might go down, but your state taxes might go up. What you make up on the Ferris wheel you lose on the merry-go-round.

Interest on the debt: 5.31 percent of the budget, $186.9 billion

This is pretty much the same as the minimum payment on your credit card. This is how much the government has to pay to banks and holders of Treasury bonds for the money we've already borrowed—and to keep the door open to borrow more.

This category actually went down in 2009, falling from $252.7 billion in 2008. That's one of the only positive things you can say about the world financial crisis: when every other investment on the planet seemed to be tanking, everybody rushed to buy Treasury bonds, one of the few safe havens that was left. Since everybody wanted them, the government could sell them with hardly any interest at all. But don't get cocky, because this isn't going to last. As other investments recover, and as the U.S. government's borrowing continues to skyrocket, this category will get ugly. The Office of Management and Budget projects interest payments on the debt will more than double by 2012.

But what about everything else? What about all that foreign aid, the space shuttle, welfare? Have another look at the pie. See all those very narrow slices? That's where all that spending is, from national forests to disaster relief, from weather satellites to interstate highways. It just goes to show that the most obvious government functions aren't necessarily the biggest ones.

Just because these programs are small proportions of the federal budget, doesn't mean they ought to be kept going. Government waste is real enough. Some programs don't work, some programs should be lower priorities than they are. But you can't get very far in tackling this problem without knowing where the money is.

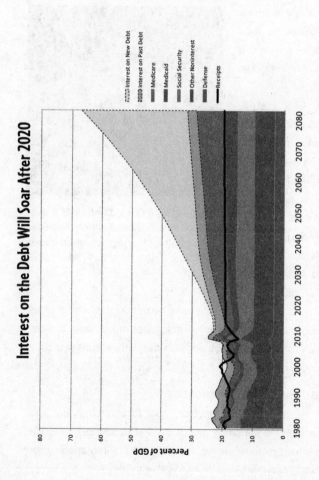

Interest on the Debt Will Soar After 2020

Percent of GDP

Interest on New Debt
Interest on Past Debt
Medicare
Medicaid
Social Security
Other Noninterest
Defense
Receipts

If we don't raise more money or cut spending, the only other option the government has is to borrow. And the government's own projections show that unless we change course, it's going to become increasingly difficult to even keep up with the interest on the money we'll need. Source: U.S. Treasury Department, "A Citizen's Guide to the 2009 Financial Report of the U.S. Government"

Prime Cuts or Deli Slices?
What It Takes to Make a Dent in the Deficit

Some government programs, like some people, are just inherently annoying. Nearly everyone has some government function that they think is a waste of money or just plain wrong. If all those programs were cut, surely the deficit would go away. Right?

Well, let's test it. When we do focus groups on the deficit, people are quick to come up with suggestions of things to cut. Here are a few of the ones we hear regularly. Let's walk through them. Check off any you think should go and we'll total them up at the end. And

Astronaut Pete Conrad unfurls U.S. flag on the moon. Spending on science, space, and technology takes up about 1 percent of the budget. *Credit: NASA Photo*

to make the cuts as deep as possible, we're taking on whole slices of the budget pie, eliminating entire categories of spending. In other words, we've thrown the baby out with the bathwater. If you cut a category, you're cutting all of it.

SCIENCE, SPACE, AND TECHNOLOGY

We rarely seem to get any Trekkies in our focus groups, because the space program is usually one of the first to be jettisoned. The basic argument is "Why are we shooting rockets into space when there are so many problems to be dealt with here?" Defenders of government research funding, particularly "basic research" that doesn't have a short-term payoff, say it expands human knowledge and pays off in the long run. For our purposes here, we're throwing in the entire science budget, including the National Science Foundation, which ranges from physics to social sciences to biology. Some medical research funding lies elsewhere in the budget.

Total savings: $29.4 billion, less than 1 percent of the budget

THE ARTS AND HUMANITIES

The beauty of the National Endowment for the Arts is that if it ever wants to get into trouble, it has a simple way of doing it: just fund something avant-garde. During the 1990s, the agency's support for Robert Mapplethorpe and other push-the-envelope artists made it a favorite target of conservatives. The National Endowment for the Humanities has been less controversial over the years. Supporters of these programs say the arts enrich our lives and even provide economic benefits to communities. But many argue that the government shouldn't be in the business of funding museums, symphonies, artists, writers, linguists, and historians. Artists should get their money from the private or nonprofit sectors.

Total savings: NEA, $152 million, NEH, $151 million, together 0.009 percent of the budget

FOREIGN AID AND INTERNATIONAL RELATIONS

Average Americans rarely have much good to say about foreign aid. After all, we have lots of problems at home. And there are many critics who say aid programs are poorly run and often wasted in corrupt countries. There are a lot of people we could quote on this, but we've always been partial to the cartoon show *Pinky and the Brain,* about a superintelligent lab mouse bent on world domination. In one episode, the Brain cons the U.S. government out of billions in foreign aid by pretending to lead the strategic country of "Brainania." At the check ceremony, the Brain announces: "Mr. President, I thank you for your friendship and for this $19 billion aid check. The friendship I will cherish; the money I will spend on polo ponies and cruise missiles."

Advocates of foreign aid don't have a cartoon for their point of view, but they do point out that the United Sates gives less proportionally than many other wealthy countries, while the poor in places like Africa and Asia are far poorer than even the most needy American (fully 1 billion people in the world live on $2 a day or less). Plus, foreign aid buys us goodwill, which is a useful asset in diplomacy and often in short supply. For our purposes, we're being hard-core and cutting all international relations funding—not just the aid, but shutting down all the embassies and the State Department itself.

Total savings: $37.5 billion, 1.1 percent of the budget

And it all adds up to? A grand total of less than 3 percent of the budget.

Not a big dent, is it? Granted, this isn't solely about saving money. It's perfectly all right to get rid of a program just because most Americans think it's a waste of time or that the money can be put to better use. And in other cases, a program should be kept because it's important, even if it's costly. But we're worried about balancing the budget here, and while every little bit helps, cuts like these aren't going to do the job. It's just not going to be this easy.

The Fortunes of War: Why Bringing the Troops Home Won't Balance the Budget

When we conduct focus groups on government finances, one of the first things we often hear people say is "If we weren't in Iraq, we wouldn't have a deficit." Or, depending on their viewpoint, "We have to be in Iraq and that costs money, so we have to put up with the deficit." In other words, wars are expensive, emergencies are emergencies, and wartime is no time to worry about the deficit.

But now that the war in Iraq appears to be winding down, can we take the money we have been spending there and use it to solve our budget problems? Well, not exactly.

As you know if you took (and memorized) the pop quiz up front, the Congressional Budget Office estimates Congress has authorized $1.1 trillion for military and diplomatic operations in Afghanistan, Iraq, and the rest of the global war on terrorism between 2001 and 2010. At least 65 percent of the total has been allocated to Iraq, according to the CBO.[4] Because of the way the government breaks out its billing, it isn't clear how much of that the Pentagon has actually spent, but government officials estimate the monthly "burn rate" about $11 billion in 2009.[5]

It certainly is a lot of money.

But the total deficit over the same period—from 2001 to 2010—was about $4.9 trillion—about five times as much as the wars cost. Even if we never spent a single penny in Iraq, we would still have added trillions to the national debt.

---

[4] "Funding for Operations in Iraq and Afghanistan and for Related Activities, The Budget and Economic Outlook: Fiscal Years 2010 to 2020," Congressional Budget Office, January 2010, www.cbo.gov/ftpdocs/108xx/doc10871/Chapter1.shtml#1099353.

[5] "The Cost of Iraq, Afghanistan and Other Global War on Terror Operations Since 9/11," Congressional Research Service, Sept. 28, 2009, http://opencrs.com/document/Rl33110/.

What about the future? President Obama's 2011 budget request asked for $159.3 billion for military spending for Iraq, Afghanistan, and Pakistan in 2011. Meanwhile, the president's budget projects a $1.4 trillion deficit in 2011.[6] So, even if we lived in a world where we could withdraw from Iraq and Afghanistan overnight, with no winding-down period, where just red-penciling the two wars out of the budget would make it go away, it still wouldn't close the deficit. And it wouldn't do anything about the long-term problems caused by the aging of the boomers and the rise in health care costs.

And, of course, in the real world we can't just walk away from those two wars, at least not if we want to leave those countries in some semblance of order. In 2009, there were about 220,000 U.S. personnel deployed in the two theaters of war. The CBO estimates that if we reduce the number of troops in the two theaters of war to 60,000 by 2015, it would reduce spending by about $550 billion through 2020. If we cut back to 30,000 troops by 2013, we'd cut spending by $900 billion. That's a lot of money, but the CBO also projects total deficits through 2020 totaling $6 trillion.[7]

So while President Obama's goal to wind down the wars may well save us money, that doesn't doesn't affect the fundamental fact that bringing the troops home, by itself, isn't going to solve the financial problem. Peace is certainly cheaper than war, but not cheap enough to make the books balance—at least not in this case.

[6] Budget of the United States Government, FY 2011, February 1, 2010, www.white house.gov/omb/factsheet_department_defense/.

[7] "Funding for Operations in Iraq and Afghanistan and for Related Activities, The Budget and Economic Outlook: Fiscal Years 2010 to 2020," Congressional Budget Office, January 2010, www.cbo.gov/ftpdocs/108xx/doc10871/Chapter1.shtml#1099353.

The Argument for the Bailouts and the Stimulus–Do You Have to Spend Money to Make Money?

In *Butch Cassidy and the Sundance Kid*, there's a scene where Butch and Sundance are trapped at the edge of a cliff, with a posse closing in behind them and a deep river gorge ahead. Butch says their only chance is to jump, but Sundance doesn't want to do it. They bicker for a while and finally Sundance blurts out "I can't swim!"

Butch bursts out laughing. "Are you crazy?" he asks. "The fall will probably kill you!"

As far as we know, there are no buddy movies featuring economists, and if you frequently hang out with economists, you already know why. But when they talk about how much the U.S. government has been spending to prop up the economy, most of them seem to view the Wall Street bailout and economic stimulus in similar terms to Butch Cassidy: the jump is worth the risk.

First things first: the bailout and the stimulus are different

People often mix up the bailout and the stimulus, as if they're the same thing. In fact, they work in different ways, have different goals, and the impact on the budget is different. Even within those broad categories, there are a lot of different programs.

The "bailout" covers a number of programs, but generally we're talking about short-term spending initiated by the Bush administration to shore up the financial system and key industries (like automakers). When all those bad mortgages came home to roost and Wall Street investment banks started to topple, the financial world did something that struck a cold chill into economists and businesspeople everywhere. It stopped lending. And if there's no lending, there's no business, not even short-term "commercial paper" loans that even blue-chip firms use to cover their cash flow while they're waiting for payments to come in. That's what the financial writers meant when they talked about "frozen credit markets." Remember the movie *The Shining*? Even the crazed killer, Jack Torrance, finally met his end frozen to death in the maze outside the Overlook Hotel. For modern economies too, having a frozen credit market is one of the worst things that can happen.

The biggest part of the bailout is the Troubled Asset Relief Program—TARP as it is often called—some $700 billion used by the government injects money into teetering big businesses by purchasing preferred stock in investment banks like Goldman Sachs, traditional banks like Citigroup and Bank of America, insurers such as AIG and automakers GM and Chrysler. The intention was that eventually, when the economy improved, these companies would buy their stock back from the government. And the good news is that most of these businesses have been able to do just that. As a result, the Congressional Budget Office estimates TARP will end up costing the government about $66 billion. That's still a lot of money and the final numbers may be different, but there's no question the government is getting most of that $700 billion back.[8]

But there were other parts of the 2008 bailout. The Federal Reserve, the nation's central bank, used its emergency powers to provide a range of loans to keep financial institutions afloat. But since these are loans, the Fed is mostly holding its own financially.[9] The Federal Deposit Insurance Corp., the agency that's been backing up your bank account since the Great Depression,

---

[8] Congressional Budget Office Director's blog, "CBO's Latest Projections for the TARP," August 10, 2010, http://cboblog.cbo.gov/?p=1322.

[9] Committee for a Responsible Federal Budget, "The Extraordinary Actions Taken by the Federal Reserve to Address the Economic and Financial Crisis," June 2009, http://dev.trellon.org/newamerica/document/extraordinary-actions-taken-federal-reserve.

used its own revolving funds to shore up banks as well, costing about $74 billion by mid-2010. Finally, the government put the two federally chartered mortgage backers, Fannie Mae and Freddie Mac, into conservatorship in 2008, shoring them up at an estimated cost of $389 billion.[10]

The stimulus is supposed to lessen the pain

In contrast, the stimulus, one of the first actions taken by the Obama administration in 2009, is designed to deal with a different problem: creating new jobs, keeping existing jobs if possible, and mitigating the pain of the Great Recession with tax cuts and direct assistance.

All told, the stimulus package (officially known as the American Recovery and Reinvestment Act, but nobody ever calls it that), is projected to cost the government $862 billion spread out between 2009 and 2019. The CBO says the stimulus only added $200 billion to the $1.4 trillion deficit in 2009 and was expected to add $404 billion to the deficit in 2010.[11]

What does it include and why is it so spread out? Extending unemployment benefits ($58 billion in 2009–10), giving states extra money for Medicaid health insurance for the poor ($74 billion), and to stabilize local school budgets ($43 billion) can be done quickly. Tax credits are also pretty fast ($35 billion in 2009–10).

But the stimulus also included transportation construction projects designed to provide jobs. These can take more time. There were relatively few "shovel-ready" projects when the bill was passed, and if you're going to go to the trouble of building

---

[10] Congressional Budget Office, "Background Paper; CBO's Budgetary Treatment of Fannie Mae and Freddie Mac, January 2010, www.cbo.gov/ftpdocs/108xx /doc10878/01-13-FannieFreddie.pdf.

[11] Congressional Budget Office, "The Budget and Economic Outlook: Fiscal Years 2010 to 2020," Appendix A, January 2010, www.cbo.gov/ftpdocs/108xx /doc10871/AppendixA.shtml#1097121.

a new overpass, it's worth spending some time planning where it should be. There's a similar dynamic in the stimulus spending devoted to developing new energy projects, part of the Obama administration's plan to double renewable energy use and create new "green jobs." As a result, those transportation and energy projects don't really start kicking in until 2011 through 2019.

And what about the results? During the second quarter of 2010, the contractors and other recipients of stimulus money reported about 750,000 jobs created. The CBO, however, says that when the impact on the rest of the economy was factored in, the total was somewhere between 1.4 million and 3.3 million more workers employed. Put another way, the stimulus reduced the unemployment rate by about .7 to 1.8 percent.[12] In July 2010, the unemployment rate was 9.5 percent, according to the Bureau of Labor Statistics.[13]

There's no shortage of criticism over the bailout and the stimulus. Angry that the Wall Street suits kept their jobs and even handed out bonuses, while your tax dollars saved them from their own malfeasance? Go with it. Wondering whether this is really the best way to create jobs? Or maybe you think the government didn't go far enough and should have spent even more to get the economy back on its feet.

But if you're thinking that the government shouldn't have done any of these things, that it should have kept its money in its pocket and tried to balance the budget in the past couple of years, there we'll have to stop you. There are economists who think the government should have done more and some who think it should have done less, but very, very few who think it should

[12] Congressional Budget Office, "Estimated Impact of the American Recovery and Reinvestment Act on Employment and Economic Output From April 2010 Through June 2010," August 2010, www.cbo.gov/doc.cfm?index=11706.

[13] Bureau of Labor Statistics, Labor Force Statistics from the Current Population Survey, www.bls.gov/cps/, accessed August 29, 2010.

have done nothing at all. Even the toughest budget hawks aren't saying the government could or should have tried to balance the budget at the expense of stabilizing the financial system or propping up the economy.

If the financial crisis had been allowed to "work itself out," there's a good chance the federal budget would have been as badly off or worse than it is now, because bankrupt businesses and unemployed people don't pay taxes. That's what they basically did in the early 1930s; it was called the Great Depression, with 25 percent unemployment. Whether you like the bailout and stimulus or not, at least we avoided *that* this time.

Our budget problems are very real, but sometimes you're faced with two bad options; you've just got to deal with the one that's more urgent. If there's a drought and your house is on fire, you don't skimp on water. You put the fire out and go back to the drought later. Or, as Butch and Sundance realized, sometimes you've just got to grit your teeth and take the scary jump.

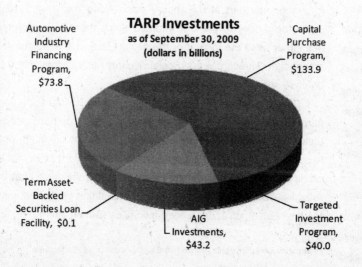

TARP Investments
as of September 30, 2009
(dollars in billions)

Automotive Industry Financing Program, $73.8

Capital Purchase Program, $133.9

Term Asset-Backed Securities Loan Facility, $0.1

AIG Investments, $43.2

Targeted Investment Program, $40.0

PLAYING DEFENSE: HOW MUCH DOES IT TAKE TO BE SAFE?

For a lot of people, national defense is the first responsibility of government, and the last place that ought to be cut. An extreme example of this comes from Ron Swanson, the libertarian department director in the sitcom *Parks and Recreation.* He enthusiastically advocates eliminating his own department and just about every other government agency, but there's a limit.

> "My idea of a perfect government is one guy who sits in a small room at a desk, and the only thing he's allowed to decide is who to nuke," Swanson says. "And women are brought to him, maybe . . . when he desires them."[14]

There are a few countries in the world that get by without an army, like Costa Rica and Lichtenstein, but they haven't had our responsibilities—or our enemies. A strong military has been a fundamental part of U.S. policy since World War II, and we've spent the money to make it happen. Since the 1940s, defense has either been the largest or the second-largest slice of the federal budget (In recent years, Social Security has regularly matched defense spending or overtaken it).

Our investment in defense is even more striking if you compare our military to others internationally. The comparisons get tricky, but there's no question that since the Soviet Union got what it deserved, the United States has outspent every other nation on defense by huge amounts. Estimates generally agree that the roughly $660 billion a year we've been spending lately is at least ten times as much as both our major allies (Britain and Japan) and

---

[14] http://tvcomedies.about.com/od/funstuff/a/ronswansonquotes.htm.

potential adversaries (China and Iran).[15] There are countries that have more troops under arms, but they don't have our high level of technology and training. To some extent, that's the price of being the only superpower. For some people, there's some comfort in having a generous safety margin on military spending. After all, there's no prize for coming in second in a war.

TWENTY YEARS ON THE WASTE AND FRAUD WATCHLIST

That said, at least some of this spending is just enriching government contractors, not necessarily making us safer. The Pentagon is often Washington's poster child for wasting money—the Defense Department has never lived down the $600 hammers it bought in a notorious procurement scandal during the 1980s.[16] Most Americans are probably hoping that a blunder like this would lead to dramatic reform, but the Government Accountability Office has cited defense acquisitions on its list of programs at "high risk" for waste and fraud since 1990. Yes, that's right: *for twenty years*. In 2008, the Pentagon's average R&D cost for weapons systems ran 42 percent above original estimates, and average delivery was 22 months behind schedule.[17]

The military is also spending more on personnel, something most Americans tend to support. Aware of the strain the wars have placed on service members, Congress has tried to improve military pay and family support over the past few years. In addition, the rising cost of health care hits military medical services as well as

---

[15] See, for example, GlobalSecurity.org, "World Wide Military Expenditures," accessed May 15, 2010, www.globalsecurity.org/military/world/spending.htm, and Congressional Research Service, "Comparisons of U.S. and Foreign Military Spending: Data from Selected Public Sources," Jan. 28, 2004, www.fas.org/man/crs/RL32209.pdf.

[16] Actually, the hammer only cost $15; it's just that the contractor was tacking on hundreds of dollars of overhead. See Government Executive, "The Myth of the $600 Hammer," Dec. 7, 1998, www.govexec.com/dailyfed/1298/120798t1.htm.

[17] U.S. Government Accountability Office, "Defense Acquisitions: Charting a Course for Lasting Reform," April 30, 2009, www.gao.gov/new.items/d09663t.pdf.

everyone else. As a result, the Congressional Research Service estimates that uniformed personnel cost 40 percent more per capita than they did in 1999, even after adjusting for inflation.[18]

And yet, despite the vast sums we're spending, the U.S. military is feeling the strain of the long-running wars in Iraq and Afghanistan, with the Pentagon forcing "stop-loss" orders to keep troops from leaving when their enlistments are up, and asking them to undergo multiple combat tours. That raises some worrisome new questions about whether our money is going to the right places. The American military can take out just about any conventional military force on the planet, as Saddam Hussein found out (twice). But does that mean that we have the right tools for an insurgency? Do we need to put money into new ships and advanced fighter planes when our main challenges will be what defense planners like to call "asymmetrical warfare": fighting terrorists and insurgents who don't have aircraft carriers, but do have roadside bombs?

Defense Secretary Robert Gates himself has said that the debate over what the military really needs will become even more critical, because the federal budget's problems—all the issues we've been talking about here—mean that the Pentagon will have to live within tighter constraints. In a speech in May 2010, Gates listed a number of areas where the military has everything it needs but is under pressure to buy more.

HOW MANY WARSHIPS DO WE NEED?

"Does the number of warships we have and are building really put America at risk when the U.S. battle fleet is larger than the next 13 navies combined, 11 of which belong to allies and partners?" Gates asked. "Is it a dire threat that by 2020 the United States will

---

[18] Congressional Research Service, "Defense: FY2010 Authorization and Appropriations," Dec. 14, 2009, http://opencrs.com/document/R40567/2009-12-14/download/1013/.

have only 20 times more advanced stealth fighters than China?"[19]

The trouble is, of course, that Gates isn't the first defense secretary to talk that way, and so far the status quo usually wins. There are a lot of vested interests around defense spending; defense contractors are major employers, as are military bases. Members of Congress generally defend defense spending in their district until someone throws a rope around them and hauls them off someplace. New weapons systems, even ones that are over budget and trouble-plagued, have proven hard to cancel. There are even cases where military officials say they don't even want a system, and yet it lives to fight another day, so to speak. And at least so far, it's been so much easier, from a Washington point of view, just to let the buying go ahead. After all, as a member of Congress, are you *sure* we don't need some more C-17 transport planes? Suppose you vote against them, and then the military is caught short handed down the road. It's a campaign attack ad in the making.

And there are jobs at stake.

Given the magnitude of the budget problems facing the nation, we're not going to be able to leave defense spending untouched. Defense spending isn't going to drive our budget problems the way that health care and the aging of America will. But defense is also the largest part of the federal budget that isn't going to increase automatically, the way that Social Security and Medicare are designed to do.

Which is all the more reason to ask the fundamental questions: what wars are we likely to fight, and against whom? What are the real threats, both now and on the horizon? Unless we get smart answers to those questions, we risk spending far too much money on the wrong kind of defense.

---

[19] The Hill, "Gates: Military spending should be subjected to harsher scrutiny," May 8, 2010, http://thehill.com/homenews/administration/96801-gates-military-spending-should-receive-harsh-scrutiny-.

CHAPTER 6

Social Security and Medicare— and Why Closing the Deficit Isn't Enough

I'm not trying to cause a big sensation
(Talkin' 'bout my generation)
I'm just talkin' 'bout my generation
(Talkin' 'bout my generation)

—*Pete Townshend*

We've said it before, and we'll say it again: Social Security and Medicare are pay-as you-go programs. Payroll taxes collected from those of us who work cover retirement and health care for those of us who are old. That's how these systems were designed decades ago. Unfortunately, an arrangement that has worked very smoothly for quite a while is about to encounter some mammoth bumps in the road. Here's why.

No. 1: The boomers are about to go on Social Security. The baby-boom generation is a lot larger than generations after

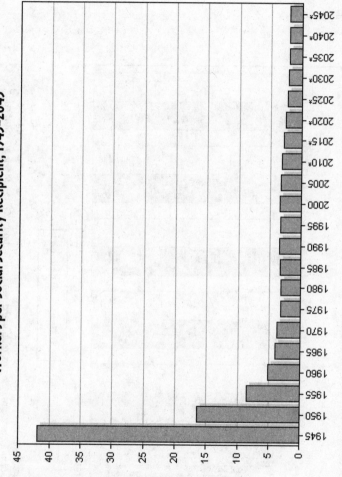

Workers per Social Security Recipient, 1945–2045

Social Security is designed as a "pay-as-you-go" system. But the problem is that if not enough people are paying in, the system won't go. And the proportion of workers to each Social Security recipient is falling. *Source: Social Security and Medicare Trustees Report, 2006*

it (even with the twin beds and all, couples managed to make a lot of babies back in the 1950s), so fairly soon there will be a lot more people collecting Social Security and a lot fewer paying into it. You can see how this could cause a problem.

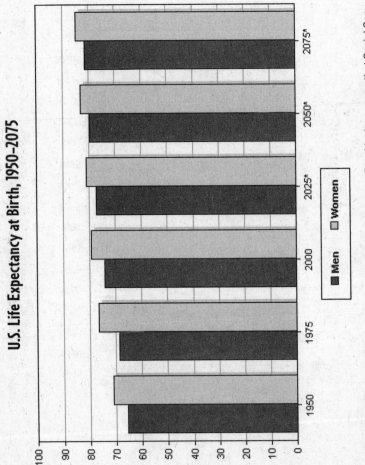

U.S. Life Expectancy at Birth, 1950–2075

Don't get us wrong, this is good news: people are living longer. But this does mean that Social Security and Medicare costs are going to keep rising. *Source: National Center for Health Statistics, CDC*

No. 2: People are living longer. When Social Security began in 1935, there were only about 7.5 million Americans over age 65. Today, there are about 36 million Americans over 65.[1] Or to put it another way, the average life expectancy in 1940 was a little under 64 years. A child born in 2006 can expect to live 77.7 years.[2] This is not brain surgery. When more people live longer, collect Social Security, and get health care paid for by Medicare, it costs more money.

No. 3. Health care costs are rising. No news here—health care costs are famous for rising faster than the rate of inflation, and that's for everybody, not just the government. But the numbers are beginning to be a little scary when it comes to Medicare—scary enough to alarm experts who worry about these things. In 2009, Medicare spent more than $430 billion for health care for older people (yes, just in that one year, lots and lots of money). With more people eligible for Medicare and rising health care costs, the program's annual expenses are expected to jump to over $650 billion by 2015.[3] As you can imagine, this is not good for the budget.

No. 4: Every year there's more health care to buy. One reason Medicare costs go up so quickly is that there are always new tests, treatments, machines, and drugs that can help people live longer and more comfortably—the miracles of

[1] Statement of Social Security commissioner Jo Anne B. Barnhart, released by the Social Security Administration, States News Service, August 11, 2005.

[2] National Vital Statistics Reports, Volume, 57, Number 14: Deaths, Final Data for 2006, April 17, 2009, www.cdc.gov/nchs/fastats/lifexpec.htm.

[3] Budget of the United States Government: Historical Tables Fiscal Year 2011, Table 3.1—Outlays by Superfunction and Function: 1940–2015, www.gpoaccess.gov/usbudget/fy11/hist.html.

modern medicine. We expect Medicare to cover these new inventions because if they can help people, it would be un-civilized not to. Even so, this costs a lot of money.

No. 5: We've expanded benefits. Over the years, the country has added improvements to both programs (see "Social Se-curity and Medicare: A Quick History," page 131). The most recent example is the prescription drug coverage Congress added to Medicare in 2003. Since a lot of elderly Americans were having trouble paying for drugs, Congress passed leg-islation to help them—legislation supported by Democrats, Republicans, and nearly nine in ten members of the public.[4] The drug plan, which is available to every Medicare recipient regardless of income, is expected to add about $445 billion to the cost of Medicare between 2004 and 2014.[5] Providing drug coverage for all Medicare recipients—not just those with lower incomes—was also supported by most Americans.[6]

---

[4] According to a Princeton Survey Research Associates/Pew survey, in June 2001, 89 percent of Americans favored making prescription drug benefits part of Medicare. Just 8 percent of Americans opposed it. "The vast majority of Americans say they favor making prescrip-tion drug coverage part of Medicare and three-quarters say it should be a top priority." Public Agenda Online (www.publicagenda.org/issues/major_proposals_detail.cfm?issue_type=medicare&list=3), accessed March 4, 2007.

[5] Centers for Medicare and Medicaid Services, "The 2010 Annual Report of the Boards of Trustees of the Federal Hospital Insurance and Federal Supplementary Medical Insurance Trust Funds," Table V.E8, "Operations of the Part D Account in the SMI Trust Fund (Cash Basis) during Fiscal Years 2004–2019," www.cms.gov/ReportsTrust-Funds/downloads/tr2010.pdf.

[6] According to a CBS/*New York Times* poll in June 2001, 62 percent of Americans wanted to make the coverage available to all Medicare recipients versus 35 percent who wanted to provide coverage for only low-income Americans. Cited from Public Agenda Online (www.public agenda.org).

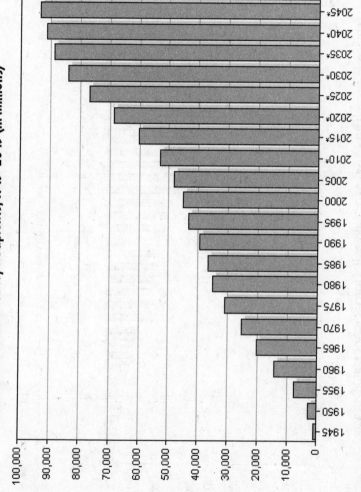

Number of Social Security Recipients, 1945–2045 (in millions)

This is probably no surprise, but the chart brings it home—more and more people are getting Social Security. *Source: Social Security and Medicare Trustees Report, 2006*

Rise in Annual Social Security Spending, 1970–2009 (in billions of dollars)

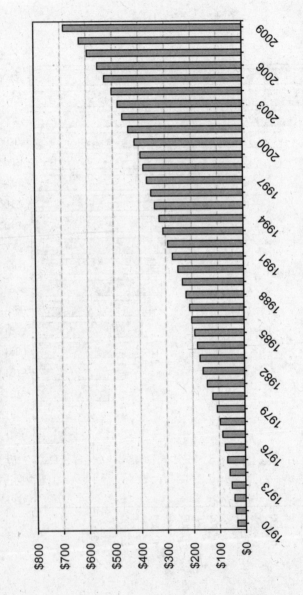

Social Security spending has been on a steady upward track for decades. *Source: Social Security and Medicare Trustees Report, 2010*

Together, these trends are going to put a real squeeze on Social Security, Medicare, and the federal budget. There's really no way around it.

DIDN'T SOMEONE THINK OF THIS?

Since it's been obvious for years that the baby-boom generation is gigantic, that Americans are living longer, and that health care costs are rising, you might have thought that the big "they" would have planned for this. Congress did take a stab at it back in the 1970s and 1980s.

In 1977, anticipating the money crunch to come, Congress almost doubled the payroll taxes workers and employers pay for Social Security and Medicare.[7] Some years later, the retirement age was raised from sixty-five to sixty-six for people born after 1943, and to sixty-seven for people born after 1960.[8] The idea was for the country to get a little ahead while most of the baby boomers were still working and paying taxes into the system. The "extra" money would be held in the Social Security and Medicare "trust funds" to be available when the boomers began to retire. A smart idea on paper, but that's not what happened.

TRUST FUND OR SLUSH FUND?

In fact, the money collected for Social Security and Medicare is not "held" anywhere. In effect, the government uses *all* of its income—including Social Security and Medicare

---

[7] Keith Melville, "The National Piggy Bank: Does Our Retirement System Need Fixing?" *National Issues Forums*, 1996, p. 3.

[8] Social Security Online, Retirement Planner, "Retirement Benefits by the Year of Birth," available at www.socialsecurity.gov/retire2/age reduction/htm.

taxes—to pay *all* its expenses. There are "trust fund" accounts, of course, and, on paper at least, the Social Security trust fund looks reasonably healthy—in good enough shape to cover projected benefits for seniors until 2037.[9] (We're not talking about Medicare in this section because even on paper it's already in trouble.) But as your mom always told you, appearances can be deceiving. Over the years, the government has dipped into the Social Security account to cover other kinds of expenses and to avoid having to raise taxes. The government gives the trust fund Treasury bills in return for what it "borrows."

The problem is that Social Security is going to start needing more and more of the money it has lent out to other parts of government starting in about 2014,[10] and the U.S. government itself is in the hole for megabucks. It's like you took money from your retirement savings to lend to your good friend Sylvester, and he's given you IOUs in return. Sylvester's a decent guy, and his word has always been good, but every year he spends more than he makes, and he's already maxed out his credit cards. He'll pay you back, but the question is how.

REMEMBER THE "LOCKBOX"?

When Social Security starts to redeem a lot of its Treasury

---

[9] Social Security and Medicare Board of Trustees, Status of the Social Security and Medicare Programs, A Summary of the 2010 Annual Reports, "A Message to the Public," www.ssa.gov/OACT/TRSUM /tr10summary.pdf.

[10] Ibid. Social Security spending temporarily exceeded revenues in 2010 because of the recession (fewer people working means fewer people paying Social Security taxes) and some technical accounting adjustments. The real problems, however, will kick in starting about 2014.

bills (which it will have to do to pay benefits it has promised to people who paid their taxes into the system for years), the government will have to cut other expenses, raise taxes, or borrow even more money—and probably more and more of it from abroad.

Over the years, some experts urged the government to invest the money in the "trust fund" in the stock market, or to allow workers to invest the "extra money" in personal accounts, but these ideas never caught on. When Al Gore was running for president in 2000, the then vice president argued so repeatedly and earnestly for keeping the "extra" money in a "lockbox" (a concept backed by some Republicans as well, including the then Texas governor George Bush)[11] that some comedians began to make fun of him. When the *Boston Herald* organized a focus group of typical voters to watch the vice president debate Governor Bush, the newspaper reported that "Gore appeared to bore viewers with his repetitive comments about a Social Security 'lockbox.'"[12] And given the sheer size of the coming Social Security shortfall and the tendency of politicians to wriggle around arrangements they don't like, some experts said the lockbox idea wouldn't make much difference anyway.[13] Whatever the case, "surplus" Social Security money has routinely been available to cover other government expenses. So when it comes to the Social Security trust fund, there's really not that much "there" there.

---

[11] CNN.com, "Bush, Gore Continue Heated Debates on Private Social Security Accounts," AllPolitics, May 16, 2000, available at http://archives.cnn.com/2000/ALLPOLITICS/stories/05/16/campaign.wrap/index.html.

[12] Steve Marantz, "Focus group unmoved by debate," *Boston Herald*, October 5, 2000.

[13] See for example, Maya MacGuinas, "Lock Boxes Are Too Easily Unpicked," *Financial Times* (London), August 18, 2000.

THE POLITICAL EQUIVALENT OF CATNIP

For most elected officials—regardless of their political party—being able to "borrow" based on the "surplus" in the "trust funds" to cover expenses other than Social Security and Medicare is like catnip to a cat. They don't have to ask Americans to pay higher taxes to pay for things like the space program or food stamps or money for special education or agricultural subsidies. Quite the opposite; they can cut taxes and enjoy all the political popularity that brings.

So here we are. Even now, all those boomers are starting to retire in bigger numbers. They (or we, as the case may be) are going to start needing hip surgery and walkers and blood pressure medicine. There will be fewer younger Americans working and paying taxes. So what's a country to do?

Up to now, the country has shown few signs of grappling with the real solutions, which will require some form of trimming benefits and/or raising taxes—or some combination of the two. And if we don't face up to the problem soon, the country is going to get itself into a horrendous financial and political mess.

COMING SOON: THREE SERIOUSLY BAD CHOICES

So let's say we just sit back and wait for the worst to happen. Here are the three seriously bad choices we'll face.

Choice One

To have enough money to cover the promised Social Security and Medicare benefits for the boomers, we could slash nearly everything else in the budget—college loans, national parks, the Centers for Disease Control, even homeland security and defense. Some experts, including the

Government Accountability Office, have calculated that as early as 2019, if we do nothing, nearly 92 cents of every tax dollar collected will be needed to pay for Social Security, Medicare, Medicaid, and interest on the national debt.

Choice Two

We could place really punishing taxes on working people. These will be people who are trying to raise families, send their kids to college, and pay off the mortgage. And the taxes would have to be very high.

Choice Three

Or we could—suddenly and in a big financial panic—cut the benefits older people have been counting on. These will be people who have themselves paid Social Security and Medicare taxes for decades. Many will be too old to go back to work, even as a greeter at Walmart. Many will be sick and frail.

It's a bleak scenario, but if we can get our collective heads out of the sand, we have the time and the resources to avoid all this. The real question is whether we can stop the sloganeering and electioneering, positioning and gamesmanship, long enough to make some sensible decisions about what to do.

Setting Out the Welcome Mat : Could Immigration Solve the Problem?

Theoretically, one way the United States could produce some extra revenue is by bringing more immigrants into the country to work and pay Social Security and Medicare taxes. We're now living in one of the great eras of immigration, with the Census Bureau estimating that almost 13 percent of Americans are foreign-born.[14] So the country probably wouldn't have any trouble attracting more people if it wanted.

In the mid-1990s, PBS's *Think Tank* host Ben Wattenberg proposed bringing in an extra 16 million immigrants (about twice the population of New Jersey) to create an "artificial genera-tion of young adults" to help pay the retirement and health care costs of the boomers.[15] Wattenberg's idea is logical enough. Since our problem stems from the fact that the boomer genera-tion is huge while subsequent generations are a little skimpy by comparison, increasing the number of younger workers would make sense.

But would the American public ever support this kind of solu-tion, even if the experts all agreed on the numbers? According to polls, fewer than one in five Americans supports increased immigration.[16] Surveys show that a lot of the public ire about immigration is directed at illegal migrants, rather than lawful im-migrants who "play by the rules," but there's not much evidence of a groundswell to throw the doors open even wider.[17]

What many people don't realize is that, financially speaking at least, the Social Security system is already benefiting from illegal immigration. Since you can't get a legitimate job without a Social Security number, lots of illegal immigrants buy fake Social Security cards with made-up or stolen numbers. They

[14] Elizabeth M. Grieco, "Race and Hispanic Origin of the Foreign-Born Population in the United States," U.S. Census Bureau, Janurary, 2010, page 3, www.census .gov/prod/2010pubs/acs-11.pdf.

[15] Ben Wattenberg, "The Demographic Deficit," *Baltimore Sun*, December 15, 1995.

[16] Gallup Poll, June 5–July 6, 2008, "Thinking now about immigrants—that is, people who come from other countries to live here in the United States: In your view, should immigration be kept at its present level, increased or decreased?" Increase: 18 per-cent; decrease: 39 percent; present level: 39 percent; unsure: 3 percent.

[17] "Red Flags on Immigration," Public Agenda Online, www.publicagenda.org/citi-zen/issueguides/immigration/publicview/redflags, accessed April 25, 2010.

cost about $150 on the streets of Los Angeles. Since their Social Security numbers aren't real, they can't actually claim benefits, but the money still gets deducted from their paycheck and used. [18]

It's not clear exactly how much money this adds up to, but the Social Security Administration says in 2002 there were 9 million W-2 forms filed with incorrect Social Security numbers. Some are no doubt simple mistakes, but Social Security officials estimate three-quarters of them might be illegal immigrants. That accounted for $6 to $7 billion in Social Security revenue and another $1.5 billion for Medicare.

The IRS also believes it's getting a fair bit of revenue from illegal immigrants. The agency offers an Individual Taxpayer Identification Number to allow foreigners who don't have a Social Security number to pay taxes. The IRS issued 1.5 million ITINs in 2006, and agency officials think many of these went to illegal immigrants who believe paying their taxes helps keep them out of trouble in the United States. Between 1996 and 2006, the total tax liability of ITIN holders accounted for about $50 billion.[19]

The debate over what to do about fake Social Security cards and ITINs tells you something about how divisive an "immigration solution" would be. Some support using these filings to track down illegal immigrants and deport them. Those who want a more open immigration policy say it's unfair to make illegal immigrants pay taxes for a system that will never give them benefits. From a purely financial point of view, both arguments have problems: deporting illegal immigrants out of the country would take some

---

[18] "Illegal Immigrants Are Bolstering Social Security with Billions," *New York Times*, April 5, 2005, www.nytimes.com/2005/04/05/business/05immigration.html and "Editorial: How Immigrants Saved Social Security," *New York Times*, April 2, 2008, www.nytimes.com/2008/04/02/opinion/02wed3.html, accessed April 25, 2010.

[19] "Illegal Immigrants Filing Taxes More Than Ever," *Associated Press*, April 13, 2007.

ghost Social Security taxpayers out of the system; legalization would allow more beneficiaries in.

What's more, there are massive disputes among experts about the numbers of immigrants and how much money they would actually bring into the system, not to mention the long-term advantages and disadvantages of changing their status. In 2005, the Social Security Advisory Board concluded that increased immigration would be helpful, but "does not view immigration as a panacea—or free lunch—for saving Social Security."[20] When it looked at the controversial immigration bill put forward in 2007, the Congressional Budget Office estimated it would "exert a relatively small net effect on the federal budget balance over the next two decades." Yes, more tax money would come into Social Security, but that would be largely offset by increased spending on immigration enforcement and other areas.[21]

Our best advice on this? Regardless of what you think about the larger immigration debate, don't hold your breath waiting for immigration to get us out of our Social Security and Medicare predicament.

---

[20] Social Security Advisory Board, "Issue Brief No. 1: The Impact of Immigration on Social Security and the National Economy," December 2005.

[21] Congressional Budget Office, Cost Estimate, June 4, 2007; Senate Amendment 1150 to S. 1348, the Comprehensive Immigration Reform Act of 2007, as amended by the Senate through May 24, 2007 (www.cbo.gov/ftpdocs/81xx/doc8141/05-23-Immigration.pdf).

SOCIAL SECURITY AND MEDICARE: A QUICK HISTORY[22]

1930   Only 15 percent of workers are covered by retirement plans, many of which collapsed during the Great Depression.

1935   President Franklin D. Roosevelt signs the Social Security Act at a time when the average life expectancy is sixty-one.

1939   Children of retired workers and surviving children of deceased workers become eligible for benefits.

1954   Social Security is expanded to include agricultural and self-employed workers.

1956   Coverage is extended to disabled workers. Women become eligible for certain benefits at age sixty-two, rather than having to wait until they are sixty-five.

1961   Men become eligible for early retirement benefits at age sixty-two.

1965   President Lyndon B. Johnson signs Medicare into law at a time when only 56 percent of older Americans have health insurance.

1972   Social Security is adjusted, ensuring that benefits rise with the cost of living. Medicare benefits are extended to some people under sixty-five with disabilities.

1977   As costs rise, Congress slows the growth of benefits

---

[22] Adapted with permission of the National Issues Forums and Public Agenda, "The National Piggybank: Does Our Retirement System Need Fixing?" by Keith Melville, 1996.

and nearly doubles the payroll taxes that support these retirement programs.

1983   Congress increases the retirement age in several phases by 2027, from sixty-five to sixty-seven.

1993   Congress increases the Medicare payroll tax by making all earnings taxable rather than just the first $135,000.

2003   President Bush signs a bill adding prescription drug coverage to Medicare.

2009   The Trustees of the Social Security and Medicare trust funds reiterate what they have reported before—the long-term costs of the two programs are "not sustainable" as they are currently designed.[23]

2010   Congress passes and President Obama signs health care legislation that—among its many provisions—improves drug coverage for seniors, but also aims to cut nearly $500 billion from Medicare's costs between 2010 and 2019.[24]

---

[23] Social Security and Medicare Boards of Trustees, Status of the Social Security and Medicare Programs, "A Summary of the 2009 Annual Reports," www.ssa.gov/OACT/TRSUM/index.html.

[24] Department of Health & Human Services, Centers for Medicare and Medicaid Services, Estimated Effects of the Patient Protection and Affordable Care Act of 2009," Page 8, www.cms.gov/ActuarialStudies/Downloads/S_PPACA_2009-12-10.pdf.

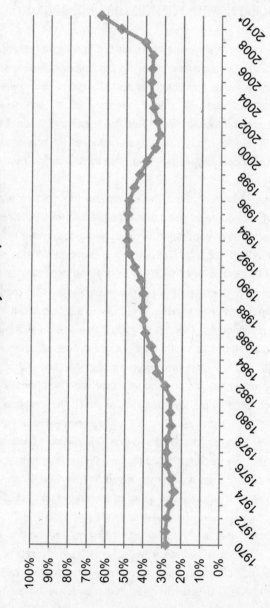

U.S. Debt as Percentage of GDP, 1970–2010

Economists say the country's debt as a percentage of the gross domestic product (GDP) is generally the best indicator of when the national debt gets out of hand. This chart covers debt held by the public (the Treasury bonds anyone can buy). This doesn't count intergovernmental debt, such as the money the government owes the Social Security trust fund. Source: *Budget of the United States Government, FY 2010*

Blinding Us with Science: The Debt and GDP

Since the point of this book is to explain the budget problems facing the country as clearly and simply as possible, we don't always use the same terms and concepts as the experts. But there is one concept that we want to draw your attention to because you may come across it when candidates and experts talk about the budget and the debt. It's a very useful concept for economists, but it can be confusing and even a little misleading to the rest of us.

Experts often talk about the deficit and the debt as a percentage of the country's gross domestic product, or GDP. This is the total amount of goods and services produced in the United States—in effect, the total size of the U.S. economy. Most economists say this is the best measure of how the debt affects the entire economy. The bigger the debt is in relation to GDP, the bigger the impact it's likely to have. This is generally true about a lot of things in economics, which is why you'll also see the GDP yardstick used in relation to health care spending, defense spending, taxes paid, and any number of other things. (And not just in the United States, either. It's a standard measure internationally.)

In fact, economists love this idea so much that not one but three independent groups—the Committee on the Fiscal Future of the United States, the Peterson-Pew Commission on Budget Reform, and the Center for Budget and Policy Priorities—have called for setting a national target based on this ratio, to provide policymakers and citizens with a way of gauging when the federal budget is on track and when it isn't.

But really, this is just a way of putting big numbers in perspective, in much the same way personal finance experts tell borrowers they shouldn't spend more than one-third of their income on housing. If your mortgage payments are higher than that, they'll eat up money you need for other things. Same thing with the national debt—if it's too big a slice of GDP, other things have to suffer.

At the end of 2009, the "debt held by the public" was about 53 percent of GDP, a pretty steep jump from 37 percent as recently as 2006. The good news is that the country's debt has actually been a bigger share of GDP in the past. Back in 1946, when the country was just starting to pay off all the money it borrowed to fight World War II, debt was at 109 percent of GDP. In 1975 it was down to 25.3 percent.

The problem, unfortunately, is that all the projections show this debt-to-GDP ratio going up at a frightening pace. The assessments vary but, for example, the Congressional Budget Office's most plausible scenario estimates debt held by the public will hit 87 percent of GDP in 2020.[25] Most projections show we'll pass 100 percent sometime in the early 2020s, meaning the federal government's debts alone will be larger than the entire American economy.

So how do we know when we're in trouble? On *Star Trek,* the producers inserted dramatic countdowns, the Red Alert siren, and the custom of having hammy actors fling themselves around the set to let us know when danger arrived. Economists aren't so helpful when it comes to debt. Basically, it depends on how much confidence everyone has in the country, its economy, and its leaders. Greece's public debt was at 115 percent of GDP when their financial crisis hit in 2010. The Greeks also had the problems of huge annual deficits, an uncompetitive economy, no control over their currency and no obvious willingness to change.[26] Argentina's

[25] Congressional Budget Office, "The Long-Term Budget Outlook," June 2010, www.cbo.gov/ftpdocs/115xx/doc11579/06-30-LTBO.pdf.

[26] International Monetary Fund, "Europe and IMF Agree €110 Billion Financing Plan With Greece," May 2, 2010, www.imf.org/external/pubs/ft/survey/so/2010/CAR050210A.htm.

debt was actually much less when its debt crisis hit in 2001, just 63 percent of GDP. On the other hand, Japan's debt is staggering, more than twice the size of its economy. But since Japan is (to be blunt about it) a better-managed country than Greece with a much more competitive economy, that debt level hasn't caused a crisis, although there's no question it's been dragging Japan's economy down and extending the problems that have dogged the nation since the 1990s.[27] As for the United States, both the Fiscal Future and Peterson-Pew panels recommended trying to stabilize the debt at 60 percent of GDP, while the Center for Budget and Policy Priorities thought it could be safely held at 70 percent.

And there's a second, even more worrisome reason to be concerned: *"Debt held by the public" isn't all the debt there is.* That doesn't include any of the "intragovernmental" borrowing the government has done from the Social Security and Medicare trust funds. It only includes the Treasury notes sold to people and institutions here and abroad. There is an actual, legitimate rationale for this. Since the government is borrowing from itself, these loans don't compete in the credit market with your mortgage and car loan. So they're treated differently, just the same way accountants treat internal loans in large corporations differently from money the business borrows from the bank.

But borrowing from the trust funds is not just some paper transaction without an impact on anybody's life. Social Security and Medicare are real, tangible obligations. People get checks every month. Hospitals and doctors have to get paid. And as we've pointed out repeatedly, pretty soon the money coming into Social Security and Medicare won't be enough to cover what's promised to go out. That's when the Social Security and Medi-

---

27 Uri Dadush, Bennett Stancil, "Is a Sovereign Debt Crisis Looming?", International Economic Bulletin, Carnegie Endowment for International Peace, Feb. 2, 2010, www.carnegieendowment.org/publications/?fa=view&id=24798.

care systems will start redeeming those Treasury bonds they've been given as IOUs. If you add the two kinds of debt together, the U.S. gross national debt exceeded 94 percent of GDP in 2010 and will probably pass 100 percent in 2012, which is much less reassuring.[28]

And when this intragovernmental debt stops being a bookkeeping maneuver and becomes a real bill, who pays for it? You do. The government will have to come up with the cash to pay back the trust funds—and you're the one it gets the cash from.

---

[28] Budget of the United States Government, Fiscal Year 2011, Table 7.1: "Federal Debt at the End of the Year: 1940–2015," www.whitehouse.gov/omb/budget/Historicals/.

CHAPTER 7

If You Think Social Security Is Bad, Wait till You Meet Medicare

As for me, except for an occasional heart attack, I feel as young as I ever did.

—Robert Benchley, American actor and writer (1889–1945)

When it comes to tackling the country's long-term financial problems, we often talk about having to "fix" Social Security and Medicare in one breath, as if the two programs were matching bookends—little public policy identical twins.

From the typical American's point of view, the two do have a lot in common. You have taxes taken out of your salary to pay for them. Almost everyone over a certain age benefits from them. They are very popular. They are both "entitlement programs," which means that Congress doesn't debate and vote on them every year the way they do on the defense and education budgets. When people who've paid into the systems

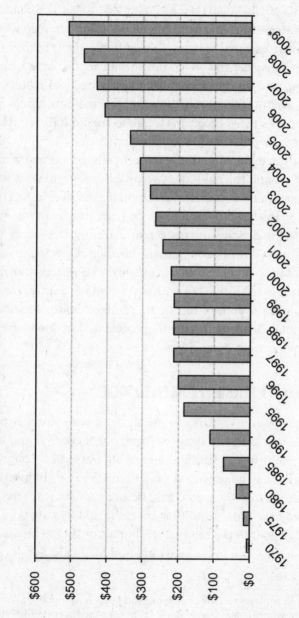

Annual Medicare Spending, 1970–2009 (in billions of dollars)

Medicare spending has risen dramatically over the last few decades because the number of older people has increased and because health care spending has gone up overall. *Source: Centers for Medicare and Medicaid Services*

reach the eligible age, they are "entitled" to get the benefits. This arrangement means older Americans don't have to watch yearly congressional debates on whether to "reauthorize" the programs they depend on (complete with all the partisanship, lobbying, and other accoutrements congressional reauthorization usually entails). That's probably a merciful thing, but it also makes these programs tough to reexamine even when there are good reasons for reexamining them.

But for experts and elected officials concerned about the budget and the debt, the two programs are in very, very different situations. When you compare the two, in fact, it's hard not to think of the 1980s comedy movie *Twins*, featuring Arnold Schwarzenegger and Danny DeVito as the world's most improbable pair of brothers. Specifically, it's hard not to think of the briefly iconic movie poster, showing the two dressed alike, but with an enormous Schwarzenegger looming over DeVito.[1] In the budget world, Medicare and Social Security are both problems, but Medicare is played by Arnold. Here's why.

MEDICARE IS A TRICKIER PROBLEM TO SOLVE

One major difference is that Medicare's costs are less predictable and far more likely to spiral out of control, and this is true even though the health care bill passed by Congress and signed by the president in 2010 made some changes designed to cut Medicare's costs. Before the law was passed, the Medicare trust fund that covers hospital costs was expected to go into the red in 2017, but according to an analysis from the Centers for Medicare and Medicaid Services, it

---

[1] We'd love to show you the poster, but you know how much that would cost? But you can see it here: www.imdb.com/media/rm1944099840/tt0096320.

will now last until 2029—getting an additional 12 years of life.[2] That's provided, of course, that all the ideas and estimates in that legislation work out as planned, and the very same report said that some of them may be "unrealistic."[3] It also assumes that Congress doesn't backtrack on the cost-cutting and revenue-raising measures that were included in the bill, such as reducing payments to doctors and hospitals and slightly increasing Medicare payroll taxes for high-income people.[4] It's a near certainty that some constituents will complain about some of these changes since this happens with almost any piece of legislation that trims expenditures and raises taxes or fees.

The dreary news we have for you here is that even if all these cost-cutting ideas that became law in 2010 work out like a dream, the country still faces a huge challenge paying for Medicare. We'll return to some of the details of the 2010 changes later, but first let's take a look at the bigger picture.

---

[2] Richard S. Foster, Chief Actuary, Centers for Medicare and Medicaid Services, Department of Health and Human Services, "Estimated Financial Effects of the 'Patient Protection and Affordable Care Act,' as Amended," April 22, 2010, page 9, http://graphics8.nytimes.com/packages/pdf/health/oactmemo1.pdf.

[3] Richard S. Foster, Chief Actuary, Centers for Medicare and Medicaid Services, Department of Health and Human Services, "Estimated Financial Effects of the 'Patient Protection and Affordable Care Act,' as Amended," April 22, 2010, page 9, http://graphics8.nytimes.com/packages/pdf/health/oactmemo1.pdf.

[4] Richard S. Foster, Chief Actuary, Centers for Medicare and Medicaid Services, Department of Health and Human Services, "Estimated Financial Effects of the 'Patient Protection and Affordable Care Act,' as Amended," April 22, 2010, page 8, http://graphics8.nytimes.com/packages/pdf/health/oactmemo1.pdf.

Medicare Spending by Category, 2009

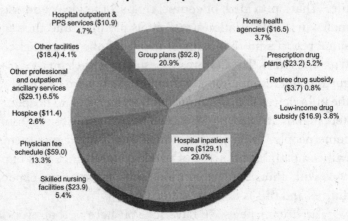

Hospital outpatient & PPS services ($10.9) 4.7%

Home health agencies ($16.5) 3.7%

Other facilities ($18.4) 4.1%

Group plans ($92.8) 20.9%

Prescription drug plans ($23.2) 5.2%

Other professional and outpatient ancillary services ($29.1) 6.5%

Retiree drug subsidy ($3.7) 0.8%

Low-income drug subsidy ($16.9) 3.8%

Hospice ($11.4) 2.6%

Physician fee schedule ($59.0) 13.3%

Hospital inpatient care ($129.1) 29.0%

Skilled nursing facilities ($23.9) 5.4%

Where does the Medicare money go? Mostly for hospital care, doctors' visits, drug coverage, and other health care needs. *Source: Congressional Budget Office*

MEDICARE'S FINANCES WILL BE HARDER TO FIX

The "fixes" for Social Security are not especially pleasant, but they probably won't put most of us in the poorhouse. No one likes the idea of raising payroll taxes, for example, and there are lots of reasons why raising Social Security taxes may or may not be a good idea (see chapters 8 and 9). But the two programs are in quite different places when it comes to raising revenue.

As of 2010, Social Security only collected taxes on the first $106,800 of salary,[5] so one widely discussed idea is to "raise the ceiling"—that is, collect taxes on the entire salaries of higher wage earners (or more of them, perhaps).

---

[5] Social Security Online, Frequently Asked Questions: "What is maximum amount of earnings subject to Social Security taxes for 2010?" www.ssa.gov/pgm/links_retirement.htm.

In contrast, the Medicare system just has much less room to maneuver. Medicare already collects taxes on nearly everything everyone earns, so there's hardly any place to go there. Older people already pay monthly premiums to cover doctors' visits (Medicare Part B), premiums that nearly doubled between 2000 and 2009.[6] As of 2010, most seniors were paying about $96 a month for this insurance.[7] But the system has also raised premiums substantially for higher-income recipients; these can go over $350 a month, depending on how much income the person has.[8] We're not trying to suggest that raising Medicare taxes, premiums, and fees should be off the table, and the increases on higher-income people affect only about 5 percent of recipients.[9] But politically speaking, the system has already been there and done that.

MEDICARE'S FUTURE COSTS ARE NOT AS PREDICTABLE

Figuring out how much money Social Security will need to pay future recipients is not as easy as you might think. The calculations can change, depending on how healthy the U.S. economy is (when people aren't working, they don't pay Social Security taxes), how many older people the country

---

[6] The Henry J. Kaiser Family Foundation, Medicare Issue Brief: The Social Security COLA and Medicare Part B Premium—Questions, Answers, and Issues, Appendix, www.kff.org/medicare/upload/7912-02.pdf.

[7] Centers for Medicare and Medicaid Services, Fact Sheet: CMS Announces Medicare Premiums, Deductibles For 2010, October 16, 2009, www.cms.gov/apps/media/press/factsheet.asp?Counter=3534&intNumPerPage=10&checkDate=&checkKey=&srchType=1&numDays=3500&srchOpt=0&srchData=&keywordType=All&chkNewsType=6&intPage=&showAll=&pYear=&year=&desc=false&cboOrder=date.

[8] Ibid.

[9] Ibid.

will have, how long they decide to work, and how long they live and collect benefits. Luckily, there are actuaries who love doing just this kind of calculating, and, in a sense, it's pretty much a closed question: a certain amount of money will come in, and the system will pay out a certain amount in benefits according to its rules and regulations.

Social Security pays people benefits that have been calculated and spelled out in advance in that nice little green-and-white newsletter you get in the mail every year (be sure to check out your own Social Security statement when it comes). Social Security doesn't pay you more if you hit hard times and need more money. That's your problem, and your kids' problem. Some people do try to cheat Social Security, of course, but it's not a program bedeviled by waste and fraud.

Medicare is a much more confusing problem. Since it pays for older people's hospital bills, surgeries, medical tests, medications, and other health care expenses, its costs are essentially linked to the country's overall health care system. And as we all read nearly every day (and as some of us are unfortunate enough to find out personally), health care costs are skyrocketing. That means that Medicare spending is not as foreseeable or easily controllable as Social Security spending. There are lots of different factors that can drive up costs.[10]

Like Social Security, Medicare's costs depend on how many older people the country has and how long they live. But its costs also depend on how sick people are. For example, the Alzheimer's Association recently raised its estimate of the number of Americans with the disease to more than

---

[10] Congressional Budget Office, The Budget and Economic Outlook: Fiscal Years 2010 to 2020, "The Spending Outlook—Mandatory Spending: What Causes Growth in Mandatory Spending?" January 2010, www.cbo.gov/ftpdocs/108xx/doc10871/Chapter3.shtml#1096746.

5 million.[11] Since caring for a patient with dementia costs Medicare about three times as much as caring for a more typical beneficiary, Medicare's costs are expected to rise as well.[12] It's a dreadful disease and a costly one as well.

But Medicare's costs can go up with good news, too. If someone discovers a new treatment that will eliminate the pain and disability of arthritis, Medicare will add it to the list of covered services. It will be a wonderful thing, but it will also drive up costs. Then there's the question of whether all the services Medicare patients receive are actually medically necessary, or whether some large portion of money is being wasted. Sometimes these questions are judgment calls—should Medicare cover cataract surgery when the patient could get by with glasses? Should Medicare drug plans cover Viagra, or, since human beings actually can live without sex (yes, there is empirical evidence showing this), should Viagra be considered a personal expense? As of 2007, Medicare drug plans can cover Viagra if the patient takes it for something like "pulmonary hypertension" but not for erectile dysfunction.[13]

Sometimes the issue is outright dishonesty, and Medicare fraud horror stories are not uncommon: The government paid over $2 million for ankle braces for people who have had a foot amputated; schemers operating a sham medical supply company used the money to buy a Rolls-Royce Phantom for themselves.[14] The Government Account-

---

[11] Jane Gross, "Prevalence of Alzheimer's Rises 10% in 5 Years," *New York Times*, March 21, 2007.

[12] Ibid.

[13] Patricia Anstett, "Medicare Limits Sex Drug Coverage," *Detroit Free Press*, January 27, 2007.

[14] Carrie Johnson, "Medicare's $869 Air Mattress Bill; Government Arrests 38 as It Cracks Down on Health Care Fraud," *Washington Post*, May 10, 2007.

ability Office has called on Medicare administrators to do more to tackle fraud, as have some members of Congress, and the FBI has joined in on the hunt as part of a Medicare Fraud Strike Force.[15] Still, like Willie Sutton, who robbed banks because "that's where the money is," thieves are likely to see Medicare as a promising target for some time to come.

THE ANSWERS TO MEDICARE'S PROBLEMS AREN'T AS CLEAR

We might not like some of the answers about how to fix Social Security, and there is a lot of "yes, it will, no it won't" bickering over whether private accounts would make the system more or less financially stable. But compared to the debate over Medicare, the debate over Social Security is a model of mathematical clarity. We could raise taxes, cut benefits, do some of both, and/or start to plan for a private accounts option in the future. The major questions we need to talk about are value questions—what solutions we think are fairest, what kind of system we really want.

But with Medicare, we could raise taxes and fees dramatically, and if health care costs continue to rise the way they have lately, the system could still be in trouble. You might be able to cut benefits some, but when older people are fragile, sick, and dying, the country is going to want to pay for whatever will help them. The big wrinkle here is that we haven't yet come up with foolproof ways to hold down health care costs without harming patients or thwarting new medical breakthroughs. In the last couple of decades, experts have pinned their cost-cutting hopes on HMOs, preferred provider plans, more preventive care, and other ideas, but health care costs have continued to climb.

---

[15] Ibid.

Some experts, including those in the Obama administration, are now placing their hopes on "comparative effectiveness research." Ideally, this research would test different kinds of drugs and treatments to find out which really do help patients recover (so that we could stop spending money on those that don't work) and, hopefully, also learn whether some less expensive approaches could be just as good.[16]

THE MEDICARE DEBATE HAS BARELY STARTED

No matter what you thought about President Bush's idea about starting private accounts in Social Security, he probably did the country a big favor by getting the Social Security issue out on the table. Soon there are going to be a lot more people retiring and fewer workers paying into the system. Most of us understand that we need to have a national debate about how to pay for Social Security, and that we're probably talking about cutbacks of some sort. In fact, the system has already been slowly pushing back the age of retirement. Those of us who can are rapidly throwing money into other kinds of retirement accounts to supplement our Social Security benefits. We've basically got the picture. The system can't continue on like this, and we've got to decide what to do.

And at least one idea, President Bush's plan for private accounts, was talked over and then shelved, at least for the time being.

But the debate over how to handle Medicare's financial

---

[16] See for example, Center for American Progress, "Better Health Through Better Information—Comparative Effectiveness Research Will Help Deliver Better Medical Care," www.americanprogress.org /issues/2009/09/cer_brief.html.

problems and keep the system solvent is not as far along, to put it mildly. The stories of people demanding "keep the government out of my Medicare" at "town hall" meetings on health care may be apocryphal, but the health care debate certainly proved that most Americans haven't got their arms around the complexity of the insurance system. What's more, the health-and-Medicare debate has the tendency to veer into much more emotional and frightening territory.[17] Until fairly recently, we just didn't talk much about the cost of Medicare at all; nearly all the debate was about what else the program should cover—not how to contain its costs to government and taxpayers. Take, for example, the addition of prescription drug coverage to Medicare in 2003. President Clinton originally proposed the idea; Democratic candidate Al Gore talked about it, too. President Bush and the Republicans who controlled Congress in 2003 made it a reality. Yet when the plan was up for discussion, the potential impact on the nation's finances barely figured in the debate. Whatever its specific merits or problems, the legislation responded to a broad public consensus that we wanted to help seniors with their drug expenses.

The question we need to ask ourselves now is whether we would have done it in quite the same way if we had been talking about the costs up front. Columnist Robert Samuelson is no fan of the drug plan. He points out that about "three-quarters of Medicare recipients already had drug coverage. The poorest had it through Medicaid; many retirees had it from their former employers and some had it through Medicare managed-care plans or private insur-

---

[17] See for example, http://slate.com/id/2224350/ or www.washington-post.com/wp-dyn/content/article/2009/07/27/AR2009072703066_2.html.

ance policies they purchased."[18] Yet the country passed a new and universal benefit—yes, Donald Trump is eligible, too—without really talking much about the cost. David Walker, the former U.S. comptroller general—essentially the country's accountant—called the prescription drug legislation "probably the most fiscally irresponsible piece of legislation since the 1960s."[19]

Have we gotten any closer to having an honest and intelligent debate about Medicare costs since then? When Congress passed the 2010 health care law, the main intent was to expand insurance for younger and middle-aged Americans, as well as control rising health care costs. Changes to Medicare are a part of that, but even though Medicare was a bit-player in the overall drama, there was still a dispiriting political sideshow that frightened a lot of seniors and confused nearly everyone. We'll need more than hot air and hyperventilating to fix Medicare.

So first, let's clear up how the 2010 health care bill actually affects Medicare—at least the main points.

★ It aims to cut about $575 billion from Medicare expenses between 2010 and 2019.

★ About half ($233 billion) will come from holding down increases in Medicare payments to doctors and hospitals. The idea is that they can and should be more efficient and can reduce their costs without reducing the quality of care.

★ Another big chunk ($145 billion) comes from reducing payments for Medicare Advantage Plans. These are

---

[18] Robert Samuelson, "Benefit Disaster," *Washington Post,* November 23, 2005.

[19] Interview with David Walker by Steve Croft, *60 Minutes,* CBS News, March 2, 2007.

special Medicare plans, sometimes HMOs, offered by private insurers as an alternative to traditional Medicare coverage. People who support this cut believe the government was overpaying the private insurers. However, nearly a quarter of seniors are in these plans,[20] and the cut may lead some Medicare Advantage companies to trim benefits or even eliminate the plans entirely. Seniors who might be affected would still be eligible for traditional Medicare coverage.[21]

★ The bill actually adds coverage in two key areas. Medicare will now pay for annual checkups (so-called wellness visits), and the much-hated "donut hole" in the drug plan will be less onerous. If you're on Medicare or have someone in the family who is, you have probably heard about the donut hole. If you're thinking we're talking Dunkin' Donuts Munchkins, there's a brief explanation below. [22]

But here's the problem. The Congressional Budget Office predicts that Medicare's expenses will come in at nearly $8 trillion between 2011 and 2020.[23] Meanwhile Medicare taxes are expected to bring in about $2.5 trillion over the

---

[20] www.healthreform.gov/reports/medicare/medicare.pdf.

[21] Peter Grier, "Health care reform bill 101: What does it mean for seniors?" *The Christian Science Monitor*, March 22, 2010, www.csmonitor.com/USA/Politics/2010/0322/Health-care-reform-bill-101-What-does-it-mean-for-seniors.

[22] Basically, the drug plan just stopped paying after you spent $2700 in one year; the coverage picked up again when your drug expenses hit $6,154. Since only people who write legislation or insurance policies could ever even conceive of a plan like this, almost everyone on Medicare is happy to see it go.

[23] Congressional Budget Office, The Budget and Economic Outlook: Fiscal Years 2010 to 2020, Table 3-3. CBO's Baseline Projections of Mandatory Spending, January 2010, www.cbo.gov/ftpdocs/108xx/doc10871/Chapter3.shtml#1096746.

same time frame.[24] So there's about $5.5 trillion of red ink there. And the cut that got everyone so excited was $585 billion, a beginning perhaps, but hardly a cure-all. And remember, some very well-informed experts worry that even that figure is exceedingly optimistic.

★ So we have our work cut out for us. We need to figure out how to make a program that millions of seniors depend on affordable and reliable over the long term. We need to shore up its finances for the millions of baby boomers who will be joining the rolls in the years to come. It's that song we've been singing since the opening pages of this book—we either have to cut spending, raise taxes and fees, or do some of both.

★ It's certainly no piece of cake, but step number one is surely to turn down the volume and actually start listening to one another. Maybe we ought to get some kindergarten teachers to come in to remind us to use our "indoor voices."

---

[24] Congressional Budget Office, The Budget and Economic Outlook: Fiscal Years 2010 to 2020, Table 4-5, CBO's Projections of Social Insurance Tax Receipts, by Source, January 2010, www.cbo.gov/ftpdocs/108xx/doc10871/Chapter4.shtml#1096749.

HEALTH CARE AND THE BUDGET:
HAVE WE GOT THE RIGHT PRESCRIPTION YET?

The debate over health care reform in 2009 and 2010 pushed just about every emotional button the public has. From a budget point of view, however, the fundamental questions about health care reform really came down to this: Could we afford to do it, and could we afford *not* to do it? And now that it's done, did we come out ahead?

The argument that we can't afford it, of course, is the roughly more than $828 billion that will be spent through 2019 on expanding insurance coverage, and it's a significant expansion. The Congressional Budget Office estimates the plan will provide insurance to more than 32 million people, raising the coverage rate to 94 percent of Americans. But for many people, the idea that we'd be expanding government costs at a moment when we're running record deficits made no sense at all. It was one of the main reasons the bill was so bitterly controversial.

The argument that we couldn't afford not to do it is rooted in the fact that rising health care costs are driving a lot of our long-term budget problems. When health care costs go up—and health costs have been steadily increasing at about 6 percent a year, double the overall inflation rate[25]—so do the costs of Medicare and Medicaid. Put another way, it is nearly impossible to do much about our budget problems unless we find ways to rein in the rising costs of health care. It drives up costs for Medicare, Medicaid, veterans' benefits, and the personnel costs of anyone who works for the federal government.

---

[25] Center for Medicare and Medicaid Services, "National Health Expenditure Data, 2009–2019," www.cms.gov/NationalHealthExpendData/03_NationalHealthAccounts Projected.asp, accessed May 23, 2010.

So for many economists and the Obama administration, the prescription was simple: control health care costs, and you go a long way toward controlling the budget. "The single most important thing we can do to improve the long-term fiscal health of our nation is slow the growth rate in health care costs," said Peter Orszag, the White House budget director at the time. "Let me be very clear: health care reform is entitlement reform."[26]

Many liberal economists go further, arguing that if you were actually able to reduce U.S. health care spending to a level comparable to Canada or most European nations, the government's budget problems could all but go away. [27]

So, given all that, how do we really stand with health care reform and the budget?

The best estimate right now is that the budget breaks even or comes out slightly ahead over the next decade—if everything goes as planned. True, we're spending $828 billion to get the system set up—and cover more Americans than we ever have before—but we're also making cuts to Medicare to offset that, and imposing new fees and taxes, such as a new tax on so-called "Cadillac" high-premium plans and penalties on employers and individuals who try to go without insurance. When Congress was considering the bill, the Congressional Budget Office calculated that it would reduce the deficit by $143 billion through 2019, and even more in the following decade, to the tune of $1 trillion.[28] If those estimates hold, that keeps it within President Obama's vow that health care reform wouldn't increase the deficit. Finally, the

---

[26] Ezra Klein, "Peter Orszag's Remarks from the Fiscal Summit," Feb. 23, 2009, The American Prospect, www.prospect.org/csnc/blogs/ezraklein_archive.

[27] See, for example, the Health Care Budget Deficit Calculator at the Center for Economic and Policy Research, www.cepr.net/calculators/hc/hc-calculator.html.

[28] Congressional Budget Office, Letter to Speaker Nancy Pelosi, March 20, 2010, "Cost estimate for the amendment in the nature of a substitute for H.R. 4872," www.cbo.gov/ftpdocs/113xx/doc11379/AmendReconProp.pdf.

Medicare actuary's office estimates the health bill is a big plus for the program's trust fund, giving it another 12 years of life (until 2029).[29]

There are a lot of "if's" in those estimates, however. Some features of the bill depend on Congress's decisions in the future, such as allowing cuts in payments to doctors and hospitals, and critics point out that Congress has usually backed away from those choices. Others say the CBO underestimates the cost of subsidies for low-income people to buy insurance. There's also about $115 billion in discretionary spending in the bill—Congress doesn't have to spend it, but if it does, that'll affect the cost.[30]

And on controlling health care costs overall? That's turned out to be one of the most contentious debates about the bill. The same Medicare actuary's report that said the bill would extend the trust fund also concluded that total national health spending would actually go up somewhat faster than originally projected by 2019 (by 0.9 percent). In many respects, the results depend on how well some of the bill's ideas, like research into the most cost-effective treatments and setting up an independent panel to set Medicare payments to doctors and hospitals, work out in real life.[31] The White House believes these are powerful ideas for controlling rising health care costs. The president's critics say the bill did almost nothing to address more straightforward cost problems like malpractice suits. Nor did the bill include the so-called public option—a government-operated insurance alter-

---

[29] Office of the Actuary, Center for Medicare and Medicaid Services, " Estimated Financial Effects of the "Patient Protection and Affordable Care Act," as Amended, April 22, 2010, www.cms.gov/ActuarialStudies/Downloads/PPACA_2010-04-22.pdf.

[30] Congressional Budget Office, Director's Blog, "Discretionary Spending in the Final Health Care Legislation," May 13, 2010, http://cboblog.cbo.gov/?p=835.

[31] The Hill, "Orszag: CBO Lowballs Savings from Obama's Healthcare Reform," April 11, 2010, http://thehill.com/homenews/administration/91527-orszag-cbo-underestimates-savings-from-obamas-healthcare-bill.

native that some say would have helped hold down costs. The actuary's report admitted that the actual impacts of the bill are hard to predict. Basically, the jury's still out.

So if the CBO projections hold, the health care reform bill doesn't make our budget problems worse, but it also doesn't solve them, at least not by itself. The White House's own projections show over $9 trillion in deficits between 2010 and 2019,[32] as opposed to the $143 billion in savings from health care reform. We're still going to have to do something more, and the "something more" comes down to the same options as before: spending cuts, tax increases, or a combination of both.

So what do we do now? Those who argue for repealing the Obama plan have to face the fact that we were heading for national bankruptcy with our old health care system. Returning to the status quo isn't an option. Others say the real problem is that health care reform didn't go far enough. Progressives say the only way to really control costs is with a Canadian-style "single-payer" system, while conservatives argue for replacing Medicare with a private voucher system.

Realistically, however, the nation's political system spent more than a year fighting itself to exhaustion over health care. How many politicians have the stomach for trying again? And how many Americans are ready for even more radical change?

---

[32] Office of Management and Budget, "Mid-Session Review: Budget of the United States Government, FY2011," Table S-1, "Change in Deficits From the February Budget," July 23, 2010, www.whitehouse.gov/omb/budget/MSR/.

★★★★★★★★★★★★★★★★★★★★★★★★★★★★★★

CHAPTER 8

Glib Answers to a Tough Problem

We won't acknowledge choices, contradictions, unpalatable facts. So, many problems persist for years. Throwing the bums out is a venerable tradition, but what if the ultimate bums are us?

—Robert Samuelson, Washington Post, *November 1, 2006*

The choices the country faces if we just ignore the problems facing Social Security and Medicare are so devastating that you might assume the country's leadership is talking day and night about how to avoid them. Some experts are trying to get leaders to tackle this problem more seriously. (There is a presidential commission that will be recommending options for tackling this problem just about the time this book is published. Maybe the commission report should be your next reading assignment.) But too many elected officials, not to mention talking heads and radio hosts, seem determined to stall genuine debate with sloganeering and whining.

In writing this book, we've come to believe that there are two realities the country needs to agree on so we can

Social Security and Poverty

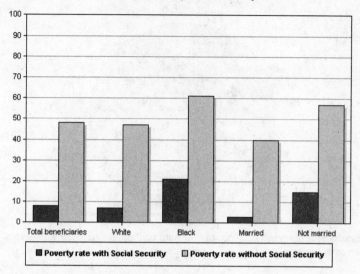

There's no question Social Security makes a difference to the people who get it. Poverty among older Americans would increase considerably without Social Security. *Source: Social Security Administration*

get down to work. They deserve to be in big bold print, so there's no mistaking them.

One is that **the American people are not going to eliminate Social Security and Medicare,** nor are we going to transform them so they're completely unrecognizable. These programs are too popular, and too many people are counting on them.[1]

---

[1] See, for example, the Gallup poll taken April 8–11, 2010: 54 percent of retirees said Social Security was a "major source" of income for them and another 32 percent considered it a "minor source." Among those who were still working, 34 percent said they expected Social Security to be a major source of income when they retired, and 46 percent said it would be a minor source. www.gallup.com/poll/1693/Social-Security.aspx.

Sources of Income for Older Americans

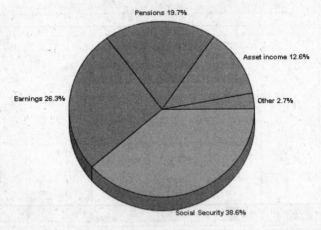

Social Security provides more than a third of the average older American's income. *Source: Social Security Administration*

The other is that **Social Security and Medicare have to change, and they may have to change substantially.** The nation cannot afford to keep them exactly and precisely the way they are right now. Nearly every expert we can find accepts both these points, as do millions of ordinary Americans. But you would never know it from some of the screaming and daydreaming that comes in via sound bites and the blogosphere.

SIX STATEMENTS THAT ARE NOT HELPING ANYBODY

Heard anything like these lately? Everyone's entitled, of course, but in our humble opinion, these six ideas aren't getting us anywhere.

No. 1: "Social Security and Medicare just aren't on the table. These benefits were promised to people." In 1940, when Social

Security first started paying out benefits, life expectancy was about sixty-three years, compared to nearly seventy-eight years today.[2] Since life expectancy has increased considerably and since the program faces financial difficulties, there's every reason to take a new look at how Social Security works. As for Medicare, health care costs are rising so rapidly and the program's financial prospects are so gruesome that there's really no choice but to change it. Surveys show that most Americans want to honor the core values of these programs—joining together to help all of us plan for retirement, making sure low-income Americans aren't destitute when they can't work anymore, ensuring that older Americans get the health care they need. Most Americans also think these programs have accomplished a lot of good, so not too many are going to go along with a slash-and-burn do-over. But that doesn't mean that Social Security and Medicare are untouchable. In fact, anyone who cares about saving them needs to open his or her mind to changes that will make them affordable again.

No. 2: "Let's just privatize Social Security right now." The idea of letting people put their Social Security payroll taxes into private accounts and invest the money as they see fit is an attractive idea to some Americans, and in the next chapter we include a proposal for gradually changing the system so people's accounts are more like 401(k)s. It's one option among many. But if you've been reading along with us, you know the downside to trying to do the private-accounts solution in a big way anytime soon—and it's a whopper. We've said it before, but it's got to be said again: Social Security

---

[2] National Vital Statistics Reports, Volume, 57, Number 14: Deaths, Final Data for 2006, April 17, 2009, www.cdc.gov/nchs/fastats/lifexpec.htm.

is a pay-as-you-go program. If people working now put all or even some of their Social Security taxes into private accounts, the country wouldn't have the money to pay for benefits for people who are old now.

And remember, Social Security is not just some generous, charitable gesture on the part of younger Americans. The older generation paid their Social Security taxes when they were working. In 2005, President Bush proposed a version of this idea in which younger workers could put a small percentage of their Social Security taxes into private accounts and invest the money. The problem is covering the hole that's left when the money moves into private accounts. The Congressional Budget Office looked at the idea and suggested that the hole would be about $270 billion just between 2011 and 2017. The Bush administration (which thought the idea would be very popular with younger workers) projected a hole of more than $600 billion in the same time period[3]—not numbers to be taken lightly. Even some who support the private accounts concept—former Fed chairman Alan Greenspan, for example—warn against moving to such a plan too quickly. "If you're going to move to private accounts, which I approve of," Greenspan testified to Congress in 2005, "I think you have to do it in a cautious, gradual way."[4]

No 3: "Social Security? What a rip-off! I could do better keeping the money and investing it myself." This is a variation on the theme above, and whether it's actually true or not may depend on where you sit on the in-

---

[3] Congressional Budget Office, "An Analysis of the President's Budgetary Proposals for Fiscal Year 2008," March 2007, available at www.cbo .gov/ftpdocs/78xx/doc7878/03-21-PresidentsBudget.pdf.

[4] Edmund L. Andrews and Richard W. Stevenson, "Greenspan Backs Idea of Accounts for Retirement," *New York Times*, February 17, 2005.

come scale (and how good an investor you are). If you're a lower-income worker, Social Security is not such a bad financial deal. You'll actually get a better return on your money than someone who earned higher wages and paid higher payroll taxes during his or her working years.[5] If you're a higher income worker and a good investor, you might well do better with the money. But this is just one piece of the puzzle. Your taxes pay for people who are elderly now. Unless we want to see huge increases in poverty and illness among older Americans and near chaos in the health care system, we need to figure out how to make these programs financially sound for the people who need them. Moving gradually to a system in which people manage their own money in private accounts may or may not be a good idea, but if you're a responsible, compassionate person, you have to admit that this debate involves more than your own financial acumen.

No. 4: "The government can't do anything right. Look what a mess they've made of this. They ought to just get out of it." There's a segment of the population that subscribes to one single political thought—don't trust the government to do anything, period. The government certainly doesn't deserve very good marks for the way it's handled Social Security and Medicare funding so far. "D minus" might be overly generous. On the other hand, Social Security probably looks reasonably good to Enron employees who lost their retirement savings when they listened to the executive-office swindlers they worked for, or airline employees whose pensions got whacked when their companies went into bankruptcy pro-

---

[5] Congressional Budget Office, "Is Social Security Progressive?" December 15, 2006, available at www.cbo.gov/ftpdocs/77xx/doc7705/12-15-Progressivity-SS.pdf.

tection, or other Americans whose private retirement plans were decimated in 2008 and 2009. It's easy to knock Social Security, but not that many Americans really can do without it.[6] As for Medicare, well, good luck with that—just try to find health insurance on your own when you're old and sick.

No. 5: "Not to worry. The Social Security trust fund doesn't run out of money for decades." Well, not exactly. We talked a little about this in the last chapter, but it's worth going over again, because it *is* confusing, and to those of us who aren't Beltway insiders, it's a little mind-boggling as well. The baby-boom generation is huge compared to the generations before it and after it, so while the boomers were (and are) working, Social Security brings in more money than it needs to pay out benefits, and that extra money is supposed to be in a "trust fund." Now, most of us hearing the words *trust fund* might think that the extra money is being invested or socked away to earn interest, that it's sitting somewhere lovingly protected by folks wearing green eyeshades working in offices with a lot of mahogany furniture. But that's just not the case. The government continually and repeatedly borrows from the trust fund to cover other government expenses. The trust fund does hold a lot of "special-issue Treasury securities,"[7] and it is entitled to redeem them. We all know about the "full faith and credit" of the U.S. government, and that's reassuring. But to pay back the money, the government will have to raise taxes, cut other government spending, or borrow

---

[6] In 2001, the Social Security Administration calculated that 48 percent of recipients would fall below the poverty line without their monthly check. See www.publicagenda.org/issues/factfiles_detail .cfm?issue_type=ss&list=9.

[7] National Academy of Social Insurance Sourcebook, "Where Do Social Security Taxes Go?" available at www.nasi.org/publications3901/ publications_show.htm?slide.

even more money (and over time this is going to be a huge, huge amount of money). So don't relax—definitely not. By the way, there is a Medicare trust fund as well, but given the skyrocketing cost of health care, no one is even suggesting relaxing on that one.

No. 6: "The government spends too much on the elderly and not enough on kids." It's because old people vote, and children can't. This one is a party favorite in some D.C. public policy circles. If you hear someone calling for more "intergenerational equity," this is basically what's bothering them. Essentially, it's a debate over who gets more, and who needs more, support from the government—the elderly or kids? According to a study from the Urban Institute, about 46 percent of domestic federal spending goes for programs that mainly serve the elderly—Social Security, Medicare, and Medicaid, which pays for nursing home care as well as care for the poor—while just 15 percent is spent on children.[8] The bulk of state and local taxes are spent on children (for public schools, mainly), but even then, the kids still don't catch up. Of course, most kids live at home with their parents, so they don't have to pay for food and housing the way most elderly people do, and children don't generally have serious health care problems the way most elderly people do. On the other side, a higher percentage of children live in poverty than elderly people. You can see how the back-and-forth on this could go on and keep on going. What bothers us here is the groupthink and the idea of setting this up as a fight between generations. People who like kids over here. People who like older folk over there. Choose your side. To our way of thinking, this just doesn't seem like a very

---

[8] Adam Carasso, C. Eugene Steuerle, and Gillian Reynolds, "Kids' Share 2007," Urban Institute, March 15, 2007, available at www.urban .org/publications/411432.html.

productive path. In fact, one of the major reasons to act now to get Social Security and Medicare on a sound footing is to make sure that we have money left to do what we need to do for our kids, especially the poorest of them.

DON'T REACH FOR THE EASY BUTTON

Our point here is that as a country, we need to start talking seriously and realistically about what to do and cut it with the manipulating and hyperventilating. These are complicated issues, and we need to listen to each other and try to get the best thinking on what will work and what won't. We're not going to get there by falling for "this is all simple if you'll just do it my way" bloviating.

In the next chapter, we'll run down some of the real choices you need to start thinking about. There are ideas for modifying the way Social Security and Medicare operate and ideas for changing the way we pay for them. They probably aren't as fun to read about as what passes for policy discussion on some cable news shows and blogs, and chances are you're not really going to be crazy about any of them. Unfortunately, there just doesn't seem to be an "easy button" for this one. But after you think about it, you can probably live with enough of them to make a real difference, enough to start getting the country back on the right financial track.

CHAPTER 9

Do We Have to Throw Granny out on the Street?

The longer we wait, the more severe, the more draconian,
the more difficult the adjustment is going to be. I think the
right time to start is about 10 years ago.

—Ben S. Bernanke, Federal Reserve
chairman, January 2007

The choices for fixing Social Security and Medicare are
not much fun, which is why politicians don't talk about
them much. Fixing the problem means cutting back benefits and/or raising taxes in some form or another, so this
is not a happy topic of conversation for people whose jobs
depend on being popular. Surveys routinely show that most
Americans want to save Social Security and Medicare, but
reject most workable solutions.

Luckily, your authors are *not* running for office, so we're
presenting for your consideration (in our best Rod Serling
voice) fifteen different ways to approach the problem. It's
not a complete list, but it will get you started. And be forewarned, reading this chapter will probably take some effort

Social Security is projected to begin paying more in benefits than it collects in taxes in 2017.
Credit: Franklin D. Roosevelt Library

and concentration. These proposals are the wheat germ, brussels sprouts, and plain yogurt of budget policy (and we know that you'd rather have the nachos).

What's more, you can't just choose one idea out of our fifteen and leave it at that. The country will have to make a number of changes on different fronts to really make a dent in the problem. And, obviously, we'll need to consider reforms to tackle both Social Security and Medicare. And while the choices in this chapter focus directly on entitlements, the country will have to make other decisions that will affect what kind of debt and economy we leave to the next generation. You can check out chapter 13 for some choices on taxes that we'll also need to be considering.

As of now, the experts haven't done all the number

crunching, computer modeling, and task force hobnobbing they need to do for us to tell you authoritatively exactly how all of these ideas would work and exactly how much each one would save in comparison to the others. And when the debate really gets going in Washington, there will be lots of variants and adaptations of what we describe here. In fact, you can probably expect an outbreak of activity like this once the presidential commission on reducing the debt issues its report, slated for late 2010. So you might want to think of these as "starter ideas," not full-fledged policy proposals. Even so, approaches like these are being talked about in government offices, think tanks, editorial board meetings, and policy conferences every day. There's no reason you shouldn't be in on this.

If you start getting a little depressed as you glance down the list, remember the dreadful alternatives facing us if the country doesn't act on the Social Security/Medicare issue (they're back in chapter 6, if you need a shot of courage). The worst choice of all is to do nothing. A list of publications and Web sites with more on these ideas and some we couldn't cover here is in the appendix. Here goes.

1. Move the retirement age up to seventy. Polls show that this is one of the least popular ways to shore up Social Security, but it would save money.[1] Americans are living longer, and people in their seventies are barely considered old now (at least not by people in their forties and fifties), so there's a commonsense argument for moving the retirement age back.

---

[1] Public Agenda Online, Social Security: Bills and Proposals, "Majorities Oppose Proposals to Raise the Retirement Age, Reduce Benefits, or Increase Taxes, but Support Limiting Benefits and Increasing Taxes for the Wealthy to Secure the Future of Social Security," available at www.publicagenda.org/issues/major_proposals_detail.cfm?issue_type=ss&list=5.

In fact, Social Security has already started edging in this direction. Despite everything you hear about sixty-five being "the age of retirement," people born between 1943 and 1954 have to wait until they're sixty-six to collect full Social Security benefits. People born in 1960 or later have to wait until they're sixty-seven.[2] But most of us don't even wait that long. Sixty-five, sixty-six, and sixty-seven may be the official ages of eligibility for full retirement benefits, but Social Security lets recipients collect benefits at reduced rates at sixty-two, so a lot of people choose that option.[3] According to the Employee Benefit Research Institute, more than 7 in 10 workers retire before the age of 65,[4] although the severe economic downturn of 2008 has led more Americans to consider postponing their retirement.[5] Most of us probably could work a few years longer without much trouble, although this might be tougher for people doing manual labor. Some jobs just get harder as you get older. To allow people to plan and adjust, Congress would probably phase in the older age over a number of years. Even done gradually, however, the Congressional Budget Office predicts that phasing in something like this could "shrink federal outlays by $7.1 billion over 5 years and by $92 billion over 10 years."[6]

---

[2] Social Security Online, Frequently Asked Questions: "Full Retirement Age," http://ssa-custhelp.ssa.gov/, accessed May 2, 2010.

[3] Social Security Online, Frequently Asked Questions: "What is the earliest age that I can begin receiving retirement benefits?" http://ssa-custhelp.ssa.gov/, accessed May 2, 2010.

[4] Employee Benefit Research Institute, Issue Brief No. 328, "The 2009 Retirement Confidence Survey: Economy Drives Confidence to Record Lows, Many Looking to Work Longer," figure 12, www.ebri.org/pdf/briefspdf/EBRI_IB_4-2009_RCS2.pdf, accessed May 2, 2010.

[5] Employee Benefit Research Institute, Issue Brief No. 328, "The 2009 Retirement Confidence Survey: Economy Drives Confidence to Record Lows, Many Looking to Work Longer," www.ebri.org/pdf/briefspdf/EBRI_IB_4-2009_RCS2.pdf, accessed May 2, 2010.

[6] Congressional Budget Office, Budget Options, Volume 2, "650-2—

2. Make people pay Social Security taxes on more of what they earn. As of 2010, Social Security taxes for you (and your employer) stop when your salary reaches $106,800.[7] If you're lucky enough to earn a salary in this range, you have probably enjoyed seeing your paycheck get quite a bit fatter the last few months or weeks of the year because Social Security taxes aren't being deducted anymore. Taxing more of people's salaries would generate more revenue for the system, and people who like this option point out that it would hit higher-income people hardest. The CBO has looked at some different options. Raising the top level to $270,000 would bring in over $668.5 billion over the next ten years; raising it to $198,000 would bring in just over $500 billion over the same time period.[8]

Currently, employee taxes are matched by employers, so if the new law continued this arrangement, this would also be a big tax increase on business. It's always nice to make "business" pay for things, but as we've mentioned before, "business" isn't the only one who ends up paying. When businesses are hit with higher taxes, they also tend to hold down salaries (we all like raises), lay people off (which hurts both individuals and communities), reduce investment in new equipment and facilities (which is bad for the economy) and/or pass the expense on to consumers (that's you and me, in case you had forgotten).

Mandatory: Raise the Normal Retirement Age in Social Security," page 145, www.cbo.gov, accessed May 2, 2010.

[7] Social Security Online, Frequently Asked Questions: "What is maximum amount of earnings subject to Social Security taxes for 2010?" www.ssa.gov/pgm/links_retirement.htm, accessed May 2, 2010.

[8] Congressional Budget Office, Budget Options, Volume 2, "Option 45: Increase the Maximum Taxable Earning for the Social Security Payroll Tax," page 234, www.cbo.gov, accessed May 2, 2010.

3. Change the way Social Security benefits are calculated. If you visit the Web site for the Congressional Budget Office, you can read about a proposal to hold down Social Security costs by linking "initial Social Security benefits to average prices instead of average earnings."[9] It's all about changing the formula for how Social Security calculates what your benefits will be when you retire. Don't worry if you find the description a little rough going. Even Social Security admits that "the benefit computation is complex."[10] And the key question is not how well you grasp the formula, but how you feel about the pros and cons of this option compared to others. As Social Security describes it, your "benefits are based on earnings averaged over most of a worker's lifetime" and "your actual earnings are first adjusted or 'indexed' to account for changes in average wages since the year the earnings were received."[11] The proposal would change the formula to base it on how much *prices* have increased, not how much *wages* have increased.[12] (Yes, there are people in Washington who have to think about these details.) The bottom line is that people retiring after the change would get lower benefits than under current rules.

---

[9] Congressional Budget Office, Budget Options, Volume 2, "650-1—Mandatory: Link Initial Social Security Benefits to Average Prices Instead of Average Earnings," page 143, www.cbo.gov/doc, accessed May 2, 2010.

[10] Social Security Online Frequently Asked Questions, Computation of Benefits. "How Are My Retirement Benefits Calculated?" (www.ssa.gov), accessed August 18, 2007.

[11] If you like math, it's at www.cbo.gov/publications/collections/social security.cfm.

[12] Congressional Budget Office, Budget Options, Volume 2, "650-1—Mandatory: Link Initial Social Security Benefits to Average Prices Instead of Average Earnings," page 143, www.cbo.gov, accessed May 2, 2010.

For example, according to the CBO, someone retiring in 2030 would get 26 percent less under the new formula than under the current one. Someone retiring in 2050 would get 44 percent less.[13] That's a big cut, but the changes would be gradual—giving everyone time to plan—and benefits would keep up with inflation because they would be tied to price increases. But in the end, people retiring in the future wouldn't get as much as people who have retired up to now.[14] Still, according to the accounting wizards at the CBO, this one idea by itself would reduce Social Security's long-term financial outlays by more than 30 percent by 2050.[15]

The downside? Reducing benefits, even gradually like this, is not popular. And it may be even less popular if it seems to be the result of some complicated mathematical calculations that nearly all of us have trouble understanding. The plan could be adjusted to provide more protection for low-income people, but middle-class people would probably have to save considerably more on their own to be as well off as retirees today.

4. Reduce Social Security and Medicare benefits for wealthier Americans.
Social Security and Medicare are available to every American who pays into the programs, no matter how high his income or how much money he has in the bank. The systems were organized that way so they wouldn't be seen as "welfare programs" and would have broad support. There's also the argument that if you pay money into these systems while you are working, you should get something back even if you are fairly well-off. Given the big crunch to come, however, some say it's time to rethink this, and polls suggest that the

---

[13] Ibid.

[14] Ibid.

[15] Ibid.

general idea of cutting back benefits for wealthier Americans has more potential support than other approaches.[16] This could play out in a lot of ways. There could be formulas allowing lower- and middle-income people to get more from Social Security and Medicare, while higher-income folk get less. You could redesign both Social Security and Medicare so that they are mainly intended for low- and middle-income people—the programs just wouldn't cover you if your retirement income from other sources was more than, say, $100,000 a year. And there, as Shakespeare put it, is the rub. How do you define "wealthy" and how do you define "middle class"? Expect to hear a lot of talk (and argument) about this approach in years to come.

5. Change the way Social Security cost-of-living increases are calculated.

Whether you're working now or you're retired and collecting a pension or Social Security, you can imagine what would happen over time if your income never went up. You might be fine at first, but after a number of years, your standard of living would really slide. That's why Social Security (and many other pensions and employee contracts) have cost-of-living increases. Social Security uses a version of the Consumer Price Index (CPI-W) to calculate COLAs (cost of living allowances) for recipients, In January 2009, people on Social Security received a 5.8 percent increase, but in 2010, because consumer prices were down in the recession, there was no cost-of-living increase.[17] Some experts

---

[16] Gallup Organization for CNN/*USA TODAY*, February 2005, available at www.publicagenda.org. See Issues/Social Security/Bills and Proposals.

[17] Social Security News Release, "Prompt Passage of Economic Recovery Act Payment for 2010 Needed, Law Does Not Provide for a Social Security Cost-of-Living Adjustment for 2010," October 15, 2009, www.ssa.gov/pressoffice/pr/2010cola-pr.htm.

say the current formula exaggerates the actual increase in people's living costs,[18] and they want Social Security to use a less-generous one. Much of the argument here is over whether the formula used now is overly generous.[19] Those who defend the current system point out that older people spend more of their income on health care, and that health care costs are rising faster than most other costs. They also argue that older people can't take on extra hours or change jobs to earn more the way a younger person could. People who reach their full retirement age (sixty-five, sixty-six, or sixty-seven, depending on when you were born) can collect Social Security plus whatever they can earn on top of it,[20] but this just may not be an option for people over a certain age. Like so much else in this debate, there are two sides to the story—if not more.

6. Privatize Social Security, but very, very slowly. It's controversial, but the idea of letting workers put their Social Security tax payments into private accounts like 401(k) plans does have some appealing aspects. One is that people would actually own and control their own accounts, so they wouldn't have to rely on the government to have the money available when they retire. Another plus is that if people had money left when they died, they could leave it to their spouse or children or pets or some other good cause. The snag, and it's a

---

[18] Congressional Budget Office, Budget Options, Volume 2, "650-4— Mandatory: Base Social Security Cost-of-Living Adjustments on an Alternative Measure of Inflation," page 147, www.cbo.gov/doc, accessed May 2, 2010.

[19] The Bureau of Labor Statistics at the U.S. Department of Labor has a good description of how the CPI is calculated and what it includes at www.bls.gov/cpi/cpi/.

[20] Social Security Online—Retirement Planner, available at www .ssa.gov/retire2/whileworking.htm.

big one, is that the government needs the money workers pay into Social Security now to pay benefits to people who are retired now. If workers put that money into a 401(k)-type plan instead, there would be a big hole. To fill it, the country would need to raise taxes, cut other government programs, borrow more money, or reduce benefits for people who are retired—none of which are very attractive prospects. Still, some privatization advocates think the idea is worth the costs if we make the changeover very, very gradually. In seventy-five years or so, these experts argue, we could have a system based mainly on private accounts that would be better than what we have now. Of course, others say the idea of taking money out of Social Security just when the boomers are beginning to retire is irresponsible, to say the least. They also worry whether people will make good investment decisions with their private accounts and what will happen to people who retire when the stock market is down. As we all now know, the stock market takes a nosedive every once in a while, and if you're near retirement when it does, it can unravel even well-laid plans. Many just don't see why we would move away from one of the most popular and effective government programs ever created for something that may or may not work as predicted.

7. Up the eligibility age for Medicare. As we explained up top, Social Security has already raised its eligibility age to sixty-seven for those born in 1960 or later, but people can still go on Medicare at sixty-five. Having the same rules for Medicare and Social Security seems like a good way to neaten up the system, and since Americans are living so much longer, it seems logical for both of these programs to kick in a bit later, especially if we decide to raise the age of retirement. Obviously, if people start collecting Medicare benefits later, the program will cost less. One option explored by the CBO

Medicare was one of the centerpieces of President Lyndon B. Johnson's "Great Society" when it was signed into law on July 30, 1965.
Credit: LBJ Library

would gradually raise the eligibility age to 70 in 2043. That would cut Medicare costs by about 10 percent by 2050.[21]

The downside? This is definitely not a winning campaign slogan.

Since people in this age range would still need insurance, employers might be hit with higher insurance premiums for older employees. Less scrupulous bosses might try to ease older workers out of their jobs to hold down their own insurance bills.[22]

---

[21] Congressional Budget Office, Budget Options, Volume 1: Health Care, "Option 17: Raise the Age of Eligibility for Medicare to 67," page 37, www.cbo.gov, accessed May 2, 2010.

[22] Congressional Budget Office, Budget Options, Volume 1: Health Care, "Option 17: Raise the Age of Eligibility for Medicare to 67," pages 37–38, www.cbo.gov, accessed May 2, 2010.

8. Increase the fees and deductibles older Americans pay for Medicare.

Anyone on Medicare (or who has a parent or grandparent on Medicare) knows that it's hardly a free program. There are premiums and fees and deductibles galore, and they are confusing, to say the least. There are deductibles for each "spell" of illness; co-payments for extended hospital care; higher deductibles for outpatient care; no deductibles at all for some things.[23] Many experts say the country needs to revamp this whole aspect of Medicare, both to make it less confusing and to save money. In its winning way with words, the CBO refers to this idea as a proposal to "replace Medicare's current cost-sharing requirements with a unified deductible, a uniform coinsurance rate, and a catastrophic limit." It might go something like this: People on Medicare would pay the first $525 of their health care costs; then they would pay a percentage of their expenses up to a cap of $5,250 per year.[24] According to the CBO, a plan like this would save more than $26 billion over a decade or so. Unfortunately, $26 billion is a pretty small amount (amazing, isn't it?), given Medicare's overall costs—about $499 billion in 2009 and projected to be over a trillion dollars in 2020.[25] The pros here are that this ap-

---

[23] Congressional Budget Office, Budget Options, Volume 1: Health Care, "Option 81: Replace Medicare's Current Cost-Sharing Requirements with a Unified Deductible, a Uniform Coinsurance Rate, and a Catastrophic Limit," page 154, www.cbo.gov, accessed May 2, 2010.

[24] Congressional Budget Office, Budget Options, Volume 1: Health Care, "Option 81: Replace Medicare's Current Cost-Sharing Requirements with a Unified Deductible, a Uniform Coinsurance Rate, and a Catastrophic Limit," page 154, www.cbo.gov, accessed May 2, 2010.

[25] Congressional Budget Office, The Budget and Economic Outlook: Fiscal Years 2010 to 2020, The Spending Outlook, Table 3-3. CBO's Baseline Projections of Mandatory Spending, January 2010, www.cbo.gov/ftpdocs/108xx/doc10871/Chapter3.shtml#1096746, accessed May 2, 2010.

proach would actually be better for "people who developed serious illnesses, required extended care, or underwent repeated hospitalizations," according to the CBO.[26] However, most people on Medicare would end up paying more in deductibles and co-pays. Still, most experts say Medicare needs to have some fees and co-pays to discourage patients from using services that aren't really necessary (or their doctors from ordering them).[27] All in all, it's likely that increased fees of some sort will be part of Medicare reform as we go forward. In fact, Medicare has already moved in this direction, increasing some premiums for higher-income beneficiaries.

9. Rethink Medicare drug coverage. When it became the law of the land, most of the headlines about the 2003 Medicare drug plan talked about how confusing it was. But the plan had another serious drawback—it was an expensive addition to the federal budget. Estimates are that it will add $445 billion to the cost of Medicare between 2004 and 2014,[28] and some budget experts say we really need to

---

[26] Congressional Budget Office, Budget Options, Volume 1: Health Care, "Option 81: Replace Medicare's Current Cost-Sharing Requirements with a Unified Deductible, a Uniform Coinsurance Rate, and a Catastrophic Limit," page 154, www.cbo.gov/doc, accessed May 2, 2010.

[27] Congressional Budget Office, Budget Options, Volume 1: Health Care, "Option 81: Replace Medicare's Current Cost-Sharing Requirements with a Unified Deductible, a Uniform Coinsurance Rate, and a Catastrophic Limit," page 154, www.cbo.gov/doc, accessed May 2, 2010.

[28] Centers for Medicare and Medicaid Services, "The 2010 Annual Report of the Boards of Trustees of the Federal Hospital Insurance and Federal Supplementary Medical Insurance Trust Funds," Table V.E8,—"Operations of the Part D Account in the SMI Trust Fund (Cash Basis) during Fiscal Years 2004–2019," www.cms.gov/Reports TrustFunds/downloads/tr2010.pdf.

look at how to reduce the program's overall costs to taxpayers. One idea is limiting the plan to low-income seniors or perhaps low- and middle-income seniors. Right now, Oprah will be eligible when she retires (provided she's been paying Social Security and Medicare taxes). Others want the government to drive a harder bargain with drug companies, and the CBO has done some calculations on one approach. Basically, it would require manufacturers of brand-name drugs to pay a "rebate" to the government or lose their ability to participate in the Medicare Part D drug program. CBO says the option could generate "substantial savings," estimated at $110 billion over the next decade.[29] The downsides are that drug makers might raise prices on new drugs to recover the money they lose in Medicare or perhaps invest less in researching and developing new drugs. As we always say, there really aren't any cost-free, "everybody's happy" solutions out there.

10. Run Medicare more like the VA. According to some experts, the Veterans Health Administration has already demonstrated some good ways to improve patient care *and* hold down costs. Columnist Paul Krugman described the VA as a "health-care system that has been highly successful in containing costs, yet provides excellent care."[30] A trio of physicians studied the VA and concluded that in the last decade or so, it had left behind its "tarnished reputation of bureaucracy, inefficiency, and mediocre care" to become

[29] Congressional Budget Office, Budget Options, Volume 1: Health Care, "Option 67: Require Manufacturers to Pay a Minimum Rebate on Drugs Covered Under Medicare Part D," page 124, www.cbo.gov, accessed May 2, 2010.

[30] Paul Krugman, "Health Care Confidential—Veterans' Hospitals Are Unsung in Delivering Excellence," *New York Times*, January 27, 2006.

a "model system characterized by patient-centered, high-quality, high-value health care."[31]

What did the VA do? It bargained with drug companies to get better prices than most private insurers. It set up computer systems so doctors and managers could pull up patient records quickly, coordinate care, and avoid prescription errors. It emphasized geriatric and outpatient care for older vets to keep them as healthy and independent as possible for as long as possible. In recent years, the challenges faced by the VA have changed. Previously, the veterans hospitals primarily served aging vets from World War II, Korea, and Vietnam. But the wars in Iraq and Afghanistan have created a new wave of seriously disabled younger vets, and the VA has been criticized for not offering the quality of care these people deserve. [32]

Despite its current problems, some say that the VA was on to something. The agency used the power of a large, centrally managed system to change the way care is delivered much the way some European-style health care systems do. In fact, the VA is essentially a government-run health care system. So, is that a good thing or a bad thing? Well, it's something you'll need to consider for yourself as the debate on how to reform Medicare heats up.

---

[31] Jonathan B. Perlin, MD, PhD, Robert M. Kolodner, MD, and Robert H. Roswell, MD, "The Veterans Health Administration: Quality, Value, Accountability, and Information as Transforming Strategies for Patient Care," *American Journal of Managed Care*, November 2004.

[32] See for example, Charles M. Sennott, "For Veterans in Rural Areas, Care Hard to Reach," *Boston Globe*, April 29, 2007, and Erika Bolstad, "Improving Rate of Vets' Survival Stresses System; Head Injuries and Post-Traumatic Stress from Combat Missions in Iraq and Afghanistan Are Presenting a New Set of Challenges Back Home," *Miami Herald*, April 6, 2007.

11. Redesign Medicare so older people choose among different insurance plans.
Most of us take whatever health insurance our employer de-
cides to give us, but current and retired federal workers can
choose from over two hundred different health insurance
plans from a range of providers.[33] The Federal Employees
Health Benefits Program has a fearsome acronym—FEHBP—
but some say a plan like this might work well for Medicare. In
FEHBP, the employer (the government) provides a set amount
for health insurance, but how much employees have to contribute depends on which plan they choose. If they choose a more
expensive plan, they have to pay more themselves. FEHBP's
costs have risen some lately, according to the GAO, but so have
insurance costs overall, and FEHBP's costs have not risen as
quickly as those of some similar plans. Those who want Medicare reorganized this way say insurance companies would
hold their costs down to attract seniors to their plan and that
there would be less bureaucracy and waste. Others point out
that this approach would allow seniors to choose the kind of
plan that's best for them. It might be an HMO, or a plan with
a very high deductible upfront, but lower costs overall, or a
plan that operates more like traditional Medicare. That's the
idea—it would be their choice, not the government's.[34]

But opponents aren't as optimistic. For one thing, elderly
Medicare recipients would have to choose among competing

---

[33] Testimony of John E. Dicken, "Federal Employees Health Bene-
fits Program: Premiums Continue to Rise, but Rate of Growth Has
Slowed Recently," United States Government Accountability Office,
May 18, 2007 (www.gao.gov/new.items/d07873t.pdf).

[34] See for example, Edmund Haislmaier, "Health Care Reform: Design
Principles for a Patient-Centered, Consumer-Based Market," The
Heritage Foundation, April 23, 2008, www.heritage.org/Research/
Reports/2008/04/Health-Care-Reform-Design-Principles-for-a-
Patient-Centered-Consumer-Based-Market, accessed May 2, 2010.

health insurance plans (just picture it—the let's-choose-from-a-zillion Medicare drug plans scenario reloaded). Opponents also worry this won't really save money because private insurance companies—unlike Medicare—need to make profits and pay for advertising to compete for customers. Unfortunately, there's not really much research on how something like this would work with an older, sicker population. As the CBO dryly puts it, there's not much "experience on which to base long-range estimates of the effects this approach would have on total costs or to assess its impact on beneficiaries."[35]

12. Redesign Medicare so people shop around for cost-effective health care.
Some experts want to harness the power of the consumer, not to shop for insurance policies, but to shop directly for doctors, hospitals, tests, and so on. In fact, many analysts say one of the reasons health care is so expensive is that people don't pay much of the cost themselves. Consequently, people rarely even ask about prices, much less shop around for a less-expensive doctor or hospital. There are different ways this idea could work, but one of the most talked about is medical savings accounts that are now offered by many employers. People would put money into the accounts while they are working (and get a tax deduction for it). When they retire, they can use the money to pay for routine medical expenses. Serious illness would still be covered by Medicare (or private insurance, as in choice no. 11). Advocates say this would discourage people from going to the doctor or having tests and procedures that aren't really necessary because they would be using their own savings. They also believe it would encourage the health care industry

---

[35] Congressional Budget Office, "The Long-Term Budget Outlook," December 2005, www.cbo.gov/doc.cfm?index=6982&type=1.

to hold down costs because patients would be asking questions and shopping around.

Critics of the "shop-around" strategy worry that seniors will avoid routine care in order to save money. It's also worth asking whether Americans are psychologically ready to go with the *cheapest* doctor, even one who's not as shameless as Dr. Nick on *The Simpsons*. The good Dr. Nick does infomercials and promises any operation for $129.95—"Hi, everybody! Call me at 1-800-DOCTORB. The 'B' is for bargain!" But then again, maybe seniors will be savvier medical consumers than anyone thinks.

13. Encourage seniors to make living wills and and use hospice care more.

It's not easy to know exactly how much Medicare spends on "heroic measures" for terminally ill patients[36]—especially since people have different definitions of what counts as "heroic" care. Still, there is very little doubt that it is billions of dollars every year. Consequently, some policy experts are suggesting, very gingerly, that Medicare needs to encourage older Americans to think carefully about the kind of care they need and want when they are near death and to consider whether they want every possible medical treatment and technology used to extend their lives even if their quality of life is limited.

Right now, there are surprisingly wide variations in the care dying people receive. When doctors at Dartmouth Medical School looked at this question, they found that patients in New York spend about thirty-five days in the hospital and see thirty-five doctors in their last six months of life.

---

[36] Daniel Altman, "How to Save Medicare? Die Sooner," *New York Times*, February 27, 2005; Mary Ann Roser, "Should Cost Be a Factor in a Case Like Emilio's, Which Exceeded $1.6 Million?" *Austin-American Statesman*, May 28, 2007.

In Oregon, the average is eight days and fourteen doctors.[37] Americans don't necessarily agree on which approach is better. Some worry about getting *too much* medical care near the end of life; some fear getting *too little*. In many respects, this is part of our society's larger ethical struggle about what constitutes "a good death."

No one is suggesting that Medicare would stop covering care to ease pain or make patients more comfortable, but some say the program shouldn't pay for procedures and treatments that have almost no chance of success. In many cases, they say, patients and families don't even want all this health care near the end of life—they just don't know about options like hospice care and living wills and can't stop hospitals and doctors once they switch into gear.[38]

During the 2010 health care debate, the idea of allowing Medicare to cover office visits where seniors could discuss signing a living will (or "advance directive") with their doctor was bitterly disputed. The story that the health care reform plan included "death panels" that would decide who would get care and who wouldn't is flatly untrue, but the reaction to it showed how emotional any discussion of this issue can be.[39] Some critics feared that seniors might be encouraged to enter hospices rather than have access to drugs and procedures that might extend their lives, however slight that hope might be. Some worried that seniors would be pushed into decisions that didn't really reflect their own beliefs and values—all in the name of saving money for Medicare. One point that is often omitted from the dis-

---

[37] Stephanie Saul, "Treatments: Need a Knee Replaced? Check Your ZIP Code," *New York Times*, June 11, 2007.

[38] See, for example, Anne Applebaum, "How We Die: Choice and Chance," *Washington Post*, March 30, 2005.

[39] See, for example, Factcheck.org, "Palin vs. Obama: Death Panels," Aug. 14, 2009, www.factcheck.org/2009/08/palin-vs-obama-death-panels/.

cussion is whether hospice care is cheaper than hospital care, and this isn't actually a clear-cut case. The National Hospice and Palliative Care Organization (which advocates hospice care) cites research saying that hospice care saves up to $8,800 per patient, depending on the illness.[40] But a RAND Corporation study reached different conclusions, saying hospice patients cost Medicare slightly more than traditional care, although for certain types of cancer there were significant savings.[41]

But for many Americans, the question is not about money. For them, the thought of not doing everything humanly possible to extend life is unthinkable—even for people nearing their end. Nearly every one of us knows an older person who seemed like they were about to die and yet rallied back to life. Sometimes this person only lived a few more months, perhaps a year. Yet the extra time can be profoundly precious to those who love that person. Consequently, this approach is unsettling to think about, ethically and emotionally.

Still, 42 percent of Americans say they would want to stop treatment if they had a terminal illness with no hope of improvement, one that made it difficult to function in their daily lives, while 43 percent would want doctors to do every-

---

[40] "Hospice Costs Medicare Less and Patients Often Live Longer New Research Shows," press release, National Hospice and Palliative Care Organization, September 21, 2004 (www.nhpco.org/i4a/pages/Index.cfm?pageid=4343); B. Pyenson, B. S. Connor, K. Fitch, and B. Kinzbrunner, "Medicare Cost in Matched Hospice and Non-Hospice Cohorts," *Journal of Pain and Symptom Management*, September 2004.

[41] "RAND Study Finds Choosing Hospice Care Raises Medicare Costs for the Last Year of Life," press release, RAND Corporation, February 16, 2004 (http://www.rand.org/news/press.04/02.16.html); Diane E. Campbell, PhD, Joanne Lynn, MD, Tom A. Louis, PhD, and Lisa R. Shugarman, PhD, "Medicare Program Expenditures Associated with Hospice Use," *Annals of Internal Medicine*, February 17, 2004.

thing possible to save their life.[42] As a public, we seem to be evenly divided on what kind of care terminally ill patients really want and need—and whether the government should be involved in this decision at all—so maybe it's time to talk about this more.[43]

14. Pass a national VAT to help pay for Social Security and Medicare. Even if we give Social Security and Medicare quite a few nips and tucks, and even if we go back to the income tax rates we had under President Clinton, the country may still need more money coming in to make these programs affordable. That's how huge this Social Security and Medicare challenge is. That's why some experts are saying that it's time to start a kind of national sales tax called a VAT to help get our financial house in order.[44] VAT stands for **v**alue **a**dded **t**ax (If you've been shopping in Paris or Madrid, this is similar to those value-added taxes you would have been entitled to get back. If you had actually filled out the forms. And mailed them to Paris or Madrid.) We've listed some places where you can find some more extensive definitions of the

---

[42] Princeton Survey Research Associates for Pew Research Center. November 9–27, 2005: "Question: Now I'm going to describe a few medical situations that sometimes happen, and for each one, please tell me what you would want YOUR OWN DOCTOR to do, if you could make the choice. Would you tell your doctor to do EVERYTHING POSSIBLE to save your life (43%), or would you tell your doctor to STOP TREATMENT so you could die (42%)? It depends, 5%; Don't know, 10%."

[43] For a nonpartisan look at both the ethical and financial issues around end-of-life care, visit Issues/Right to Die at www.publicagenda .org/issues.

[44] See for example, Henry J. Aaron, William G. Gale, and Peter R. Orszag, "Meeting the Revenue Challenge," *Restoring Fiscal Sanity: How to Balance the Budget*, ed. Alice M. Rivlin and Isabel Sawhill (Brookings Institution Press, 2004).

VAT,[45] but basically it's applied to products at various stages of their coming to life—when the raw materials are bought, when it's manufactured, etc.—and the cost is passed on to—you guessed it—the consumer. Some economists believe that VATs are less likely to discourage investment and entrepreneurship, although others worry that these kinds of sales taxes are tougher on low-income and working people. Others say we shouldn't be raising taxes at all.

If a VAT proposal (or even a more familiar sales tax idea) moves to the head of the class in terms of the national debate, you'll have plenty of chances to think about the pros and cons, but do keep a close eye on the details. Sometimes VATs are discussed mainly as ways to simplify the current tax system—not to bring in more money.[46] This isn't necessarily a bad idea, but if you care about the problem we are discussing here—the habitual red ink and the coming money crunch on Social Security and Medicare—you need to keep your eye on the bottom line. If the sales or value-added tax doesn't bring in extra money, it won't help us get out of the financial hole we are so busily digging. By the way, VAT is not the only new tax that could play a role here. Another idea is to put a "carbon tax" on oil, coal, and other forms of energy that contribute to global warming, so you may be hearing more about that option as well.

15. Expand Medicare to cover all Americans. When the country was debating health care reform in early 2010, a group called

---

[45] Answers.com has definitions of the VAT from the *Small Business Encyclopedia*, *Columbia Encyclopedia*, Wikipedia, and other sources; see www.answers.com/topic/value-added-tax.

[46] See, for example, Michael J. Graetz, "100 Million Unnecessary Returns: A Fresh Start for the U.S. Tax System," *Yale Law Journal*, September 2004 (www.law.yale.edu/graetzhome/extra/YLJ_Graetz%20essay.pdf).

Physicians for a National Health Program published an "open letter" to President Obama calling for "Medicare for all." The idea is to change Medicare from a program just for the elderly to one that covers everyone. There would still be private doctors and hospitals, but when they delivered care, they would submit the bills to Medicare for payment—just the way it works for seniors now. Writing for the group, Dr. Margaret Flowers argued that taking private insurers out of the picture would reduce spending on "activities that have nothing to do with health care, such as marketing, administration and high executive salaries and bonuses." [47]

If that sounds like Medicare would turn into a European or Canadian-style national health insurance plan, that's because it would. And if Medicare's already in financial trouble, why would we expand it? For one thing, since Medicare would be the "single payer" (another name for this idea), advocates say it could bargain with doctors, hospitals, and drug companies for better prices. Obviously, Medicare's costs would go up substantially because it would be insuring almost everyone, but advocates say the combination of lower overhead and negotiating power would control costs overall. As the CBO has repeatedly emphasized, rising health care costs are "the single greatest challenge to balancing the federal budget."[48]

And the drawbacks of single payer? This chapter is not

---

[47] Dr. Margaret Flowers, MD, "There is Still Time For Real Reform, Listen to the American People: Open Letter to President Obama on Health Care Reform," Op-Ed News, January 28, 2010, http://pnhp. org/news/2010/january/there-is-still-time-for-real-reform-listen-to-the-american-people.

[48] Statement of Douglas W. Elmendorf, Director, Congressional Budget Office, "Options for Expanding Health Care Coverage and Controlling Costs," February 25, 2009, http://www.cbo.gov/ftpdocs/99xx/doc9911/02-25_HealthIns.htm.

exactly chock-full of popular ideas, but broad public skepticism is a major downside here. In 2009, about 7 in 10 Americans said they opposed "a single-payer system" with government as national insurer.[49] Many Americans recoil at any additional government involvement in health care,[50] and private insurers would surely take a major financial hit and probably lay off employees if Medicare insured almost everyone.

Would this really control health care costs? Other countries with single payer systems do have significantly lower per person costs than we do, but they are also struggling to pay for new medical procedures and drugs that treat diseases that simply didn't exist before. The question here is whether a single payer system offers a better chance of holding costs in line overall or whether private insurers competing for business have a better shot at it.

---

[49] Ipsos/McClatchy Poll by Ipsos Public Affairs. November 19–22, 2009, Pollingreport.com, www.pollingreport.com/health3.htm.

[50] Surveys do show more support for something like Medicare as an option that would compete with private insurers: 62 percent of Americans said they would favor "the government offering everyone a government-administered health insurance plan—something like the Medicare coverage that people 65 and older get—that would compete with private health insurance plans." CBS News Poll, October 5–8, 2009, also at Pollingreport.com, www.pollingreport.com/health3.htm.

CHAPTER 10

Waste Not, Want Not

It is a popular delusion that the government wastes vast amounts of money through inefficiency and sloth. Enormous effort and elaborate planning are required to waste this much money.

—P. J. O'Rourke, "The Winners Go to Washington,"
Parliament of Whores, *1991*

Donald R. Matthews is a fortunate man. He lives in a nice house in a suburban subdivision, where the federal government subsidizes his backyard.

Every year, this retired asphalt contractor from El Campo, Texas, gets $1,300 in agricultural subsidies from the federal government. Never mind that he isn't a farmer. Never mind that he never even said he wanted to be a farmer. The fact is, his house *used* to be part of a rice farm, and that's good enough for the government.

Matthews feels guilty about this, according to the *Washington Post*. He even tried to give the money back to the government, but was told the government would just give it to somebody else who lives on a former rice farm. So he gives the money to local scholarship funds. "Still, I get money I don't think I'm entitled to," he said.

The federal government has sent $1.3 billion in crop subsidies since 2000 to people who don't farm anything, the *Post* reports.[1] And if that's not mystifying enough for you, this came about because of changes to the law that were supposed to *reform* the crop subsidy program—even phase it out over time.

You can go post that angry blog entry or that furious e-mail to your member of Congress now. We'll wait.

Stories like that leave people with the impression that the U.S. government, that marvel of checks and balances, the inspiration for freedom fighters for generations, is nothing but an enormous pork-delivery system. And there's plenty of evidence for that view if you decide to go looking for it.

★ The Federal Emergency Management Agency (FEMA), which did such a "heck of a job" responding to Hurricane Katrina, became infamous for buying trailers that storm victims never got to use, but that wasn't all. Audits showed that the agency racked up nearly $2 billion in waste and fraud in funds allocated for Katrina victims.

★ The "Bridge to Nowhere" has a romantic ring to it, but this $223 million bridge linking a small island in Alaska to the mainland has become a symbol for wasteful and surreptitiously "earmarked" federal spending. Unfortunately, there seem to be other communities in line for bridges that hardly any of us will ever use. There's a $27 million appropriation for a bridge linking Lone Star with Rimini, two towns in South Carolina that have barely two thousand

---

[1] "Farm Program Pays $1.3 Billion to People Who Don't Farm," *Washington Post*, July 2, 2006.

people between them. Nowhere must be a popular destination these days—lots of people want to get there fast.

★ Between 1997 and 2003, the Pentagon bought $100 million in refundable airline tickets it didn't use, and somehow they never got around to asking for refunds. On top of it, they spent another $8 million mistakenly reimbursing employees for tickets the Pentagon had purchased itself.[2]

★ In the business world, corporate credit cards are notorious temptations for big spenders ("Lemme just put this on my expense account, baby"). So why should the government be any different? One audit found 15 percent of all the Agriculture Department credit card accounts examined were being abused, with $5.8 million spent on purchases such as Ozzy Osbourne tickets, tattoos, lingerie, and tuition at bartender school.[3]

★ If you'd like to get your blood pressure up sometime, we recommend the *Congressional Pig Book Summary* from Citizens Against Government Waste, available on Web site, www.cagw.org. In 2009, there were 9,129 projects tucked into appropriations bills that met their definition of "pork," costing $16.5 billion.

Infuriating, isn't it? If we could just get rid of all that pork, if we just had an honest, efficient government, then we wouldn't have budget problems. Right?

Unfortunately, no. Waste is a problem, but it's not *the* problem. We're not going to call chasing waste and fraud an "easy answer"—that does an injustice to anyone who has devoted their life to fighting city hall. It's rough work, and not for the squeamish. In fact, we think anyone who has

---

[2] "The Top 10 Examples of Government Waste," Heritage Foundation Backgrounder, April 4, 2005.

[3] Ibid.

successfully battled government waste and fraud deserves the equivalent of a national standing ovation.

But the harsh fact is that if we somehow found enough people who were incorruptible, smart, and really, really cheap with other people's money to staff the entire government, we'd still have an enormous budget problem to solve. Simple honesty isn't going to be enough.

Waste *does* matter. But maybe not the way you might think.

THE TRIFECTA OF THROWING AWAY MONEY

As the examples above prove, there are lots of ways to waste government money. People are creative that way. But it's helpful to define some terms. If you're going to leave this chapter angry, you ought to know exactly what you're mad at.

There are basically three categories of government money gone wrong.

★ *Fraud and abuse,* which pretty much means stealing
★ *Waste,* which can best be summed up as bungling
★ *Pork,* which is politically motivated spending designed to keep an officeholder's supporters and constituents happy

Each happens for a different reason and demands a different solution.

Category No. 1: Fraud and Abuse—or, At Least We're Doing Better than Ghana

Outright corruption pretty much speaks for itself. But another way of characterizing corruption is when people in government do things they have absolutely no right to do. Stealing government money to buy things for yourself is a pretty clear example. Those Agriculture Department workers charging tattoos and lingerie to the government knew what they were doing was wrong. Bribes, kickbacks, bid rigging, influence peddling, and all the rest of it are pretty obvious.

It's hard to put a figure on how much all this costs the taxpayers since we only know about the pilferers who get caught. And while we don't mean to be Pollyannas about this, the United States is far from a "kleptocracy" where *nothing*, not even the most routine business, gets done without a payoff. There are places like that in the world, and Transparency International's list of most- and least-corrupt countries is a good conversation starter, if controversial, at www.transparency.org. In 2009, Somalia came in at number one for corruption, with Afghanistan and Myanmar close behind. New Zealand, Denmark, and Singapore were deemed the most honest nations on earth.[4] We've sat in focus groups with immigrants conducted by Public Agenda, the nonprofit organization we work for. For more than a few, the sense of relief at living under a government where they didn't have to bribe every cop every day was palpable.

Money for Nothing and Chicks for Free

Corrupt government employees who steal our money for themselves undoubtedly deserve their own ring in Dante's *Inferno*—and Dante was pretty clever with his punishments.[5] But frankly, lots of people outside the government find that ripping off taxpayers comes pretty easily. Tens of thousands of Americans suffered terribly from Hurricane Katrina, but for others, the disaster turned out to be a let's-get-crazy opportunity.

---

[4] Transparency International, Corruption Perceptions Index 2009, www.transparency.org/policy_research/surveys_indices/cpi/2009/cpi_2009_table, accessed May 16, 2010.

[5] Hordes of literature majors just raised their hands. Yes, Dante put crooked officials in Circle Eight. And it's pretty gross.

FEMA handed out debit cards so people displaced by the storm could get what they needed. And after a trauma like that, who's to say you don't need a Caribbean vacation? Or porn to get you through those lonely nights in the motel? And if the government is foolish enough not to check on whether you're collecting motel money and rental assistance at the same time, is that your fault? It's the sort of thing we expect criminals and people with me-first ethics to do whenever they get the chance. If the government's giving out "free" money, why not file a claim on the vacant lot next door. (Some people did this.)[6]

But lots of otherwise ordinary people seem to think it's OK to rip off large, anonymous institutions, and there's none bigger or more anonymous than the U.S. government. Kramer from *Seinfeld* is a man whose mind-set costs American taxpayers and consumers a lot of money. This, for example, was Kramer's stance on mail fraud.

KRAMER: Jerry, all these big companies, they write off everything.
JERRY: You don't even know what a write-off is.
KRAMER: Do you?
JERRY: No. I don't.
KRAMER: But *they* do. And *they're* the ones writing it off.

Regrettably, the federal government is a frequent patsy for people who think this way. For example, getting a student loan is a rite of passage for many Americans, with

---

[6] Government Accountability Office, "Hurricanes Katrina and Rita Disaster Relief: Improper and Potentially Fraudulent Individual Assistance Payments Estimated to Be Between $600 Million and $1.4 Billion," June 14, 2006.

the Department of Education processing about 14 million loan applications every year. In 1992, Congress specifically amended existing legislation to allow students to use government financial aid to study abroad,[7] so no one at the Department of Education thought twice when three students put in for loans to attend the prestigious Y'Hica Institute for the Visual Arts in London.

They should have. It doesn't exist.

Oh, sure, Y'Hica had a Web site and a catalog, plus a letter from educational authorities in Great Britain certifying that it was an accredited institution. All of which are easily forged by anyone with a personal computer, in this case the staff of the Senate Governmental Affairs Committee, who were trying to find out how easy it would be to scam the government out of student loans. They got approval to seek $55,000 for three nonexistent students. To their credit, someone at Bank of America didn't like the looks of the application he or she received and turned it down. But both Nellie Mae and Sallie Mae swallowed the story whole. A top Education Department official sheepishly admitted the department "did not completely follow every step of the procedure."[8]

That's not the only time the government simply has failed to check on the massive amounts of applications coming in (and contracts going out). Fraud in Medicare and Medicaid has been a continuing problem even though the government has ramped up efforts to recover the money that seeps out of the system. In 2008, the Feds filed 455 criminal actions and more than 300 civil suits attempting to stop the fraud and get the money back. Among the problems they were chasing

---

[7] http://studentaid.ed.gov/PORTALSWebApp/students/english/aboutus.jsp and http://www.nafsa.org/resourcelibrary/Default.aspx?id=8328.

[8] "Fake School Reveals Holes in Loan Program," Associated Press, January 21, 2003.

down: "payments for unallowable services," "hospitals taking advantage of enhanced payments by manipulating bill-
ing," and "hospitals reporting inaccurate wage data." Some
of the rip-offs are even more brazen. One group of criminals
set up HIV clinics in Miami that got more than $2.5 mil-
lion in Medicare payments between 2004 and 2006. Their
scheme? Submitting "claims for medically unnecessary HIV
infusion and injection treatments."[9] Unfortunately, most of
the effort seems to be taking place after the horse is out of
the barn. According to an analysis from GAO, 84 percent of
Medicare and Medicaid contracts in 2008 contained errors
or omissions that left them vulnerable to just this kind of
fraud and manipulation.[10]

Category No. 2: Waste—or, Never Give a Sucker an Even Break

There are times when government behaves like a damn
fool, either doing things that don't need to be done or doing
potentially useful things in unbelievably wrongheaded
ways. Mr. Matthews's $1,300 annual rice subsidies are like
that. Crop subsidies have a purpose, or at least they used to
have a purpose. During the Depression, farmers were going
under in droves because they couldn't sell what they raised.
Many ended up just walking away and letting the bank fore-
close. (Remember the Okies of Steinbeck's *Grapes of Wrath*?
Those guys were all too real.)

---

[9] Testimony of Lewis Morris, Chief Counsel, Office of Inspector General,
Department of Health and Human Services before the Senate Subcom-
mittee on Federal Financial Management, Government Information, Federal Services, and International Security, April 22, 2009, http://oig.hhs.gov/
testimony/docs/2009/4-22-09HomelandSecurity.pdf, accessed May 16, 2010.

[10] Government Accountability Office, "Centers for Medicare and
Medicaid Services; Pervasive Internal Control Weaknesses Hin-
dered Effective Contract Management," April 28, 2010, www.gao.gov/
highlights/d10637thigh.pdf, accessed May 16, 2010.

So the government came up with the idea of buying up surplus food and then paying farmers not to grow things they couldn't sell. That way the farmers didn't go broke and didn't have to lose their farms.

Extended Indefinitely

So what started as a response to a crisis has become an agricultural way of life. Eighty years later, agriculture is much more like big business, and by the mid-1990s much of the subsidy money was going to huge agricultural conglomerates.[11] Small farmers got subsidies too, but they also got a lot of federal regulations that kept them from switching crops easily. There was a good argument to be made that the system was actually hurting small farmers, not helping them. So the 1996 Freedom to Farm law introduced simplified direct payments, with the goal of weaning agriculture off subsidies. Farmers would get the money no matter what they farmed, or if they bothered to farm at all. And after seven years, the money would stop.

But a couple of years later, farm prices dropped, and under pressure from the farm lobby Congress extended the program indefinitely—and even increased the subsidies. And since the law promises payments even if nothing is grown, a suburban backyard that used to be a farm still qualifies. Which is why Donald Matthews gets his money. In parts of Texas that used to be big in rice growing, developers actually advertise their new subdivisions as being eligible for subsidies.

This, of course, is utterly boneheaded. But the Agriculture Department just shrugs and says it's implementing the

---

[11] "Federal Subsidies Turn Farms into Big Business," *Washington Post*, December 21, 2006.

law as written. And Congress, not wishing to tick off the farm lobby (which never wanted to lose subsidies anyway), has not been inclined to change it.

That's usually the dirty little secret behind wasteful spending (and pork, which we'll talk about in a minute). It exists because somebody defends it—or at least defends the overall system, because he's afraid any changes might damage his interests.

Manila Folders at the FBI?

Lest you think that waste is all about big corporations with their hands out, let us set you straight. Sometimes government officials are plain just in over their heads.

Over at the FBI, they've been trying since 2001 to upgrade their computer systems. On TV's *Criminal Minds*, the chubby, punky computer genius Penelope Garcia can pull up complete dossiers on everyone, everywhere, without ever facing the "blue screen of death." And the team on *Without a Trace* seems to get all the computer info they need pronto, too. But there's a reason why that's called fiction. In the real world, FBI management has been famously technophobic. (In the 1990s, then-director Louis Freeh refused to use e-mail.) The old 1980s mainframe system was so bad that some agents avoided using it. The 9/11 Commission concluded the bureau's "woefully inadequate" technology and clunky policies on sharing information prevented agents from making sense of the scraps of seemingly unrelated intelligence that might have unraveled the 9/11 plot. "The FBI lacked the ability to know what it knew," the commission said.[12]

When the bureau finally started working to upgrade its

---

[12] "FBI Organization and Priorities," chapter 3, National Commission on Terrorist Attacks Against the United States, available at www.911commission.gov.

computers, the FBI's leaders did what technologically naive and computer-phobic managers everywhere do: they were vague about their requirements and then kept tinkering with them; they set overly ambitious deadlines; and they neglected to make a plan to guide purchases and implementation. At least that's what the Justice Department inspector general concluded in a brutal 2005 report.[13]

$104 Million, $425 Million, $451 Million, and Counting

By 2005, the FBI realized that one key element of the project, the Virtual Case File, was so bug-ridden and behind schedule that it was unusable. That was $104 million thrown away right there, Director Robert Mueller III admitted to Congress. In 2006, the FBI basically decided it was time to reboot, launching a multiyear, $425 million effort called Sentinel to replace its antiquated, "paper-based" filing systems (just imagine the kind of split-screen suspense that would make on *24:* Jack Bauer waiting on his cell phone while people bend over filing cabinets riffling through manila folders. They'd have to rename the show *A Week to 10 Days.*) Sad to say, the project is still bedeviled by glitches, delays, and cost overruns. In March 2010, the Department of Justice's inspector general reported that costs had already risen to $451 million, that the FBI's original schedule had been "very optimistic," and that the Department's concerns about the FBI's ability to "complete Sentinel in a timely and cost-effective manner" had "escalated."[14]

---

[13] The Federal Bureau of Investigation's Management of the Trilogy Information Technology Modernization Project, Audit Report 05-07, Office of the Inspector General, U.S. Department of Justice, February 2005, www.usdoj.gov/oig/reports/FBI/a0507/final.pdf.

[14] U.S. Department of Justice, Office of the Inspector General, Status of the Federal Bureau of Investigation's Implementation of the Senti-

Unlike some, we're not arguing that government is inherently, laughably incompetent. We even suspect that at least some of you who work in the private sector are reading these stories and nodding, saying, "I can top that." There's a reason why *The Office* and *Dilbert* are so popular. As people who've spent our lives in the private and nonprofit sectors, we've got a few scary stories of our own.

And of course, the government certainly does not have a corner on fraud. Enron, WorldCom, and subprime loan specialists who encouraged borrowers to fib about their incomes to qualify for "liar loans" prove that—and unfortunately, they're *not* alone.

But the difference is this: when Dunder-Miffin Paper Co. bungles things in *The Office*, a few employees and investors suffer. When the government bungles, we all suffer.

Category No. 3: Pork—or, Alexis de Tocqueville Has Left the Building

It's impossible to write an entire book about American politics without quoting Alexis de Tocqueville. In fact, in some states it may be illegal. We've come this far without mentioning the nineteenth-century French author who wrote one of the most famous books about the United States, but we can't hold it off any longer:

> The American Republic will endure until
> the day Congress discovers that it can bribe the
> public with the public's money.

---

nel Project, Report 10-22, March, 2010, www.justice.gov/oig/reports/FBI/a1022.pdf.

That's the best definition of "pork" right there: the government bribing you with your own money. But one of the reasons we like this quote is that de Tocqueville was clearly wrong. That day has come and gone. In fact, it probably came and went not too long after he wrote this in the 1830s. At least according to some, the term *pork*, or *pork-barrel spending*, comes from the time when country politicians would gather at the general store, use a pork barrel for a desk, and pass out favors to the faithful.

Money Works Just as Well

It doesn't work quite that way now, thanks to civil service rules, sealed competitive bidding, and the fact that fewer people buy pork products by the barrel. But the idea is the same. To get elected to office—and stay there—politicians need to knit together a coalition adding up to 51 percent of the vote. Political science professors and editorial writers might like politicians to do that using reasoned debate, passionate oratory, and enlightened policy. But in the real world, money works just as well.

Let's face it, lots of voters see the federal government as a big sugar daddy. Why not? *Someone's* getting all those federal projects. And the benefits of those projects are real. If your community needs (or would like) a new bridge, and the federal government has money to pay for bridge building, why shouldn't you ask for it? Why shouldn't you expect your member of Congress to get it for you? And if he does, hasn't that earned him another term?

There are members of Congress, plenty of them, who view getting projects for their home states as a badge of honor. Consider the late Senator Robert C. Byrd (D-W.Va.), the longest-serving senator, author, zealous defender of the balance of powers—and, by general agreement, Congress's "King of Pork." "They don't know how much I enjoy it," said Byrd of that title, in much the same tone Robert Duvall used to describe the smell of napalm in the morning in *Apocalypse Now*. "I want to be West Virginia's billion dollar industry," Byrd said on another occasion.[15]

Thanks to Senator Byrd, a slew of federal agencies that otherwise might have trouble finding Wheeling, West Virginia, on a map now have major facilities there, from the FBI and Treasury Department to the Fish and Wildlife Service and NASA. And to express the state's appreciation—and just so voters wouldn't forget their benefactor's name come election time—a lot of West Virginians see the senator's name nearly every day. There's the Robert C. Byrd Expressway, not to be confused with the Robert C. Byrd Freeway, two Robert C. Byrd Federal Buildings (call first if you're visiting to make sure you've got the right one). There is also the Robert C. Byrd Federal Correctional Institution,[16] and in 2010, the senator received an Oinker Award from the Citizens Against Government Waste for his "dogged perseverance in the mad pursuit of pork." Even in a year when the government's red ink topped the charts, the senator managed to get a $7 million earmark for the Robert C. Byrd Institute of Advanced Flexible Manufacturing Systems.[17]

In Senator Byrd's defense, if you grew up in a house with no electricity and no running water, and then pulled

---

[15] Michael Barone and Richard E. Cohen, *Almanac of American Politics, 2004* (National Journal Group, 2003).

[16] Citizens Against Government Waste, "Words of Wisdom from the King of Pork," www.cagw.org/site/PageServer?pagename=news_byrd droppings, accessed December 3, 2006.

[17] Citizens Against Government Waste, "Pig Book Oinkers of 2010," www.cagw.org/reports/pig-book/2010/oinkers.html, accessed May 16, 2010.

yourself up to represent one of the poorest states in the Union, you might feel obligated to bring home the bacon, too. The people of West Virginia seemed happy with the deal—Byrd served as his state's senator from 1958 until his death at age ninety-two in 2010.

Does Anyone Really Need This?

So, defenders of pork ask, where's the harm? For example, NASA's Mission Control Center is in Houston for one reason: then vice president Lyndon Johnson was from Texas. NASA was going to build the center somewhere and Houston was as good a place as any. It hasn't done the space program any harm to have it there.

But there's a big difference between channeling needed projects to your home state, when and where you can, and proposing projects that aren't needed, just to get more federal money into your state. To our way of thinking, this is one of the two big signs that pork has gotten out of control: when you hear about a project and can't imagine why *anyone* needs it or why it's the federal government's job to pay for it.

We haven't got anything against teapots or the people who collect them, but honestly, how many Americans really wanted their tax dollars spent on the Sparta Teapot Museum in Sparta, North Carolina? That got half a million dollars in the 2006 federal budget. How many of us are worried about increasing the number of wild turkeys (nope, they're not endangered)? The National Wild Turkey Federation got $234,000.

Are "Earmarks" Really on Death's Door?

The practice of a lawmaker putting special provisions into larger spending bills so they don't get the normal budget review has been around a long time, but their use exploded in the 1990s. Citizens Against Government Waste (CAGW) has calculated that between 1991 and 2010, there were nearly 110,000 earmarks costing taxpayers a total of more than $300 billion.[18] In the 2006 elections, the practice finally emerged as a political issue, and the new Democratic majorities in the House and the Senate promised to put some brakes on their use. There have been some changes (more about this in chapter 12), and according to CAGW, the number of pork projects dropped by about 10 percent in 2010. Even so, the practice (which serves members of Congress from both parties so well) is far from dead.

IT'S JUST SO INFURIATING

So how much does all this actually add to the deficit? Most of the examples of waste, fraud, and pork we've talked about are counted in the millions of dollars, or even thousands of dollars, not billions. Obviously, it would be better to save that money rather than waste it, but hacking earmarks out of the budget is not going to solve the country's financial problems.

Still, waste infuriates people, as much as or more than anything else the government does. Here we have to consult an expert in these matters, the late and less-than-honorable George Washington Plunkitt. Back in his day, a hundred years ago, Plunkitt was the very model of a Tammany Hall poli-

---

[18] Citizens Against Government Waste, "Pork Trends 1991–2010," www.cagw.org/reports/pig-book/#trends, accessed May 16, 2010.

The man who gave us the idea of "honest graft": Tammany Hall politician George Washington Plunkitt. *Credit: projects.ilt.columbia.edu*

tician: paunchy, mustachioed, genial, and blatantly out for himself. Mustaches are out of style in Washington nowadays (although not paunches), but Plunkitt's spiritual descendants are still around. Plunkitt's important not because of jobs he held (he never rose above state senator) or bills he wrote. He's important because of a phrase he coined: "honest graft."

Graft, as you know, means politicians profiting from their connections with government. But Plunkitt prided himself on making a pile of money without breaking the law. "Dishonest graft" to him was actual bribery, embezzlement, or shaking people down, and he had contempt for it. "Honest graft" was another matter. Plunkitt's favorite scheme was to get advance information on where public works were being built, such as a new park, and buy up the land cheap before anyone else heard about it. Then he'd sell the land to the city for a nice profit. No laws were broken and the city wasn't paying any more than it would have paid the previous owner, so the taxpayers weren't being cheated, Plunkitt argued. He was even able to get offended when anyone suggested otherwise.

"I don't own a dishonest dollar," Plunkitt declared in 1905. "If my worst enemy was given the job of writing my epitaph when I'm gone, he couldn't do more than write: 'George W. Plunkitt. He Seen His Opportunities, and He Took 'Em.'"[19]

When Tammany finally got tossed out, our friend Plunkitt figured the problem was that the voters, foolishly, didn't get the difference between honest and dishonest graft.

"They saw that some Tammany men grew rich, and supposed they had been robbing the city treasury or levying blackmail on disorderly houses, or working in with the gamblers and lawbreakers," Plunkitt said. "As a matter of policy, if nothing else, why should the Tammany leaders go into such dirty business, when there is so much honest graft lying around?"

Interestingly, a hundred years later, many Americans worry that we haven't made much progress. When our organization, Public Agenda, conducted focus groups on the federal deficit and debt in 2006, federal finances weren't the top priority for most people when the groups started. It didn't take long for the participants to become concerned, but most were cynical and pessimistic about the government's ability to do anything about it.

Why? Because of a lifetime of hearing anecdotes about bungling, wasteful, inept government. It's no surprise that an ABC/*Washington Post* poll in 2010 that asked Americans how much of their tax dollar was wasted found an aver-

---

[19] "Honest Graft and Dishonest Graft: Very Plain Talks on Very Practical Politics," by Senator Plunkitt of Tammany Hall, recorded by William L. Riordon, 1905, available at www.panarchy.org/plunkitt/graft.1905.html.

age answer of 53 cents of every dollar [20]—which by any objective estimate is way, way off the mark. Remember that estimate from the "Pig Book" people—about $300 billion worth of pork projects between 1991 and today. The numbers are from a group that's dedicated to fighting pork so they're not inclined to underestimate it. But even though $300 billion is a lot of money, it wouldn't even begin to cover the country's deficit for just last year.

"I think to get robbed is a crime," one participant said in a New Jersey focus group. "To get robbed and lose trust, I think, is more of a crime, and that's what [politicians] are doing, they're taking our trust."

So Plunkitt *saw* it, but he didn't *get* it. People should be skeptical of their government; it's the only way democracy can work. But there also needs to be a minimum level of trust to get things done. Tammany Hall fell because the name "Tammany Hall" came to represent bloated, corrupt government. Eventually, people figured they couldn't trust Tammany to do anything right.

Given the budget mess we're in, the government should hang on to every dollar it can. But no one who's studied the federal budget believes that eliminating waste, fraud, and pork is going to balance the budget. Even if it did, that wouldn't do a thing to change the long-term demographic and health care trends.

The real issue we face now is that we can't solve the budget crisis without trust—the public's trust that the government is facing the problem honestly, proposing real solutions, and that the inevitable sacrifices are fair to everyone.

---

[20] *Washington Post*/ABC survey conducted February 4–8, 2010, Q28: "On another subject, out of every dollar the federal government collects in taxes, how many cents do you think are wasted?" www.washingtonpost.com/wp-srv/politics/polls/postpoll_021010.html.

A lot of Americans may be willing to take a financial hit to ensure that Medicare is around to take care of their parents and, eventually, themselves. But why should they sacrifice if Medicare continues to let money dribble away to schemers and tricksters and outright criminals? Why should people dig into their own pockets when Congress continues spending millions of dollars on bridges to nowhere just to up the reelection chances of the already powerful?

If a group of people get lost in the wilderness, and they pool their granola bars and Oreos so that no one goes hungry, that brings out their human dignity. But if the group is rationing snack food while one guy has a roast chicken hidden in his knapsack, that makes everybody else a sucker. And nobody puts up with being a sucker forever.

THE BEST AND THE BRIGHTEST

Once upon a time (1962, to be precise), the New York Mets were so hapless, so far down in the cellar, that manager Casey Stengel once wailed, "Can't anyone here play this game?"

Sometimes it's easy to feel that way about the federal government when you hear so much about waste and mismanagement. But it's also true that lots of federal programs run pretty well, and it's worth taking note of them. A good place to start is www.expectmore.gov, which is where the Office of Management and Budget posts its ratings of how well government agencies function. The OMB has a formal assessment process that rates

★★★★★★★★★★★★★★★★★★★★★★★★★★★★★★★★★★★★★★

programs as effective, moderately effective, adequate, ineffective, or "results not demonstrated."

As of 2008, the OMB said it had assessed 1,015 programs, covering almost all of the federal government. Of those, 80 percent were rated "adequate" or better, compared to 20 percent that were ineffective or had too little information to make a judgment. Only 19 percent got the highest rating, "effective," while 3 percent were "ineffective."

So who are those top performers? It's quite a mix. Some are comforting (the Secret Service protection programs get top marks, for example). Others are functions that frankly, we never would have thought of, but as soon as they're mentioned you realize they're really important to some folks. (Best example: the Coast Guard's domestic icebreakers. Somebody's got to keep shipping moving on the Great Lakes.) And, of course, there are frequently "effective" and "ineffective" programs in the same department.

Check out the entire list for yourself, but some themes that jumped out at us include:

★ **The statisticians:** One of the main products of the federal government is statistics about American life, and the government does that extremely well. The Census Bureau, Bureau of Labor Statistics, Bureau of Economic Analysis, Bureau of Justice Statistics, and the National Center for Education Statistics all got high ratings.

★ **The researchers:** A number of programs got high ratings at NASA and the National Science Foundation, including solar system exploration, astronomy and astrophysics, information technology, basic engineering, and polar research. The Federal Aviation Administration's research on air safety is also on the list, as is the U.S. Geological Survey.

★ **People-to-people contact overseas:** The State Department gets good grades for its cultural exchanges, refugee assistance, and the consular services for Americans abroad. The Peace Corps does well, too.

SO MAYBE BILL GATES AND OPRAH COULD PAY OFF THE DEBT . . .

Nice try, but no way—not even if we vacuumed up every single dollar they have.

It's not easy to grasp how much money we're talking about here, especially for those of us who get a sinking feeling every time we think about how many years it's going to take us to pay off our measly little home mortgages. Even the massive fortunes of Bill Gates and the Walton family (the Walmart heirs) are puny alongside the federal government's numbers. Take a look at the chart below for a sobering little lesson in the numbers we're up against.

The federal government's red ink for 2009: $1.4 trillion
The combined fortunes of the 10 richest people in America: $245.9 billion[21]

---

[21] Information in this section is from "The 400 Richest Americans," Forbes.com, September 30, 2009, www.forbes.com/lists/2009/54/rich-list-09_The-400-

★★★★★★★★★★★★★★★★★★★★★★★★★★★★★★★

Bill Gates, Microsoft, Medina, WA: $50 billion

Warren Buffett, Berkshire Hathaway, Omaha, NE: $40 billion

Lawrence Ellison, Oracle, Redwood City, CA: $27 billion

Christy Walton and Family, Walmart, Jackson, WY:
   $21.5 billion

Jim C. Walton, Walmart, Bentonville, AR: $19.6 billion

Alice Walton, Walmart, Fort Worth, TX: $19.3 billion

S. Robson Walton, Walmart, Bentonville, AR: $19 billion

Michael Bloomberg, Bloomberg, New York, NY $17.5 billion

Charles Koch, manufacturing, energy, Wichita, KS $16 billion

David Koch, manufacturing, energy, New York, NY $16 billion

Total outstanding debt of the U.S. government: about $14 trillion in 2011

Combined wealth of the Forbes 400 wealthiest Americans: $1.27 trillion in 2009

And as rich and successful as they are, people like Oprah and Donald Trump couldn't even keep up with the federal government's interest payments. Oprah's fortune is estimated at about $2.3 billion. Donald Trump is at $2 billion. The federal government? In 2009, it spent about $187 billion just on interest.

Richest-Americans_FinalWorth.html, and "Special Report: The Richest People In America," Edited by Matthew Miller and Duncan Greenberg, Forbes.com, September 30, 2009, www.forbes.com/2009/09/30/forbes-400-gates-buffett-wealth-rich-list-09_land.html.

BOONDOGGLING FOR FUN AND PROFIT

Once upon a time, a boondoggle was a way of tying a lanyard or neck-erchief. Despite what you might have heard in the movie *Napoleon Dynamite,* boondoggles were never "a must have for this season's fashion." But in 1935, the New York City Board of Aldermen was somewhat nonplussed to find out that the government was paying people to make them. In fact, some $3 million of city relief funds were being spent on teaching unemployed people to dance and, as the *New York Times* put it, "otherwise amuse themselves."[22]

This was in the midst of the Great Depression, with one in five workers unemployed. It's not so much that the government felt the jobless needed to jitterbug, but President Roosevelt's New Deal strategy was that if there were no private-sector jobs for these people, the government had better come up with jobs for them, and fast. So the government set up whole agencies just to put people to work. The Works Progress Administration employed millions of people building schools, post offices, parks, and town halls across the country. The Civilian Conservation Corps planted trees and tended national parks. The Federal Writers' Project and Theatre Project funded the arts, including rising young talents like James Agee and Orson Welles.

But it fell to a crafts instructor named Robert Marshall to face the music on boondoggles.

"I spend a good deal of time explaining it," he said ("some-

---

[22] "$3,187,000 Relief Is Spent to Teach Jobless to Play; $19,658,512 Voted for April," *New York Times,* April 4, 1935.

★★★★★★★★★★★★★★★★★★★★★★★★★★★★★★★★

what sadly," the *Times* noted). It could have been worse. He appeared right after Myra Wilcoxon, who was teaching people "eurythmic dancing." The board members asked her to demonstrate a few moves, but she refused.

So the boondoggle, once a perfectly innocent technique taught to Boy Scouts, became a term for anything big, useless, and funded with government money.

When you think of a boondoggle, you may be thinking of something like this:

Way behind schedule and far over budget, the Big Dig highway project in Boston cost $12 billion more than originally projected. *Credit: Massachusetts Turnpike Authority*

It's Boston's Big Dig, also known as the Central Artery/Tunnel, a massive construction project to change Interstate 93 from an elevated roadway to a 3.5-mile tunnel under the city. At $14.6 billion, it's the most expensive highway project in U.S. history. And it came in a mere $12.1 billion over the original projections. But that's not counting $100 million the state

attorney general is trying to get contractors to give back because of shoddy workmanship. In fact, a few months after the tunnel was opened, it had to be closed again because a piece of concrete fell off and killed someone.

A boondoggle is pretty much in the eye of the beholder. Some people say farm subsidies, the international space station, and the Pentagon's missile defense plan are boondoggles, but they've all got their defenders. In this case the Big Dig is, in fact, open for business, and it's easier to get across Boston than it used to be. To us, that means it's not useless and therefore, technically, not a boondoggle. It's merely badly built and vastly over budget.

But it's a close call.

CHAPTER 11

The Liberals and the Conservatives

Blessed are the young, for they shall inherit the national debt.

—Herbert Hoover (1874–1964), U.S. president

Given the threat to the nation's finances, you might think the president and Congress—the Republicans and the Democrats, the liberals and the conservatives—would be up there wheeling and dealing, looking for areas of agreement and compromise. Research conducted by the organization we work for, Public Agenda, shows that most Americans believe that we will have to compromise on this issue.[1] Compromise has an honorable tradition in American government, and politicians are generally pretty good at horse trading.

Logically, after all, the main options for closing the budget gap are tax increases or spending cuts, so the debate in Washington ought to be about how much of each

---

[1] Public Agenda, *It's Time to Pay Our Bills: Americans' Perspectives on the National Debt & How Leaders Can Use the Public's Ideas to Address the Country's Long-Term Budget Challenges,* April 2006, www.publicagenda. org/research/pdfs/facingup_leaders_report.pdf.

to apply, right? There are few issues more amenable to a practical, pragmatic approach than the federal budget. You'd think.

But we haven't heard much talk of compromise in Washington in recent years. Instead, what most of us hear most of the time is a battle of the sound bites—usually over-heated, over-the-top sound bites.

As you no doubt realize by now, we think all sorts of ideas should be on the table, and that in the end, we'll have to come at this problem from many different directions—that includes spending cuts, tax increases, and changes in the way that Social Security and Medicare are organized. In chapter 9, we tossed in a list of ideas, including a VAT and a whole bunch of proposals for changing Social Security including pushing back the retirement age and trimming benefits for upper income Americans. We think it's time for people to start considering these ideas with an open mind and accept that it's time to talk turkey and do a deal. But how many Americans are ready to stop fuming and sit down and solve this thing? Sometimes we're not so sure.

Here's what we found about the idea of a VAT on a Web site for people supporting former Alaska governor Sarah Palin (www.conservatives4palin.com):

> An enormous European-style VAT to cement the transformation of America into a country we won't be able to recognize is something he [President Obama] has been planning all along. . . . If Obama is successful in passing the VAT, the days of America's status as a military and economic superpower will be numbered.[2]

---

[2] www.conservatives4palin.com/2010/04/obama-moving-forward-on-vat.html.

And here's how a liberal blogger reacted to the idea of Social Security reform. "The Plot to Kill Social Security," the headline screams. Here's what follows:

> Each new day brings a fresh call to "reform en-titlement programs"—Social Security, Medicare, etc., (in Congress, the word "reform" now means to eliminate, or drastically reduce) . . . The newest liberal recruit to the destruction of Social Security is Thomas Friedman, the influential columnist for *The New York Times* . . . For political hacks like Friedman—and there are thousands of them—the ONLY solution to curing the U.S. deficit is cutting social services in general, while specifically target-ing Social Security and Medicare.[3]

Whew! We're sure that both President Obama and Tom Friedman can take care of themselves, but it this kind of rhetorical fire-breathing really getting us anywhere? A VAT is not going to obliterate America's influence in the world, and there are plenty of ways to modify Social Se-curity that—rather than "killing" it—would give it the fi-nancial stability it needs to keep its promises to the older Americans who rely on it.

Maybe it's the political equivalent of the old "hellfire and damnation" sermons—designed to scare the congrega-tion into repenting. Sometimes it reminds us of Bill Murray forecasting doom in *Ghostbusters:* "This city is headed for a disaster of biblical proportions . . . Human sacrifice! Dogs and cats living together! Mass hysteria!" Of course, in the

---

[3] Shamus Cooke, "The Plot to Kill Social Security," Counterpunch.org, February 24, 2010, http://www.counterpunch.org/cooke02242010.html, accessed May 2, 2010.

movie, New York faced destruction at the hands of an evil Sumerian god shaped like a gigantic Stay-Puft Marshmallow Man. Definitely a crisis worth getting excited about.

Politicians and commentators insulting each other makes for a good read and seems to improve TV ratings, but we suspect a lot of Americans are getting tired of it. We don't think it's a coincidence that polls show Congress, the presidency, and the press getting some of their lowest performance grades in recent history. Outside the Beltway, most Americans seem ready to move on, and so are we. The country's financial mess doesn't have to lead to disaster if the country stops screaming and starts working on the problem now.

Still, it's important to remember that the two sides didn't get mad at each other over nothing. For all the hyperventilating among the partisans, both liberals and conservatives bring important ideas about government and the economy to the table. So we've done for you what congressional staff members often do for their bosses. We've created a quick recap of the main points liberals and conservatives make about matters budgetary (known as "talking points" in Beltway-speak).

If you've been getting your news mostly from your own politically comforting source (be it Salon, Fox News, Ann Coulter, or *The Colbert Report*) here's your chance to refresh yourself on the other side. And even if you plan to steer a course right down the political middle, it's not a bad idea to keep the shorelines in sight.

So here are "the rules" as far as most conservatives see them:

1. Individuals and families, local governments, and the marketplace almost always do a better job of solving problems than the federal government.

2. The best federal government would be a much smaller one, covering national defense, homeland security, and a few other items that local governments or the private sector simply can't handle.

3. When the federal government tries to "help" in areas like retirement, health care, prescription drugs, education, economic development, and so on, it wastes money and mangles the job.

4. Waste, fraud, abuse, and mismanagement are rampant in the federal government today. When a government official is allowed to spend other people's money, this result is almost inevitable.

5. Social Security and Medicare take money out of workers' hands and give them unstable, unfair federal programs in return.

6. Nearly all Americans would be better off if Social Security and Medicare were redesigned as private savings programs. That would capitalize on Americans' sense of individual responsibility and judgment.

7. Low taxes lead to more investment and entrepreneurship—that helps the economy grow.

8. When people and businesses earn more, they return more to the government in taxes.

9. Keeping the economy growing is the way to improve Americans' standard of living.

10. Big government and high taxes interfere with the marketplace. When the free enterprise system is left to operate without interference, it produces the prosperity that benefits us all.

And for the liberals:

1. Government has a responsibility to try to improve people's lives and address problems like inequality and poverty.

2. Americans need more government help, not less. Number one example: the government has finally decided to help the nearly 46 million Americans without health insurance.

3. It's fashionable to complain about "big government," but Americans need and want programs like Social Security, Medicare, Head Start, food stamps, the Centers for Disease Control, and many others. They do things that need to be done and do them well.

4. Social Security and Medicare are two of the great advances of the last century. Before them, millions of older Americans lived in poverty with inadequate health care.

5. Conservative plans to "privatize" Social Security and Medicare are unworkable. Wealthy, well-educated people will benefit. Poor people, not-so-savvy investors—even people who just have a run of bad luck—will be much worse off.

6. Taxes are the way we pool our resources so government can address society's problems.

7. But taxes are not fair now. The recent tax cuts have mostly benefited the very wealthiest Americans. These tax cuts are the major cause of our current budget problems.

8. Wealthy Americans who prosper from living and working in this country should be willing to pay more. They should pay higher taxes so less fortunate Americans can enjoy some of the advantages they have had.

9. What threatens the economy isn't taxation, but leaving millions of Americans in underfunded schools, in poor neighborhoods, and without decent medical care. If those people can't find decent work and get decent services, they'll never contribute what they could to society.

10. Competition and the free market are good things, but they can't solve every problem, and they don't always work for everyone.

A LITTLE OF BOTH, PLEASE

If you read these over and find yourself agreeing with some ideas from both lists, you're not alone. Moderates and middle-of-the-roaders don't get much respect these days, but mixing and matching is totally allowed in this book. In fact, we're convinced that a little mixing and matching is the only way the country is going to work its way back to financial sanity.

What you're not allowed to do is adopt a conservative "keep taxes as low as possible" stance, while blithely endorsing liberal ideas to spend money on good works. Sadly, this is a compromise that a lot of D.C. types seem willing to live with, which is unfortunate, because it's the one compromise that can't possibly work. That's when the numbers just don't add up.

CHAPTER 12

Politics, as Usual

When we got into office, the thing that surprised me most was to find that things were just as bad as we'd been saying they were.

—*President John F. Kennedy (1917–1963)*

Election politics is probably the chief reason so many candidates and elected officials don't talk about the country's financial problems and haven't started to deal with them responsibly. It's a risky business to suggest raising taxes or spending less on something people like in order to solve a problem that seems far, far away. Even the feeblest call to hike taxes or cut benefits in Social Security or Medicare is likely to be a godsend to an election opponent.

Frankly, the deficit and the growing debt haven't really been major issues in most past elections, and until recently, they didn't make it into the winner's circle in those surveys about which problems worry Americans most.

Given the dreadful state of the U.S. economy in the last couple of years, it's probably not surprising that economic issues are at the top of the list. In July 2010, for example, a CNN/Opinion Research survey showed that 47 percent of Americans named the economy as the most important issue facing the country, while 13 percent chose the federal budget deficit. Other issues were important, too: 9 percent of the public named illegal immigration; 8 percent, health care; 8 percent, the wars in Iraq and Afghanistan; and 6 percent said education.[1] We don't really see any problem with this. All these issues are important, and we would certainly expect anyone running for national office to have some sound ideas for addressing all of them.

PUBLIC OPINION LAND MINES EVERYWHERE YOU LOOK

The problem for candidates—and for elected officials once they're in office—is not that the budget issue doesn't worry people. It does. The problem is that when it comes to solutions, public opinion is just all over the map, and that makes political types nervous.

No matter what a politician does, he or she runs the risk of making a lot of potential voters unhappy. For example, Congress passed some pretty hefty tax cuts in 2001 and 2003, but in 2006, half of all Americans (51 percent) still said that cutting income taxes should be a top priority for Congress and the president.[2] Meanwhile, 80 percent of Americans say it's the government's responsibility to "provide a decent standard of living for the elderly."[3] Numbers like that strike fear

---

[1] CNN/Opinion Research Corporation Poll, July 16–21, 2010, available at PollingReport.com, www.pollingreport.com/prioriti.htm, accessed September 1, 2010.

[2] Pew Research Center for the People and the Press, "January 2006 News Interest Index, Final Topline," January 4–8, 2006, www.people-press.org/reports/questionnaires/268.pdf.

[3] CBS News/*New York Times* Poll, June 10–15, 2005: "On the whole, do you think it should or should not be the government's responsibil-

into the heart of any politician who even thinks about proposing Social Security or Medicare cuts.

More recent polls just add to the confusion (and to the danger for anyone contemplating a political career). Americans are getting angrier about the deficit, and most want something done to reduce it. Even though hardly any expert—economist, budget wonk, or politician—thought that cutting the deficit right in the middle of the 2008–9 recession was advisable or even possible, most Americans seemed to be calling for it. In mid-2009, nearly six in ten Americans said it was more important to reduce the deficit than try to stimulate the economy. But in the very same poll, over half (53 percent) said that they would not wish for "the government to provide fewer services, in areas such as health care, education and defense spending" to reduce the deficit. Even more, 56 percent, said they would not be willing to pay higher taxes to reduce the deficit either.[4]

Let's see. Can't raise taxes. Can't touch Social Security and Medicare. Can't touch defense. Can't touch education and health care. There's not all that much left in there to cut (and if you think you can stop the red ink by eliminating "waste, fraud, and abuse," you must have skipped chapter 5. Go back and read it.).

That puts a responsible candidate or lawmaker who wants to make sensible proposals in a bind. It's the political equivalent of being caught between a rock and a hard place. In Spanish, the phrase is being between "the sword and the wall," which conjures up visions of Zorro slashing a Z into

---

ity to provide a decent standard of living for the elderly?" Should: 80 percent; should not: 16 percent; unsure: 4 percent, available at www. pollingreport.com/social.htm.

[4] CBS News/*New York Times* Poll, July 24–28, 2009, available at PollingReport.com, www.pollingreport.com/budget.htm, accessed May 16, 2010.

some chubby guy's pants. It's a more menacing image, but luckily, not that many members of Congress speak Spanish.

DOES THE AMERICAN PUBLIC REALLY DESERVE ALL THE BLAME?

Let's just suppose that Americans across the country began saying that it's time to get serious about the nation's finances. And let's just say that not only do people consistently name the debt and the deficit as one of the country's chief problems, they've come to accept the inevitable conclusion: there is simply no way to solve this problem without raising taxes and/or cutting services in ways that are going to hurt. The kinds of changes we'll need to make may not signal the end of civilization itself (as some bloggers would have you believe). But they're not fun, and there's no use pretending that they are.

Would Washington step up to the plate and make some tough decisions if elected officials were getting strong signals that most Americans were ready to accept real solutions? Well, we certainly hope so, but there are a couple of other obstacles in the way. Unfortunately, there is something about the way that Washington works these days that seems to fight against Congress and the administration tackling tough issues and making needed decisions about them. There is a boomlet of analyses from journalists, political scientists, and others examining why "Washington seems mired in dysfunction," as the *New York Times*'s John Broder phrased it. In fact, anyone who spends a lot of time watching the contemporary political scene could probably list dozens of malfunctions in the way the system works today. But in our little Budget Politics 101 introductory course, we're going to zoom in on just two of them—the ones we think could really hold us up on this particular issue.

The first is that members of Congress and the administration (from both parties) listen to lobbyists. The second is that good old-fashioned bipartisan compromise does seem pretty old-fashioned these days. In our humble opinions, solving the country's budget challenges requires change in both areas. Decision makers need to remember that an assortment of special interests (represented by lobbyists) do not necessarily add up to the public interest. And they need to work with the other party and be willing to compromise. Let's take a look at what we face in each of these areas in the here and now.

THE K STREET CONNECTION

In Washington, lobbyists are affectionately known as K Street because so many of the big lobbying groups and firms have offices there. And there's no question that this lobbying business (and it's definitely a business) is really annoying to most Americans. Nearly eight in ten Americans say that political lobbyists have too much power and influence in Washington.[5] Both Republican and Democratic leaders have repeatedly promised to "do something" about it, but reforms seem to disappear or lose their teeth while the practice seems entrenched.

In a devastating 2006 portrait of contemporary K Street, Jeffrey Birnbaum of the *Washington Post* reported that Capitol Hill now boasts roughly thirty thousand registered lobbyists, about double the number there were in 2000.[6] Showcasing the "industry's simple-yet-dazzling economics," Birnbaum described one prominent lobbying firm, the Carmen Group, which bragged "that for every $1 million

---

[5] Harris Poll, February 16–21, 2010, pollingreport.com, www.polling report.com/politics.htm#h, accessed May 21, 2010.

[6] Jeffrey H. Birnbaum, "Washington's Once and Future Lobby," *Washington Post*, September 10, 2006.

its clients spend on its services, it delivers, on average, $100 million in government benefits."[7]

You probably won't be surprised to learn that major health providers spent millions of dollars on lobbying while Congress was debating the reform bill passed in 2010. According to the Center for Responsive Politics, a nonprofit organization that tracks this kind of spending, the pharmaceutical and health products industries spent nearly $268 million on lobbying in 2009.[8] Hospitals and nursing homes spent nearly $108 million; health professionals nearly $85 million, and health services and HMOs about $74 million.[9] Have you been adding this up with us? It's over half a trillion dollars on health care lobbying in just one year.

Perhaps it's understandable that a major industry would want a presence on Capitol Hill while major legislation affecting it was up for debate. If your entire business can be radically changed by a new federal law, maybe it's understandable that you would want a robust presence on Capitol Hill when a historic piece of legislation was debated and passed. But these industries—and many others—routinely invest huge sums of money to make sure that their perspectives don't get lost in the legislative shuffle. Back in 2006, a more typical year in terms of health care legislation, the pharmaceutical industry spent nearly $187 million—less than the banner year perhaps, but still an awful lot of money.[10]

---

[7] Ibid.

[8] Center for Responsive Politics, Lobbying: Top Industries, 2009, www.opensecrets.org/lobby/top.php?showYear=2009&indexType=i, accessed May 30, 2010.

[9] Center for Responsive Politics, Lobbying: Top Industries, 2009, www.opensecrets.org/lobby/top.php?showYear=2009&indexType=i, accessed May 30, 2010.

[10] Center for Responsive Politics, Lobbying: Top Industries, 2006.

There's one other thing that makes this lobbying issue so complicated—these days, nearly everyone does it. Sure, a lot of lobbying benefits corporate, banking, and oil interests, but there are also lobbyists representing consumer groups, environmental groups, women's groups, organized labor, schoolteachers, higher education, and more.

American Indians, the Sierra Club, Goldman Sachs

Maybe you've forgotten the details of the Jack Abramoff lobbying scandal or never knew them in the first place. But however much you forgot or never knew, you might recall that Abramoff was accused of ripping off American Indian tribes who thought they were hiring a topflight D.C. lobbyist to help them.[11] Like many other groups in American society, American Indians often believe they need a Washington lobbyist to watch out for their interests.

To Principal Chief Jim Gray of Oklahoma's Osage Nation, "this isn't anything new; lobbying is an exercise in free speech. It just happens to be new for Americans to see Indian Country speaking its voice in this way."[12] And just in case you've leaped to the conclusion that most lobbying for American Indian tribes focuses on casinos and gambling, the main issues are actually "sovereignty, health, and housing," according to federal records examined by Oklahoma's *Tulsa World* newspaper.[13]

---

www.opensecrets.org/lobby/top.php?showYear=2006&indexType=i, accessed May 30, 2010.

[11] James V. Grimaldi, "Abramoff Indictment May Aid D.C. Inquiry; Lobbyist's Work for Tribes at Issue," *Washington Post*, August 13, 2005.

[12] S. E. Ruckman, "Tribes Put More into Lobbying," *Tulsa World*, August 28, 2006.

[13] Ibid.

Can We Rein It In?

Lobbying is a vexing problem for people who worry about government ethics and honesty, and, unfortunately, we can't cover the question adequately here. But it's worth mentioning the major new ethics law passed by Congress in 2007, designed to close off some of the connections between lobbyists and Congress—or at least make some of these back alleys a little better lit. Among the law's provisions:

★ Lobbyists are required to disclose when they organize "bundled" campaign contributions by getting multiple people to contribute to the same candidate or party, at least when the contributions exceed $15,000 over a six-month period.

★ Members of Congress and their staffs are prohibited from accepting gifts (including meals) from lobbyists, and lobbyists are barred from knowingly giving gifts that violate congressional rules, with stiff penalties for lobbyists who break the law.

★ Candidates for the Senate and the presidency must pay charter rate for travel on private planes (previously, corporations could offer politicians a lift on the corporate jet and the pol had to reimburse only the price of a first-class airline ticket). House candidates must fly on commercial planes.

★ Members of Congress have to disclose all earmarks at least forty-eight hours before a vote (although legislative leaders are allowed to waive that rule). Members also certify that they and their families don't have a financial interest in the earmark.

★ New online databases will be set up for financial disclosures by lobbyists and members of Congress.

The Obama administration has required its appointees to sign an "ethics pledge" promising not to "accept gifts from registered lobbyists or lobbying organizations" or become involved in policymaking affecting companies or organizations they have worked for previously.[14]

But whether any of this is making a dent in lobbying seems to be a matter of opinion. Fred Wertheimer, president of the nonprofit government reform group Democracy 21, hailed the Obama rules as "a major step in setting a new tone and attitude for Washington that challenges the lobbyist, special interest culture."[15] But many of the president's critics have charged that former lobbyists are slipping through anyway. Conservatives, for example, pointed out that Secretary of Health and Human Services Kathleen Sibelius, whose department oversees policies on malpractice, spent years as head of the Kansas Trial Lawyers Association.[16] Other observers say the rule has actually backfired, keeping some highly-qualified people out of the administration.[17]

And despite tough economic times, the business of lobbying is hardly in retreat. In 2009, spending on lobbying rose to

---

[14] The White House, Executive Order, January 21, 2009, www.white house.gov/the_press_office/Ethics-Commitments-By-Executive-Branch-Personnel, accessed May 21, 2010.

[15] Dan Eggen and R. Jeffrey Smith, "Lobbying Rules Surpass Those of Previous Presidents, Experts Say," *Washington Post*, January 22, 2009, www.washingtonpost.com/wp-dyn/content/article/2009/01/21/AR2009012103472.html, accessed May 22, 2010.

[16] The Heritage Foundation, The Foundry blog, "Obama Taps Ex-Trial Lawyer Lobbyist to Lead Tort Reform," September 10, 2009, http://blog.heritage.org/2009/09/10/obama-taps-ex-trial-lawyer-lobbyist-to-lead-tort-reform/, accessed May 22, 2010.

[17] See for example, Ryan Grim, "Obama's Anti-Lobbyist Policy Causing Unintended Harm," The Huffington Post, March 5, 2009, www.huffingtonpost.com/2009/03/05/obamas-anti-lobbyist-poli_n_172244.html.

nearly $3.5 billion, a 5 percent jump over 2008.[18] As a number of commentators pointed out, the recession may have led to widespread unemployment, but apparently not for lobbyists.

So there's more to be done. To keep lobbying in line, some reformers have suggested changes like these.

- Go further in curbing campaign contributions from lobbyists and lobbying firms. For example, the watchdog group Public Citizen wants to limit contributions to less than $500 per election cycle and ban lobbyists from giving fancy parties to "honor" members of Congress, often at the political conventions.[19]
- Ban lobbying by members of lawmakers' families. There are rules governing what's allowed when you're in Congress and someone in the family is a lobbyist, but some reformers believe this is something that should be banned entirely. Changing the rules here would hit some very prominent politicians on both sides of the aisle. Republican congressman Roy Blunt (MO) and Democratic senator Kent Conrad (ND) both have wives who are lobbyists. Democratic senator Daniel Inouye (HI) and Republican Senator Orrin Hatch (UT) both have sons in the lobbying business.[20]
- Prohibit members of Congress from voting on issues in

[18] Center for Responsive Politics, "Federal Lobbying Climbs in 2009 as Lawmakers Execute Aggressive Congressional Agenda," February 12, 2010, www.opensecrets.org/news/2010/02/federal-lobbying-soars-in-2009. html, accessed May 22, 2010.

[19] "Senate Has Failed to Deliver Effective Lobbying and Ethics Reform," *Public Citizen*, March 29, 2006, available at www.citizen. org/pressroom.

[20] Sharyl Attkisson, "Family Ties Bind Federal Lawmakers to Lobbyists," CBS Evening News, June 25, 2010, www.cbsnews.com/stories/ 2010/06/25/eveningnews/main6618973.shtml.

which they have investments or hold stocks, suggests law professor and commentator Jonathan Turley in an excellent op-ed for *USA TODAY*.[21] He suggests that members of Congress put their assets in blind trusts the way judges and officials in the executive branch have to do.[22]

- Ban earmarks entirely. The 2007 ethics bill made the earmark process more open and Citizens Against Government Waste, the people who conduct the annual earmark count, reported that number of earmarks dropped about 10 percent from 2009 to 2010. As the group's president, Tom Schatz, noted, earmarks are widely detested by Americans in general, and it is "popular to posture as an anti-earmarker." But earmarks can still produce good vibes in the home district. As Schatz notes, "most members of Congress still aren't willing to eliminate the practice."[23] That's why we'll be surprised if Congress acts on the boldest of Jonathan Turley's recommendations (and the one that most voters would probably support if they could)—ban earmarks entirely.[24]

Clearly, some of these ideas are worth thinking about, as are others, but not everyone is convinced changes like these will be effective. *New York Times* columnist David Brooks favors more disclosure about lobbyists' campaign contributions and a longer moratorium between leaving office and assuming the lobbyist's mantle. But he thinks the

---

[21] Jonathan Turley, "A Question of Ethics," *USA TODAY*, November 14, 2006.

[22] Ibid.

[23] Citizens Against Government Waste, "Earmark Spending $16.5 Billion in CAGW's 2010 Congressional Pig Book," April 14, 2010, www.cagw.org/newsroom/releases/2010/earmark-spending-165.html. Accessed May 22, 2010.

[24] Turley, "Question of Ethics."

results of trying to control the nice dinners out and flights on corporate jets will be negligible: "The bans on lobbyist-financed gifts, meals and travel are unimportant," Brooks wrote. "Few legislators are corrupted by a steak or even a ride in a Gulfstream."[25]

Frankly, we think government might improve some if elected officials had to foot the bill for their own steaks and sit in the middle seat back in coach with the rest of us. But even if lobbying could be scrubbed clean, having thirty thousand people running around Washington working hard for the "special" interest of the people who pay them means that the common interest of all of us can get lost in the process. Let's face it: how many of those thirty thousand people are out there lobbying for fiscal sanity?

We can all think of places where we want the government to spend more. We can all think of places where we'd like the tax laws changed so we don't have to pay as much. The problem is that when professional lobbyists begin pushing to spend more on this and ease taxes on that, the whole thing goes haywire. In some ways, it's like overfishing in the North Atlantic. From the point of view of every fishing boat captain, the best thing to do is to catch as many fish as possible, even though it's common knowledge that the fish stocks are being depleted. Unless the dynamic changes, unless some broader interest takes hold, people just keep doing what benefits them the most.

ENOUGH BIPARTISANSHIP TO FILL A THIMBLE

So is there any way to get elected officials to pay more attention to the general interest and take on the important

---

[25] David Brooks, "Mr. Chips Goes to Congress," *New York Times*, January 21, 2007.

issues with the tough choices? One way, at least historically, has been the grand bipartisan compromise. Both parties join in; neither gets exactly what they want; since elected officials on both sides of the aisle have to put their name to the less-than-perfect solution, they all get a little political cover. But based on national politics of the last decade or so, bipartisanship and compromise are beginning to look a little like the bald eagle—a noble American symbol that's on the endangered species list.

Once upon a time, Washington was considered "cozy" and "clubby." Now it's almost a cliché to call the current political climate "hyperpartisan" and "poisonous." And it would be easy to get into a long, angry, depressing argument over why this happened and whose fault it was. You could, if you wanted, follow it back to the disputed 2000 election or the Clinton impeachment or the confirmation hearings for a dozen all-but-forgotten political appointees, and, for all we know, the time that Stephen slapped Irene on *The Real World: Seattle*.[26] Tracing it all would take another book, and we don't have time for that now.

The important point for our purposes is that members of Congress used to be able to fight it out on the floor and during the campaign, and then sit down and cut deals on legislation over drinks afterward. It's not that Republicans and Democrats never cooperate on anything. The No Child Left Behind education law, the 9/11 Commission, the Iraq Study Group, and the 2007 immigration bill were all examples of some Republicans and Democrats getting together to do something together. But even bipartisanship doesn't seem to keep the peace or guarantee progress. These bipartisan efforts were and are still controversial;

---

[26] Not that we ever watched that show.

in fact, we'd be inclined to say that immigration has now leaped into the stratosphere of partisan politics.

"You can't reach across the aisle today," said former Republican senator Warren Rudman. "I am told that some members of Congress feel you're almost a traitor if you approach the other side to work with major legislation. People want to block that. Well, that is not the way most major legislation, domestic or foreign, has been made in our history. It's always been bipartisan. The amount of bipartisanship left on the Hill, you could put in a thimble right now."[27]

Not surprisingly, Washington's inability to focus on the public interest and solve problems most Americans really care about has soured public attitudes. A recent survey by the Pew Research Center reveals widespread "cynicism about politics and elected officials," with 76 percent of the public saying that "elected officials in Washington lose touch with the people pretty quickly." Half of Americans (51 percent) say that "people like me don't have any say about what the government does."[28] But we can't put all the blame on Congress and the president. The American public seems to be growing more divided in its views. The Pew Research Center has tracked public thinking about 48 "values questions" for more than two decades. During that time, Pew reports, "the average difference between the opinions of Democrats and Republicans has grown from nine percentage points as recently as 1997 to a new high of 16 points

[27] Panel discussion, Concord Coalition Economic Patriots Dinner, November 1, 2005, www.concordcoalition.org/images/event-transcript/2005-patriotdinner/panel-discussion-transcript.html.

[28] Pew Research Center for the People and the Press, Trends in Political Values and Core Attitudes: 1987–2009, Section 8: Politics and Political Participation, May 21, 2009, http://people-press.org/report/?pageid=1523, accessed May 22, 2010.

today. In many cases, already existing partisan divides have increased in size."[29] As we've pointed out throughout this book, our leaders have been letting us down, but we haven't actually been doing our part as citizens, either.

So how can we begin to turn the tide? First, we urge you to check into and support the work of some of the groups trying to clean up politics. There's a list to start with in the appendix. Even more important—and it's basically the point of this whole book—we need to start demanding that elected officials stop the spinning and the blaming and the finger-pointing and get down to work making the tough decisions—and the compromises—needed to make headway on this problem. And we need to be realistic ourselves about what it will take to sort this financial mess out.

When our organization, Public Agenda, conducted focus groups on federal finances in 2006, most people grasped the magnitude of the problem after just a little discussion.[30] Most immediately saw that compromise would have to be part of the solution. Most were also pretty skeptical about politicians, wondering whether they would ever act, given all the incentives to continue with business as usual. At some point, however, someone in nearly every group would suggest that leaders in Washington would never let it really get out of hand because that would be so "insane."

That certainly would be insane. But that brand of insanity has struck governments before. The historian Barbara Tuchman wove a compelling and disturbing book *(The*

---

[29] Pew Research Center for the People and the Press, Trends in Political Values and Core Attitudes: 1987–2009, Section 11: Growing Partisan Gaps and Centrist Independents, May 21, 2009, http://people-press.org/report/?pageid=1526, accessed May 22, 2010.

[30] Public Agenda, *Facing Up to the Nation's Finances: Understanding Public Attitudes about the Federal Budget,* December 2006, available at www.publicagenda.org.

March of Folly) out of examples of governments that stuck to policies contrary to their own best interests. Remember, there are powerful forces pulling on political leaders to skim over the budget problem. The "business-as-usual" mentality is very hard to fight. Unfortunately, just assuming that elected officials will wake up and smell the coffee on their own could be the most insane assumption of all.

Here's our goal for what needs to happen: every time an elected official sits down with a lobbyist to discuss what his or her client wants, and every time he or she is tempted to get on a "my way or no way" hobbyhorse, there should be a little voice in the back of their head asking, "What does this mean for the country's financial future? And what will voters at home do if I don't start acting responsibly on the country's budget problems?"

The Politically Dead and Departed

Given how unrealistic so many voters are about taxes and spending—and given what a rough game politics is—what happens to candidates who suggest that we might have to make some tough choices to get our financial house in order? Remember these men?

Back in the 1990s, H. Ross Perot launched a brief but notable political career urging Americans to take the federal budget deficit seriously.[31] Perot was a wealthy man who didn't have to raise money to run for office, so he had more freedom than most candidates to campaign on the issue that concerned him most. For a while, he attracted a sizable following, but his campaign eventually fell apart. Most observers think his downfall had more to do with Perot's personality than his position on the budget. "Prickly" and "eccentric" are words that often come up in connection with Mr. Perot.[32]

Despite Perot's ability to attract a fairly significant political following by talking tough about the budget deficit, his experience is the exception. The conventional political wisdom—and it's pretty entrenched—is that candidates who want to win had better talk about cutting taxes and spending more money on things voters like—preferably both. Calling for higher taxes and/or cuts in popular programs like Social Security and Medicare is definitely not recommended. Recent political history is littered with some very promising candidates—established leaders with broad ex-

---

[31] Steven A. Holmes with Doron P. Levin, "The 1992 Campaign: Independent Perot's Quest—a Special Report; A Man Who Says He Wants to Be Savior, If He's Asked," *New York Times*, April 13, 1992.

[32] See for example, "Hat in Ring, Head to Follow," *Rocky Mountain News* (Denver), October 2, 1995; see also "James Urges Republicans to 'Fight All the Pee-rows,'" *Birmingham News*, January 14, 1996.

perience and strong backing—who fell by the wayside when they disobeyed "the rules."

Running for office is a complex, dicey affair, and there is generally more than one reason why a candidate wins or loses—money, personality, stands on issues, ability to get the vote out, cried during the campaign, didn't cry during the campaign, got a picture taken windsurfing, and many others. Yet anyone mulling a run for office has to consider the scary list of candidates who said the "wrong" things about taxes or spending and ended up making a concession speech when all the votes were counted.

This is where we the voters come in for our share of the blame. Why would we expect candidates to tell us the unvarnished truth given what generally happens when they do? It's really no wonder that most politicians today decide that their best bet is to avoid going out on the "how to balance the budget" limb.

Here's some of the political history that's gotten us where we are today.

★ **Vice President Walter Mondale** took what he himself called "a helluva shellacking"[33] in the 1984 presidential campaign, which he lost to President Ronald Reagan. Political columnist Tom Wicker summed up the campaign efficiently: "When

Vice President Mondale said he would raise taxes to cut the deficit. He lost his presidential bid. *Credit: U.S. Senate Historical Office*

---

[33] Dan Balz and Milton Coleman, "Mondale Is Back, at Practicing Law; Defeated Candidate Admits Failings, Sees Signs of Vindication," *Washington Post,* April 8, 1985.

Walter Mondale pledged a tax increase to cut the deficit, he lost forty-nine states—to a Republican president who had run up that deficit and doubled the national debt"[34] Mondale himself recognized what had gone wrong. Interviewed later, he said: "If you look at the campaign in retrospect, I looked like a person who was always talking about problems, about tough steps that were needed to solve problems. While my opponent was handing out rose petals, I was handing out coal."[35] Mondale's political demise was not lost on future presidential candidates. In fact, the headline on Wicker's column chronicling Mondale's defeat just about summed up the moral of the story politically speaking. "Death Wish and Taxes" is all most politicians really need to know.[36]

The first President Bush suffered politically when he agreed to a budget compromise that included tax hikes. *Credit: Library of Congress, David Valdez, Photographer*

★ We give **President George H. W. Bush** a lot of credit for his role in the 1990 bipartisan budget compromise—one that set the nation on a more solid financial path for some years. But whatever the merits of Bush's budget-minded decision making, he, too, got caught in the "death wish and taxes" quicksand. When he ran for office in 1988, he promised, "Read

---

[34] Tom Wicker, "In the Nation: Death Wish and Taxes," *New York Times,* December 14, 1986.

[35] Balz and Coleman, "Mondale Is Back."

[36] Wicker, "In the Nation: Death Wish and Taxes."

my lips, no new taxes."[37] When he got in office and faced up to some painful budget realities, he decided that tax hikes had to be part of the overall picture.[38] When the next election came round, President Bush became a one-term president despite having an 89 percent approval rating right after the Persian Gulf War.[39] President Bush also got caught glancing at his watch during a TV debate with Bill Clinton,[40] and his staff ended up assuring people that he had indeed been inside a grocery store "a year or so ago . . . in Ken-

nebunkport," even though the president marveled at seeing the kind of price scanner commonly used at checkout counters at a manufacturing convention.[41] The man was just not having his best campaign. Still, there is little doubt that his decision to raise taxes while in office was a serious political wound.[42]

★ Some candidates get caught on the other side of the ledger. **Senator Bob Dole** tripped up on the spending side in his unsuccessful run against Bill

Many voters feared Senator Bob Dole might cut Medicare. *Credit: U.S. Congress, House Committee on Veterans' Affairs*

---

[37] Quotes of Note; the Best of '88, *Boston Globe,* December 31, 1988.

[38] Andrew Rosenthal, "Bush Now Concedes a Need for 'Tax Revenue Increases' to Reduce Deficit in Budget," *New York Times,* June 27, 1990.

[39] The Pew Research Center, "Modest Bush Approval Rating Boost at War's End; Economy Now Top National Issue," April 18, 2003.

[40] B. Drummond Ayres Jr., "The 1992 Campaign: Campaign Trail," *New York Times,* October 30, 1992.

[41] Andrew Rosenthal, "Bush Encounters the Supermarket, Amazed," *New York Times,* February 5, 1992.

[42] Roberto Suro, "Viewing Chaos in the Capital, Americans Express Outrage," *New York Times,* October 19, 1990.

Clinton in 1996. After the Clinton team fired a series of volleys suggesting that Dole would cut Medicare and raise Social Security taxes to pay for broad income tax cuts, the candidate was politically on the run. News reports described him as "brimming with frustration" in a West Palm Beach elderly center. "The last lady I talked to as I left," Dole complained, "this lady said, 'Why are you cutting my Medicare?' The lady pushing the wheelchair said, 'That's all she hears all day long, the Clinton ads, that you're going to cut Medicare, cut Medicare, cut Medicare.'"[43] Despite Dole's claims that he, too, would protect programs for the elderly, Clinton trounced him in the election. Dole even ended up aggravating some prominent conservatives like David Frum, then at the Manhattan Institute.[44] For Frum, "Dole's passionate declaration of his support for Medicare and Social Security only fortified the false notion that these programs are in fine shape." Frum complained that Dole, rather than advancing the debate on entitlement spending, had actually reinforced the political belief that Social Security and Medicare are untouchable. "There are worse things in politics than losing," Frum wrote.[45]

---

[43] Katharine Seelye, "Politics: The Republican; In Blistering Attack, Dole Says Clinton Is Using Scare Tactics," *New York Times,* September 27, 1996.

[44] Until 2010, Frum was a resident fellow at the American Enterprise Institute but was apparently fired after criticizing conservatives' unwillingness to work with Democrats on health care reform. You can still keep up with his views at www.davidfrum.com/.

[45] David Frum, "The Big Scam of 1996," *New York Times,* November 6, 1996.

When to Be Afraid, Very Afraid

It is easy to get confused about what they are up to in Washington when the billion—and trillion-dollar guesstimates combine with the "I have an advanced degree in economics, and you don't" jargon. But baffling statistics and expert gobbledygook are only part of it. Politicians have some very clever ways to cloud the issue while they push us deeper in debt. During elections, candidates tend to scurry around the hard facts as much as possible, but you need to keep an eye on politicians between elections, too. When it comes to the budget and the debt, our elected officials have not been doing us any favors lately. Here are the most popular ploys to look out for.

They promise popular new programs without saying how to pay for them. Americans used to fall for this all the time, which is one of the reasons the nation is now approaching $15 trillion in debt and counting. Surveys suggest that most Americans still want the government to spend more on health care and education rather than reduce the deficit. Even so, this is the one area where we see a sliver of hope. It's a mini advance, we know, but the fact that members of Congress kept hitting the pause button waiting for CBO cost estimates during the 2010 health care debate is an infinitesimal step forward. In 2003, when Congress added drug coverage to Medicare, and when it voted money for the war in Iraq during the early Bush years, the problem of how to cover the cost without adding to the debt barely came up. But times have changed on Capitol Hill. Even the health care bill's staunch supporters who believed it was unconscionable to continue living with some 46 million uninsured had to face up to the cost. One major issue now that the bill is law is making sure that the tax increases and other changes designed to pay for it don't get watered down when push comes to shove. Even so, this time around, the rules were different. More and more Americans don't like the idea of adding billions of dollars to the budget without including ways to cover the cost. It's a trendlet we hope to see continue.

They promise tax cuts without saying where the money will come from. Taxes don't make people happy, especially when they apply to you personally, so cutting them is a staple of the campaign trail. Politicians who propose tax cuts may talk vaguely about "smaller government" or "making government more efficient" or "cutting waste and bureaucracy." Lately the argument has been that tax cuts will make the economy grow. The problem is that Congress passes tax cuts, the president signs the bills into law with a big flourish, and the government just keeps on spending and spending. As for the economy, any boost that tax cuts might offer now has to be weighed against threats posed by the huge amount of money we owe. Nearly every budget expert we could find—including well-respected conservative ones—says that we need to put the days of tax cuts without spending cuts to match behind us.

They put the costs in a "supplemental" spending bill. Sometimes Washington seems to operate on the same principle as many dieters: "if no one sees you eat that pint of chunky chocolate fudge with walnuts, the calories don't count." To avoid getting blamed for record-breaking deficits—and so they won't really have to tell the public how much things cost—politicians sometimes put major expenses in "supplemental budgets." Congress votes on these separately from the main budget (which is already huge), so it's harder for people to focus on the bottom line. Sometimes they string out really big budget items—like much of the money for the war in Iraq—into a series of supplemental appropriations: $70 billion here, $90 billion there; it's just so much easier than adding billions of dollars more to budgets that are already billions of dollars in the red.

They hide pet projects in "emergency" spending bills. When something terrible happens, a catastrophe like September 11 or Hurricane Katrina, Congress often passes emergency spending bills to address the problem. There is nothing wrong with this. Some things can't be predicted. We're a wealthy and compassionate country, and we want to help when our fellow citizens face tragedy and loss. But the definition of "tragedy" is elastic in Washington, as is the definition of "emergency." Hurricane Katrina was both tragic and an emergency, beyond doubt. A 2006 emergency spending bill to provide money for Hurricane Katrina victims and the war in Iraq also contained money for higher education, relocating railroad tracks, and a "seafood promotion strategy."[1] You can decide for yourself whether these are good ways to spend taxpayer money, but it's hard to call them actual emergencies.

Sometimes aggressive reporting and a subsequent public outcry force politicians to back away from "now you see it, now you don't" budgeting and even renounce some of the odder spending projects tucked away in bigger pieces of legislation. Still, the takeaway message here is that you just have to watch these folks all the time.

They promise to slash big government and get spending in line. You might think this slogan would get our "both-thumbs-up" rating. After all, we've just spent pages describing infuriating examples of government waste and the insane way decisions get made in Washington. But we also believe that political leaders have to be frank with the American people. "Slashing" government spending

---

[1] "New Criticism Falls on 'Supplemental Bills,'" *New York Times,* April 25, 2006.

is definitely going to hit things that plenty of Americans care about. Take the idea of "eliminating" the U.S. Department of Education. Fine, but if that's your idea, you need to admit that local school systems will not be getting money from the federal government to help pay for special education and beef up spending in low-income schools. Millions of American families count on having low-cost college loans that come through the U.S. Department of Education. It's absolutely fair to propose bold ideas for cutting government—and the Department of Education should be on the block along with everything else. But it's double-dealing to make the promise and then neglect to mention what it means. That's why we give credit to people like the Cato Institute's Downsizing the Federal Government project. They believe in smaller government and are pretty specific about what that means. Cato in fact does advocate eliminating the Department of Education, and they are utterly frank about what will disappear (www.downsizing government.org/education). We're not endorsing their plans, but proposals that include the details advance the dialogue even when you don't like all their ideas. What we object to are politicians who pretend that solving our budget problems will be simple and won't involve sacrifices. Just vote for me, they claim, and all our deficit and debt problems will painlessly disappear.

CHAPTER 13

The Taxman Cometh

Should five per cent appear too small,
Be thankful I don't take it all.

George Harrison, "Taxman"

Most Americans feel that our political leaders have pretty much led us down the garden path when it comes to budgetary matters. And you won't get an argument on that from us. But complaining is not enough. And frankly, complaining isn't even all that helpful unless you have a basic understanding of what our options are. We looked at some choices for tackling the mega-problems facing Social Security and Medicare earlier. We also looked at the possibilities for spending cuts in other areas, especially the defense budget. Now it's time to bring up that eagerly-awaited topic we all love so much—taxes.

Unless you dozed off repeatedly during the first two hundred and some pages of this book (and if you did, we're sorry. There's just not many ways to get sex and vampires into a book about the budget), you know that in 2001 and 2003, President George W. Bush signed about a dozen different tax cuts signed into law. Nearly all of them were designed to expire on one red-letter date—December 31, 2010. Congress may have extended some of them (at least temporarily) while this book was being printed and shipped around in boxes. But whatever has happened so far, we're almost positive that for the next few years, the country is going to be debating which is better: President Bush's approach to taxes or something that's *closer* to what President Clinton did and President Obama has talked about. Yes, it's the Republican versus the Democratic approach to taxes.

So to help you decipher the sloganeering to come, let's just review what President Bush did and what kinds of choices we have going forward.

According to projections by the Department of the Treasury, extending President Bush's tax cuts to 2020 would mean about $3.7 trillion in lost revenue.[1] Since the youngest baby boomers will be collecting Social Security and on the verge of getting Medicare by this time, the country's financial choices (if we're honest about them) will be grim.[2]

If we don't put more money into the system (raise taxes) and/or stop the money from flowing out (cut government programs), the red ink will just hemorrhage from here on out. This financial reality is not really in dispute. The Congressional Budget Office says it. The U.S. Government Accountability Office says it. Former U.S Comptroller General David Walker and former secretary of commerce Pete Peterson say it. Financial guru Warren Buffett says

---

[1] Tax Policy Center, "Department of the Treasury Revenue Estimates for Extension of 2001 and 2003 Tax Cuts and the Administration's High-Income Tax Proposals Impact on Tax Revenue ($ billions), 2010–20," July 29, 2010, www.taxpolicycenter.org/numbers/displayatab.cfm?DocID=2785.

[2] Remember, Medicare kicks in at age sixty-five, but if you're willing to accept reduced benefits you can get Social Security at age sixty-two.

it. Former Federal Reserve chairman Alan Greenspan says it, and so does the current chairman Ben Bernanke. The editors of the *New York Times*, *Washington Post*, *Washington Times*, and about a gazillion other major newspapers say it. Blue-ribbon panels like the Committee on the Fiscal Future say it. President Obama says it and even set up a Commission on Fiscal Responsibility and Reform to propose ways to solve it. If we were making a speech at the Academy Awards, the music would come on, and we could still keep adding names of knowledgeable people who are sounding the alarm. Nearly everyone who knows anything about this issue says we have big, big trouble on the way unless we act.

WHEN BUSH COMES TO SHOVE—WHAT DO WE DO ABOUT TAXES NOW?

There is very little in today's political chatter leading us to believe that we're now going to have a sensible "let's look at the facts" discussion about raising taxes and how to do it so that it doesn't damage the economy and is as fair and equitable as possible.

We do expect that there will be plenty of political maneuvering and fancy dancing as elected officials try to avoid hard choices on the budget. We can confidently predict you'll hear some of the same old, same old political rhetoric—liberals insisting on rolling back the Bush tax cuts because they "just benefit the rich"; conservatives insisting on keeping all of them because "taxes are bad for the economy." We bet there will be some wearisome knock-down, drag-outs over whether letting a particular cut expire is actually a tax "increase" or not—complete with "yes, it is, no, it's not" screaming all over cable television. And since the actual decisions will revolve around tax brackets, tax credits, deductions, filing status, percentage restrictions, and the "uniform definition of a child," a lot of us will get bleary-eyed reading the details. Some Americans will take a "tax cuts, good, tax increases, bad" attitude, and never rouse themselves to think about anything beyond that.

However, please believe us when we tell you that willful ignorance is the worst possible choice you can make. The dilemma we face now is that it would be virtually impossible to address the country's budget and debt problems through spending cuts alone. You

President Bush signed a series of tax cuts into law. Keeping them all will cost trillions of dollars in the next decade. *Credit: White House Photo by David Bohrer*

can try it yourself in chapter 15, but unless you really plan to live "off the grid," it can't be done. Plus, we are going to have to do a deal that Republicans and Democrats, liberals and conservatives sign on to. The notion that you can do that focusing only on cutting spending or only on raising taxes is—well, dream on if you must.

So we'll lay out the highlights here. By the way, we're giving you a very, very simplified introductory version. Much more detailed information and analysis can be found in the CBO's "Budget Options Publications"[3] and at the IRS Web site at www.irs.gov (we know you just can't get enough of the IRS).

---

[3] You can find them at www.cbo.gov.

Choice 1: What should we do about income taxes?

When President Bush first ran for office in 2000, he was elected at least in part on his promise to cut taxes—and for most people, that means income taxes. Over the next few years, he made good on his word, signing legislation that reduced rates on individual taxpayers at different income levels, including those who earn at the very top levels. Republicans (and others) argue that these tax cuts have helped the U.S. economy by putting more money into people's hands to invest and spend, and that people from all walks of life have benefited. But given the country's mounting debt, and the problems we face on Social Security and Medicare, others want Congress to let some or all of these cuts expire and basically return to the tax rates we had under the Clinton administration. Democrats have generally criticized the Bush tax cuts as mainly benefiting the wealthy. When President Obama was running for office in 2008, he proposed eliminating these tax cuts for families earning more than $250,000 a year. Since the economy was in a whopper of a recession in 2009, he signed nearly $300 billion in tax cuts aimed, as the administration puts it, at 95 percent of working families.[4]

The choice is two-fold. We need to decide what is a sensible and appropriate income tax rate is given the massive debt we've allowed to build up, and the second is how a tax increase will affect the economy. Naturally, experts tend to nuke it out on these very questions, so all we're going to do here is to try to give you some perspective and some key facts.

One key fact is that income tax rates are low by historical standards (You might want to peek back to page 65 at our chart showing the top tax rates over time). The other

---

[4] Recovery.gov., www.recovery.gov/Pages/home.aspx, accessed May 8, 2010.

key fact is that nearly everyone paying income taxes is at least muddling along, financially speaking. Nearly half of Americans earn so little or get enough tax credits that they don't actually owe income taxes (although they do pay other kinds of taxes).[5] It is really hard to think of yourself as lucky when you're watching the money go out the door to the IRS, but in some respects, it's true.

So what would some possible tax hikes mean for helping us with the problem we're tackling here—getting the federal budget under control? Luckily, those clever numbers crunchers at the CBO have put together some choices for us.[6] Here are just a few of them:

Proposal	What it would bring in between 2010 and 2019
Raise all tax rates on ordinary income by 1 percentage point	$454.8 billion
Raise the top tax rate by 1 percentage point. This would be the rate for the very richest people filing taxes	$73. 5 billion. Yes, that is a bit of a bummer, isn't it? It would be so nice to get more out of only hiking taxes on the really filthy rich.
Raise the top four tax rates by 1 percentage point	$200 billion
Raise the tax rate for families earning over a million dollars and individuals earning over $500,000 by 5 percentage points	$222.6 billion

[5] Tax Policy Center, Tax Topics: Who Doesn't Pay Federal Taxes, www.taxpolicycenter.org/taxtopics/federal-taxes-households.cfm, accessed May 9, 2010.

[6] Congressional Budget Office, Budget Options, Chapter 3: Revenue Options, Option 1, page 175, www.cbo.gov/, accessed May 9, 2010. The CBO describes eight different options in this category.

That last option might seem tempting to most Americans, but here's where the downsides come in even if you aren't the one who actually has to pay the tax. Raising taxes, especially if you do it suddenly and/or get carried away, can reduce investment—which you need for a healthy economy—and consumer spending—which you also really need for a healthy economy. And while soaking the rich sounds good to many people, you also have to worry that they might decide to pick up and live in one of their houses in the Cayman Islands or an apartment in Bahrain—then we might not get much out of them. On the other hand, the economy has also thrived in times past when income taxes were somewhat higher (the 1990s, before the Bush tax cuts were passed, were pretty prosperous, and people were hardly fleeing into exile).

Choice 2: What about the estate tax?

Like the hero in the Frank Sinatra song, "That's Life," the estate tax has been "up and down and over and out" in the past few years. In 2001, estates worth over $675,000 were taxed at a rate of 60 percent of the amount over that.[7] In other words, if you inherited $1 million, you didn't pay any tax on the first $675,000, and the remaining $325,000 faced a 60 percent tax rate. President Bush passed legislation phasing it out by 2010, and its status is still up in the air as we go to press. As you might expect, not too many Americans actually pay taxes on inherited estates. According to the nonpartisan Tax Policy Center, "99.8 percent of deaths trigger no estate tax." Even so, about half of Americans (48 percent) say that they would be more likely to vote for a candidate

---

[7] Tax Policy Center, Tax Topics: Estate and Gift Taxes, www.taxpolicy center.org/taxtopics/estatetax.cfm, accessed May 9, 2010.

who opposes the estate tax, so the issue does have political currency, so to speak.[8] Those who want to repeal the estate tax permanently often refer to it as "the death tax." They argue that the person who originally earned the money paid taxes on it in his or her lifetime, so it's not right to tax it a second time. People on the other side of the debate typically say the country shouldn't be offering another windfall for the very wealthiest Americans at a time when we have routine deficits and face huge expenses for Social Security and Medicare. Some opponents of repealing the estate tax have started calling it the "Paris Hilton Benefit Act."[9]

Whether Congress decides to let the estate tax come back to life, or whether there's a move to repeal it permanently, may depend on which party has power. Democrats tend to see the estate tax as a fair way to raise money from wealthy heirs. Republicans tend to see this as a government taxing someone's hard-earned lifetime wealth yet a second time. One question raised by estate tax critics is how to handle inheritances that are actually small family businesses or farms (which can easily be worth a couple of million dollars), although an analysis by FactCheck.org suggests this is a relatively small slice of the issue.[10] Still, if Congress were in a mood to compromise, it might try to

---

[8] NBC News/*Wall Street Journal* Poll, June 9–12, 2006, from the Polling Report (www.pollingreport.com/budget.htm).

[9] E. J. Dionne credits Michael J. Graetz and Ian Shapiro, authors of *Death by a Thousand Cuts*, for coming up with the phrase in his column, "The Paris Hilton Tax Cut," *Washington Post*, April 12, 2005.

[10] Congressional Budget Office, "Effects of the Federal Estate Tax on Farms and Small Businesses," July 2005 (www.cbo.gov/ftpdocs/65xx/doc6512/07-06-EstateTax.pdf). See also "Estate Tax Malarkey: Misleading Ads Exaggerate What the Tax Costs Farmers, Small Businesses and 'Your Family,'" FactCheck.org, June 6, 2005 (www.factcheck.org/article328.html).

work out some ways to exempt inheritances in this category or reduce the tax's impact on them. But realistically, it's up to us whether Congress is of a mind to compromise or not.

Choice 3: What about taxes for married couples?

Before the tax changes ushered in by President Bush, many Americans complained that the tax system was unfair to married couples—that there was a "marriage penalty" in the law.[11] To address this concern, the Bush tax package instituted two changes that are pretty helpful to married couples. One change raised the standard deduction for married couples and the other allowed low-income married couples to earn more before having to pay the lowest tax rate (you can check into the details at the IRS Web site).

On the face of it, you might assume that any change that reduced a "marriage penalty" would just automatically benefit middle-class taxpayers—at least the married ones. However, there was a healthy debate when this legislation was proposed about whom it was really helping and whether it was removing a "penalty" on marriage or giving a "bonus" to some married couples.[12] According to an analysis by the Tax Policy Center, changes to reduce the marriage penalty tend to benefit the prosperous among us. Someone in the top fifth of the income curve would get a benefit of more than $1,000 in 2010, while someone in the middle of the curve gets a benefit of less than $100.[13]

---

[11] See for example, Eric Pianin, "House Votes for Reduction in 'Marriage Penalty' Tax; Plan Covers Millions More Than Clinton's," *Washington Post*, February 11, 2000.

[12] Ibid. See also Iris J. Lav and James Sly, "Conference 'Marriage Penalty' Relief Provisions Reflect Poor Targeting," Center on Budget and Policy Priorities, July 21, 2000 (www.cbpp.org/7-21-00tax.pdf).

[13] Tax Policy Center, Tax Topics: Marriage Penalty, www.taxpolicy center.org/taxtopics/Marriage-Penalties.cfm.

Can two live more cheaply than one? Should married people be able to pay taxes at the same rate they would if they were still single? Should government try to make marriage a more appealing lifestyle through its tax policies? Is this fair or not? In the next year or so, you may be hearing this debate again.

Choice 4: What about the higher tax credits for children and deductions for child care?

The tax code is filled with deductions and credits for this and that, but President Bush's tax packages included two that are especially helpful to families with children—a higher tax credit for each child and higher deductions for child care. The child tax credit is aimed mainly at middle- and low-income families; the credit is reduced for couples with incomes over $110,000 or single parents with incomes over $75,000.[14]

Families in which parents work and pay someone else to watch children also benefit from the higher deductions for child care. Again, the largest deductions go to those in the lower income brackets, but even more affluent families can deduct 20 percent of their child care expenses.[15] It does seem fairly hard-hearted to think of eliminating these tax benefits for families. After all, children are expensive. Most politicians will probably avoid this category like the plague when it comes to looking at tax hikes. Even suggesting reducing the deductions for child care for top-income people would probably result in a headline like "Senator So-and-so Calls for Tax Hikes on Families," so we don't expect much political push to change these.

---

[14] Internal Revenue Service, Publication No. 972, Child Tax Credit.

[15] Internal Revenue Service, Publication No. 503, Child and Dependent Care Expenses.

Choice 5: What about tax rates on capital gains and dividends?

Capital gains taxes apply to the profit people earn when they sell property or stocks, bonds and dividends (payments profitable companies make to shareholders). Republicans typically believe these taxes discourage investment, which they see as the powerhouse of a strong and growing economy. Democrats typically support higher taxes on capital gains and dividends since in their view the fact that you even have a capital gain or dividend is a sign that you're reasonably well-off. In 2003, Congress voted to simplify the taxes (if you don't know, don't ask) and cut them substantially.[16] The rates are generally lower for lower-income people, and right now, they are set to go up in 2011 unless Congress votes to extend or change the current rules.[17] Congress seems to be voting on capital gains taxes fairly often, and whenever the subject comes up, you can expect partisan fireworks. In 2006, Congress extended the lower rates, and then Speaker of the House Dennis Hastert said the vote signaled "a day of celebration for the American people."[18] Florida representative Alcee Hastings, a Democrat, complained, "Now millionaires have the right to have all the money they can," which gives you an idea of how controversial this particular tax area is.[19] Extending the current capital gains tax rates

---

[16] "Phase-in and Expiration Schedule of Key Bush Tax Cuts under Current Law," Joint Economic Committee—Democrats, CBO Confirms that the Bush Tax Cuts Are Skewed Toward the Rich, August 2004, p. 5, www.senate.gov.

[17] Turbo Tax, Summary of Federal Tax Law Changes for 2009–2017, http://turbotax.intuit.com/tax-tools/tax-tips/irs-tax-return/5519. html, accessed May 9, 2010.

[18] Sheryl Gay Stolberg, "House Votes to Extend Investor Tax Cuts for 2 Years," *New York Times*, May 11, 2006.

[19] Ibid.

until 2019 will reduce revenues by about $350 billion,[20] so you can also see why they're arguing over this.

PUTTING THE BUSH TAX CUTS IN PERSPECTIVE

If you have this book in your hand along about March or April in any given year, chances are that the prospect of any tax hike whatsoever will seem extremely unpleasant. But it may also be worth considering a little historic perspective. Even if all of President Bush's tax cuts went away, that would only put taxes back where they were in the 1990s, under President Clinton. Extending all the tax cuts would cost the government an additional $3.7 trillion through 2019, a huge chunk of money to lose when our budget problems are so sizable. On the other side, we have to be realistic about what can be accomplished if we just focus on the Bush tax cuts. According to CBO projections, even if Congress were to let all of the Bush tax cuts expire, the country would still face a big long-term budget problem. We still couldn't meet the commitments we've made on Social Security and Medicare. As Federal Reserve chairman Ben Bernanke testified to Congress in 2007, allowing *all* the Bush tax cuts to expire does "not come anywhere close to balancing the budget over the long run."[21]

---

[20] Congressional Budget Office, Budget Options, Chapter 3: Revenue Options, Option 3, page 180, www.cbo.gov/, accessed May 9, 2010.

[21] Testimony of Ben S. Bernanke, chairman of the Federal Reserve Board of Governors, before the House Committee on the Budget, February 28, 2007, www.access.gpo.gov/congress/house/house04ch110.html.

THE BIG WRINKLE: WHAT SHOULD WE DO ABOUT THE ALTERNATIVE MINIMUM TAX?

There's another big tax decision that comes up repeatedly. It's what to do about the alternative minimum tax (aka the AMT), a Byzantine set of tax rules originally passed in 1969 to ensure that very wealthy people wouldn't be able to weasel out of their share of taxes by using a lot of deductions. When the law was passed nearly forty years ago, it targeted people with incomes over $200,000, which would be about a cool million in today's dollars.[22] And that's the problem with the AMT. Unlike a lot of other parts of the tax code, it wasn't indexed to account for inflation, so now you have a lot of not exactly poor, but hardly wealthy, people paying this tax. Basically, if you have an upper-middle-class income, several children or multiple mortgages and live in a high-tax state, you might need to worry about this. The AMT is very complicated, and if you don't know the gory details personally, count yourself lucky. If you've had to pay it in the last couple of years, you're probably seething. Nearly everyone in and out of politics wants to fix the AMT, but putting this section of the tax code on a more rational footing will send red ink splashing every which way, like a Jackson Pollock painting. According to the Congressional Budget Office, modifying the AMT would cost almost $450 billion in lost revenue between 2010 and 2019. Eliminating it entirely would cost over $625 billion during the same time frame. It may be a ghastly creation, but fixing it or getting rid of it would put us even further in the hole and by big numbers.[23]

---

[22] David Cay Johnston, "It Doesn't Pay to Be in the A.M.T. Zone," *New York Times*, February 12, 2006.

[23] Congressional Budget Office, Budget Options, Chapter 3: Revenue

Debates about the Bush tax cuts sometimes skip over consideration of the AMT, but you shouldn't. We need to think through the whole thing together. Are there taxes we should raise, or, put another way, taxes we should return to the levels they were under President Clinton? Are there credits and deductions we need to reconsider? Are there taxes that should be lower for reasons of fairness or because of their effect on the economy? If so, what other taxes should be higher or what cuts should we make so that the numbers begin to balance out? Recommendation number one from our point of view—be flexible and prepared to compromise, because it is extremely unlikely that Americans will all see these questions exactly the same way. Just ask a single person and a married person about the "marriage penalty," and see how much seeing eye-to-eye you get.

For us, our great hope is not that these issues get resolved according to our own personal preferences, but rather that our leaders will conduct the big tax debate with an eye to the future, not just what seems most popular and convenient at the time.

Options, Option 5, page 184, www.cbo.gov/doc, accessed May 9, 2010.

★★★★★★★★★★★★★★★★★★★★★★★★★★★★

CHAPTER 14

Tackling the Long-Term Problem One Bite at a Time

In the movie *Annie Hall*, Woody Allen sums up his philosophy of life with two dreadful old Borscht Belt jokes.[1] Luckily for you, we're only going to use one bad joke to explain what the country needs to do to tackle its federal budget problems.

The Question: How do you eat an elephant?
The Answer: One bite at a time.

Solving the budget mess is actually quite similar to having to eat an elephant—there's really no way to do it in one sitting.

For most political leaders, the gargantuan size of the problem seems to provoke more artful dodging than genu-

---

[1] Don't want to rent the DVD? Here they are: (1) Two old ladies are in a hotel in the Catskills. "Boy, the food at this place is really terrible," the first says. "Yes, I know," says the second, "and such small portions." (2) "I wouldn't want to belong to any club that would have someone like me for a member."

ine thought. And that's partly our own fault. Voter grati-tude for taking even baby steps on this issue is practically nonexistent. The risks of suggesting a comprehensive deficit-and-debt reduction plan are downright scary to anyone who's chosen a career in politics. Offer up a list of concrete ideas—things to cut, taxes to raise—and you'll have so many people mad at you that your next campaign will be over before it starts.

But sooner or later—by choice or because we no lon-ger have a choice—the country has to get moving on this problem, and it's likely to be a complicated, messy, lengthy, conflict-ridden affair. We didn't get ourselves into this situa-tion in a year or two, and we're not going to be able to get out of it in a year or two either. Still, **if we break the problem down into smaller, manageable pieces, the country can make progress. But we have to be frank about what the pieces are and work up the nerve to take the first bite.**

As we said before, the country will face countless deci-sions on how to address the budget issue, and we'll have to make these decisions over and over again for many years. So what should we be debating? Where should we put our political energies? How do you even begin to think about a problem as big as this? Well, in fact, there are some choices about where to start—some backed broadly by experts, some more controversial, and at least some, in our view, that would be a bit of a detour. Here are the top contenders.

SHOULD WE GO COLD TURKEY ON DEFICIT SPENDING?

Before the U.S. economy plummeted into recession in 2008, many deficit hawks would have said that going cold turkey on deficit spending and deciding to balance the budget no matter what was the right first step. But that was then and

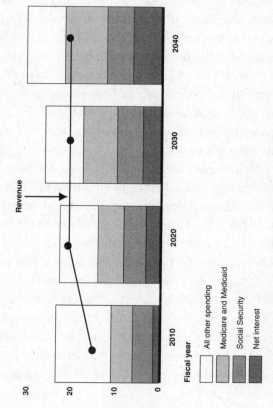

The Scary Projections on Revenues and Spending

Fiscal year

- All other spending
- Medicare and Medicaid
- Social Security
- Net interest

The country will soon need to use nearly every tax dollar collected to pay for Social Security, Medicare, Medicaid, and interest on the debt. *Source: Government Accountability Office*

this is now. Most mainstream economists believe that there are times when the country simply has to spend what it takes and run a deficit, and the worst recession since the Great Depression surely qualifies. We had some really dark days, and even unwavering small government advocates like Wisconsin congressman Paul Ryan voted for the TARP legislation that "bailed out" the big banks (As Ryan says: "We were on the cusp of a deflationary spiral which would have created a depression. I think that's probably pretty likely"[2]). Given how much tax revenues fell during 2008 and 2009, and that the government frantically dispensed cash on emergency measures like the TARP and the stimulus, balancing the budget wasn't possible, and probably isn't possible for a few years.

But that doesn't mean we shouldn't be thinking about what this would mean. President Obama asked the nonpartisan Fiscal Commission he set up in 2010 to come up with a plan to balance the budget (aside from interest on the debt) by 2015. The Center for American Progress, generally seen as a moderate, but left of center think tank, has proposed a more "gradual" process that would stipulate "a fully balanced budget in 2020, an intermediate target for 2014, and benchmarks along the way." CAP argues this would "send a strong signal to financial markets and the world that we are serious about addressing federal budget deficits," and "create a necessary discipline for Congress and the president."[3]

---

[2] Jon Ward, "Paul Ryan Explains His Votes for TARP, Bailouts and Tax on AIG Bonuses," *The Daily Caller*, February 15, 2010, http://daily caller.com/2010/02/14/paul-ryan-explains-his-votes-for-tarp-auto-bailouts-and-tax-on-aig-bonuses/#ixzz0ogUuUanxhttp://dailycaller. com/2010/02/14/paul-ryan-explains-his-votes-for-tarp-auto-bailouts-and-tax-on-aig-bonuses/#ixzz0ogTycLOK, accessed May 22, 2010.

[3] Michael Ettlinger, Michael Linden, Lauren D. Bazel, "A Path to Balance: A Strategy for Realigning the Federal Budget," Center for

Conservative experts like the Heritage Foundation's Brian Riedl have called for "government-wide spending caps [that] would set a simple and predictable annual growth rate."[4] And of course, there are those who've been advocating for years in favor of a constitutional amendment to force the federal government to balance its books every year.

Unfortunately, just balancing the budget every year isn't going to cut it. The country is approaching $15 trillion in debt, and we have massive expenses coming up with the boomers getting long in the tooth. So stopping the deficit spending isn't much more than putting your finger in the dike. We need to take some additional steps, and we need to take them soon. Here are some alternatives about where to start first.

Fix Social Security First

Some experts say getting Social Security on a sound financial footing should be the first step. People generally understand how Social Security works. Millions of Americans depend on it (if for no other reason than to keep Grandma from moving in), so generating the political will to fix it should be doable. Guaranteeing the program's future might relieve a lot of the voter anxiety that makes the budget issue such a political hot potato. Compared to its sister program, Medicare, Social Security is, according to most experts, the "easier problem," so maybe we should tackle it first.

There are dozens of alternatives combining relatively

American Progress, December 14, 2009, www.americanprogress.org/issues/2009/12/path_to_balance.html, accessed May 22, 2010.

[4] Brian Riedl, "Raise Debt Limit, But Attach Spending Caps," WashingtonTimes.com, December 8, 2009, www.washingtontimes.com/news/2009/dec/08/riedl-raise-debt-limit-but-attach-spending-caps/, accessed May 27, 2010.

acceptable cuts in benefits with relatively acceptable increases in taxes that could essentially solve the Social Security problem for a very, very long time. Plus, if the country could take this first step successfully, maybe we would be encouraged to move on to more daunting budget issues. The only hurdle here is whether the country can really negotiate a solution, or whether liberals who consider Social Security untouchable and conservatives who never liked the program in the first place will make compromise impossible.

Fix the Tax System First

Maybe you may think taxes are too high, or maybe you may think the country has gone overboard cutting taxes in recent years. But whatever you think about how *much* we pay in taxes, chances are you want tax cheaters to pay up and would love to see the tax system simplified. If the country really has to consider raising taxes to get its financial house in order, some people say we ought to fix the tax system first. We need to nab the cheaters and reduce the mind-boggling complexity of the tax code. We've actually heard of a few people who say they would be happy to pay even more in taxes if they just didn't have to spend the first half of April scurrying around the house looking for bank statements and rummaging through shoe boxes of receipts.

At least, we top Greece when it comes to getting taxpayers to pay what they owe. The Greeks are so used to rampant tax cheating that when the government proposed requiring taxi drivers to give receipts to keep track of their income, the drivers went into the streets to protest.[5] Even

[5] Eric Westervelt, "Greece's Bottom Line: Too Many Tax Cheats," National Public Radio, March 25, 2010, www.npr.org/templates/story/story.php?storyId=125125500&ft=1&f=1001, accessed May 22, 2010.

here though, collecting taxes that have "gone missing" could bring in another $290 billion a year, according to IRS estimates. The idea of finding "extra money" in the system without actually having to raise taxes has become so enticing to Congress that it gave the IRS additional funding in 2009 to update and monitor the extent of the "tax gap." The nub of the issue for the IRS is how to "maximize revenue collection" without "imposing unreasonable compliance and enforcement burdens" on most people and businesses that are already obeying the law.[6] For example, more IRS audits might bring in more cash, but it's not hard to see why politicians might shy away from this in a campaign season ("Vote for Smith. He'll Boost Your Chances of Being Audited").

Making the tax code simpler is another "sounds good, but . . ." idea. Treating different kinds of income differently and having all sorts of deductions makes the system extremely complicated and cumbersome, but there are lots of people ready to scream their heads off if their favorite deduction is touched. In 2005, President Bush asked political powerhouses Senator John Breaux of Louisiana and former Florida senator Connie Mack to head up the President's Advisory Panel on Federal Tax Reform to devise a plan to simplify taxes. When the commission issued its ideas in late 2005, the U.S. Conference of Mayors objected to eliminating deductions for state and local taxes,[7] the National Association of Realtors said proposals to change the home mortgage deduction would cause real estate prices to plunge,[8]

---

[6] Department of the Treasury, Update on Reducing the Tax Gap and Improving Voluntary Compliance, July 8, 2009, www.irs.gov/pub/newsroom/tax_gap_report_-final_version.pdf, accessed May 22, 2010.

[7] U.S. Conference of Mayors Statements on the Report of the President's Advisory Panel on Federal Tax Reform, US Newswire, November 1, 2005.

[8] "Now the Debate Begins on Tax Reform," *Omaha World-Herald*, November 5, 2005.

and the National Retail Federation said changes in the way businesses deduct the cost of imported goods would in effect mean a 30 percent tax increase for retailers.[9]

More recently, former Federal Reserve chairman Paul Volcker headed a panel of experts that proposed a number of ways to make the tax code simpler and more straightforward; you can take a look at it yourself at www.whitehouse.gov/blog/2010/08/27perab-tax-task-force-report. Simplifying taxes might be a good idea in concept, and maybe we should pursue it (we talk more about it ourselves in chapter 4), but the country could lose an awful lot of time working on the budget problem while all the various constituencies duke it out over the tax code. It's just a lot easier said than done.

Get a Grip on Health Care Costs First

Hang on, you're probably saying. Didn't we just *do* this? Well, yes. The massive health care reform plan passed in 2010 has a number of features designed to control the rise in Medicare costs in particular and health care in general, including insurance exchanges where people can shop around for coverage, pilot programs where doctors and hospitals can experiment with more cost-efficient care, and research on more effective ways to provide treatment. (see the sidebar on "Health Care and the Budget: Have We Got the Right Prescription Yet?" on page 152 for more).

But controlling health care costs is critical if we're going to get the budget and national debt under control. The U.S. government spends mega-dollars on health care every year. In fact, in 2008 government dollars covered 47 percent of all the health care spending in America.[10]

---

[9] Ibid.

[10] Center for Medicare and Medicaid Services, National Health Care

There's a double-whammy problem here. The number of older Americans is increasing. Added to that, health care costs are rising faster than inflation. According to a 2010 report from the Government Accountability Office, this isn't just a federal budget problem, "the continued rise in health care costs also poses challenges to American businesses, families, and societies as a whole."[11] That's one of the reasons why the Obama administration argued tackling health care was vital.

Fair enough. But it's also fair to ask whether the plan does enough to control costs, fast enough. The country did take some initial steps to curb Medicare costs in the 2010 health reform legislation, about $575 billion worth between 2010 and 2020. It generated a lot of screaming and shouting, but these decisions have actually given the Medicare trust fund an additional 12 years of life[12]—which is not nothing. That assumes that everything works out as planned (which is not a sure thing) and that Congress doesn't get cold feet and restore some of the cuts when people start to complain (also not a sure thing).

But most of the broader changes in the bill are phased in over the next decade, as the national debt is projected to rise to nearly the size of our total economy. There's furious debate over whether the cost measures will do

Expenditure Data, www.cms.gov/NationalHealthExpendData/down loads/dsm-08.pdf, accessed May 28, 2010.

[11] U.S. Government Accountability Office, "The Federal Government's Long-Term Fiscal Outlook," January 2010 Update, www.gao.gov/new. items/d10468sp.pdf.

[12] Richard S. Foster, Chief Actuary, Centers for Medicare and Medicaid Services, Department of Health and Human Services, "Estimated Financial Effects of the Patient Protection and Affordable Care Act, as Amended," April 22, 2010, page 9, http://graphics8.nytimes.com/packages/pdf/health/oactmemo1.pdf.

better or worse than projected. In addition, the reform plan passed up on some alternatives for controlling costs, like a government-run "public option" insurance plan to compete with private insurers, or reforming medical malpractice laws.

Basically, there's no way to get out of our budget problems without getting health care spending under control. We know, everyone's exhausted from arguing on this topic. But we need to watch this problem closely and see how well the health care plan works in the real world, as opposed to the world of projections. The country's health care costs are just not sustainable given how quickly they are rising, whether it's government, business, or individuals paying them.

Improve the Congressional Budget Process First

If you remember those "how a bill goes through Congress" charts from junior high, you might think the process Congress uses to decide how to spend taxpayer dollars is logical and straightforward. But not in today's Washington. Congressional rules and procedures regarding the budget are elaborate, convoluted, and slippery to boot.

It's hard for most of us to keep track of what actually happens to our money given all the clever ways Congress has to confuse things. That's bad enough, but the process has gotten so bad that even *Congress* doesn't actually know how much it's spending. For example, most of the cost for Iraq wasn't included in the regular budget for the first several years of the war (see "The Fortunes of War" in chapter 5). The requests for money for the war were submitted in "supplemental" spending bills that bypass the usual appropriations process. War costs are also spread out in various places in the defense budget, which, as the Iraq Study Group points out, means you have to be a professional budget analyst to figure out how much the war costs. And maybe you can't figure it out even then.

Then there are those tasty little earmarks—"tasty" and "little" to people in Washington, that is. In 2007, Congress passed legislation that makes it easier to know who's sponsoring earmarks and why. The practice does seem to be a little less brazen than it once was. Even so, like bacteria that mutate and no longer respond to antibiotics, a lot of earmark-type spending seems to be slithering through anyway.[13]

The question is whether Congress can make good decisions given the Byzantine process it has now. There are plenty of ideas for fixing the problem—and some of them are almost as complicated as the processes they would replace. Check out David Bauman's explanation of a recent reform plan that included "line-item enhanced rescission, budget caps, sequestration, biennial budgeting, commissions, the kitchen sink, 2007 draft picks and a provision to be named later" to see what we mean.[14]

But there are some relatively straightforward steps many budget experts think are essential. Put everything in the budget; stop hiding things away in "supplemental" or "emergency" spending bills. Get rid of the earmarks—bring all spending out in the open and subject it to debate. Build on sites like USAspending.gov and Recovery.gov, and publish a complete list of every spending item Congress approves and every member who voted for it and put it on the Internet for easy access (it's called "transparency"). Adopt an enforce-

---

[13] John Solomon and Jeffrey H. Birnbaum, "In the Democratic Congress, Pork Still Gets Served," *Washington Post*, May 24, 2007, www.washingtonpost.com/wp-dyn/content/article/2007/05/23/AR2007052301782.html.

[14] "Budget Reform, Yet Again," *National Journal*, July 21, 2006.

able pay-as-you-go system where Congress can't add new spending without raising taxes or cutting existing programs to pay for the addition. A real pay-go system would also prevent Congress from cutting taxes without cutting spending enough to stay out of the red ink.

Are changes like these blindingly obvious? Yes. Are they necessary? We think so, and for two reasons. One is that they probably would help ensure that taxpayer dollars are used more carefully. And second, if the rest of us are going to have to make some sacrifices, we think it's only fair that Congress clean up its act, too.

Set a Target First

Despite all the energy spent on arguing over the federal budget, most of the political debate is caught up in the weeds over a particular tax or spending bill, and not stepping back to look at the big picture. Over the last couple of years, a number of blue-ribbon panels and budget experts have started arguing that the United States should have an official budget target: a goal that shapes everything else the government does. You can't get anywhere until you know where you're going, these people say, and a formal target could take the government out of the realm of "muddling through" and force the nation to have an actual plan.

There are a couple different ways you could do this. Two different panels, the Peterson-Pew Commission on Budget Reform and the Committee on the Fiscal Future of the United States, have called for a budget target based on a ratio of national debt-to-GDP, or basically how much money we owe compared to the total size of the American economy. They even picked the same number: 60 percent of GDP. Another organization, the Center for Budget and Policy Priorities, also favors the idea but says that target's too low, calling for a target of 70 percent. All three groups argue that controlling the debt at that level would be tough, but would allow us to pay for what we need without letting the debt get out of control.[15]

President Obama gave his deficit commission a somewhat different target: to balance the budget by 2015, not counting interest (and as you know, interest payments are a big chunk of the budget. But Obama also asked the panel to look at stabilizing the debt as well.

There are a couple of advantages here. One is that setting a target sends a signal to our bondholders, both at home and abroad, that we're serious about this problem, and helps keep them confident in our government (and also keeps them lending us money). The other is that a target could help frame our debate in a more nonpartisan way. The Fiscal Future committee, for example, offered four different alternative paths to meet its budget target, ranging from a small government/low tax option to a big government/high tax approach, with a couple of ways in between. That's a point worth remembering, that this doesn't have to be about ideology; there are lots of ways to make the budget work, whether you're a conservative or a liberal.

The downside is that we still need to make all the choices needed to get to the target, and all of them are just as controversial as they ever were. A target is a tool—it's not a solution in itself.

Clean Up Politics First

When we were doing the research for this book, we went down to Wilmington, Delaware, to attend a session of the

---

[15] You can find out more about all these plans: the Peterson-Pew report is at budgetreform.org, the Fiscal Future committee is at ourfiscalfuture.org, and the Center for Budget and Policy Priorities is at cbpp.org.

Fiscal Wake-up Tour. The Wake-up Tour is a traveling road show that includes panel presentations from former Comptroller General David Walker and budget experts from think tanks like the Heritage Foundation and the Brookings Institution, and representatives from the Concord Coalition. Each of the presenters talked about the crisis the country could face if we don't begin to face up to some financial realities.

When the time came for audience Q & A, we were surprised by the number of questions that focused on how to fix the political system rather than on ideas for cutting spending or raising revenues. Should we reform campaign financing? What about curbing lobbying? What about federal funding of campaigns? What about term limits?

What people in the audience seemed to be saying is this: If we have to do things that are not so pleasant—pay higher taxes, postpone our retirements, cover more of our own health care costs, and so on—what can we do to ensure that the people who represent us in Washington really have our best interests at heart? How can we be sure that the solutions they vote for are fair?

This is a tough one. If you've been reading along with us, you know we're not happy with what's been going on in Washington. As a group, our elected officials really haven't been watching out for our interests. It's certainly hard to argue that the political system as it is now is acceptable. It's pretty awful, frankly.

But the question is whether the country can really afford to fix the political system *first*. Every year we lose tackling the budget issue makes the problem even worse. The debt gets higher and the time to fix Social Security and Medicare gets shorter.

What's more, people have been trying to fix up the political system for years, proposing ideas like term limits and federal funding for campaigns without much happening. Campaign finance reform is a very squiggly thing—you fix one problem, and new ones break out somewhere else. We're not saying that we think the country should just live with the political system we have now. And the country can certainly work on different problems at once. In fact, we have to—the country still has to address terrorism, jobs, energy independence, the environment, and other extremely important areas. We can't let those slide while we stop to debate the budget.

But everything we have seen and learned while working on this book leads us to one conclusion: We can't wait another year to get going on the budget mess. And saying that we have to fix the political system first could turn out to be a gigantic mistake.

So Has Anyone Got Any Bright Ideas?

There are lots of fiscal experts who say the way the U.S. government approaches budget issues is all wrong. In fact, the U.S. government doesn't really have a long-term fiscal plan, and our year-by-year process is a little loose as well. It's hard to believe, but there's no single moment when Congress votes on "the budget" for the year.

By law, the president has to submit a budget request to Congress every February, which usually includes goals and projections (recently for five years out). And while the president's request sets up much of the budget debate, Congress doesn't have to accept a single thing in it. Instead, Congress passes its annual budget resolution, which is nonbinding (and thus not subject to a presidential veto) but sets the structure for what Congress will do with federal finances that year.

But neither the president's request nor the congressional resolution is the actual budget. There are no less than thirteen separate spending bills that Congress has to pass to fund various departments and agencies, from Agriculture to Veterans Affairs. Those bills are each debated separately and may be vetoed by the president. Entitlements don't count in this. Unless Congress makes a specific decision to pass legislation affecting Social Security and Medicare, the programs clip along on autopilot without Congress or the president doing anything.[16]

Obviously, this isn't how corporations handle their budgets (although Enron and WorldCom prove there are plenty of ways to get fiscally funky in the private sector). But even in the realm of government finances, is there a better option?

The European Union does have broad outlines for member countries. To become an EU member, a country has to agree to keep budget deficits under 3 percent of the country's gross domestic product and the public debt at 60 percent. Unfortunately, there's a procedure for making exceptions and very little the EU can do to make a country fall in line. The European debt crisis of 2010 underscored that point, with Greece, for example, running deficits of 13 percent of GDP and a public debt at 115 percent. Countries like Italy, Belgium, Spain, and Portugal have all broken the guidelines as well.

SHOULD WE GO DUTCH?

A lot of fiscal experts like the way the Netherlands handles its budgets. Dutch governments are generally coalitions of competing parliamentary parties, and as part of putting together the coalition, the parties hammer out a budget blueprint that covers the entire four years until the next election. The blueprint includes

---

[16] Heniff, Bill Jr., "Overview of the Congressional Budget Process," Congressional Research Service, October 21, 1999.

caps for spending and rules for changing the budget if tax revenue comes in higher or lower than expected. If the budget runs a surplus, the parties agree on what percentage will go to tax cuts or paying off the national debt. Politicians being politicians, this system isn't perfect, but it does have a certain logical appeal. Given the bitterness of our own politics, the idea of Republicans and Democrats sitting down to agree on a four-year plan for what they will spend seems like a political pipe dream. On the other hand, both the first President Bush and President Clinton managed to hammer out bipartisan budget deals when they were in office, so maybe we shouldn't toss this idea out so quickly.

DO AS THEY DO IN NEW ZEALAND?

New Zealand has a different strategy, which is based on setting goals and being clear and open about the results of government policies. By law, the New Zealand government has to set long-term fiscal goals (like keeping the national debt at a reasonable level), and every year the government is required to report how it's doing in meeting these goals. Just prior to elections, the government has to report on how campaign promises will affect the budget (yes, we're trying to imagine that, too). Again, the system is not perfect, but New Zealand does consistently run budget surpluses.[17]

TIME FOR A BALANCED BUDGET AMENDMENT?

One option that's often been proposed is a constitutional amendment requiring a balanced budget. Forty-nine states have some sort of provision that their state budgets should balance. But this has never really gained a political foothold on the federal level. And it all depends on how the amendment is crafted. The state balanced-budget rules often look good on paper but aren't that rigid in practice. Many states have rules on the books but no

---

[17] Allen Schick, "Can the U.S. Government Live Within Its Means? Lessons from Abroad," Brookings Institution Policy Brief, June 2005.

provision for enforcing them.[18] And lots of state budgets over the years have been "balanced" using one-shot gimmicks and other short-term schemes that meet the law but don't address the underlying problems.

WHAT ABOUT THE LINE-ITEM VETO AND PAY-GO?

Another possible constitutional amendment would give the president a line-item veto. Again, this is a tool many state governors have that allows them to strike out portions of a bill while approving the rest. The president can only sign or veto entire bills, warts and all. A line-item veto would certainly give the president the power to strike out pork-barrel projects—or, at least, the ones that don't benefit the president's party.

Other changes don't require amending the Constitution. We've already talked about "pay-go" rules, which basically require that if Congress wants to spend more money on a program or cut a tax, it has to make up that lost money by cutting programs or raising revenue elsewhere in the budget. Pay-go legislation was a key tool in balancing the budget in the 1990s, but it was allowed to expire in 2002.[19]

A new pay-go law was signed in February 2010, and while experts say it will help, Congress can be pretty broadminded in interpreting the rules. For example, the law allows for exceptions (like "patching" the alternative minimum tax and limiting automatic cuts in physicians' fees under Medicare) and the ability to waive the rules in "emergencies."[20]

All of these budget strategies, at home and abroad, are no

[18] Ronald K. Snell, "State Balanced Budget Requirements: Provisions and Practice," National Conference of State Legislatures, www.ncsl.org/programs/fiscal/balbuda.htm, accessed May 19, 2007.

[19] "Federal Budget Process Reform in the 110th Congress: A Brief Overview," Congressional Research Service, January 22, 2007.

[20] Politico.com, "President Obama hails return to PAYGO," Feb. 13, 2010, www.politico.com/news/stories/0210/32921.html.

better than the politicians who implement them. The good news is that the raw material is there to turn this situation around. The Congressional Budget Office and the Social Security and Medicare trustees provide honest assessments of the nation's finances. And the bipartisan will to change has emerged before—not that long ago, in fact. The government balanced its budget in the 1990s in large part because President George H. W. Bush and a Democratic Congress were willing to raise taxes, and because President Clinton and a Republican Congress were willing to maintain fiscal discipline.

We can get the nation's finances under control. It's just going to require the determination—and a lot more scrutiny from the public—to get the job done.

DON'T WORRY, BE HAPPY: FOUR DISTURBINGLY SIMPLE IDEAS FOR CURING OUR BUDGET PROBLEMS

The vast majority of experts and economists accept what would seem to be an obvious truth—the only way to tackle the country's budget problems is to stop spending more than you take in. Since that means raising taxes, cutting programs, or doing some of both, plenty of people will be unhappy and some scream their heads off. And some will put their faith in the latest miracle cure.

Yes, there are people riding to our rescue who say that if we listen to them, we can avoid having to make tough choices. They're riding in from the right and the left; they're blogging, and you can easily catch them on talk radio. To us, their prescriptions fall squarely into the "it sounds too good to be true" category, but we wouldn't be doing our jobs if we didn't mention them. If you want to read more, you can check the footnotes here for places to start (although you may want to have your rose-colored glasses handy). These ideas are rejected by nearly all mainstream economists, and they pose huge risks if we pursue them, but here goes:

Miracle Cure No. 1: Print More Money. We all know that the U.S. government issues U.S. currency. What's more, the government's "ability to spend is numerically unlimited," according to Pavlina Tcherneva, an assistant professor at Franklin and Marshall.[21] Since the government can "print money," its spending is "constrained only by the inflation it can create by over-spending." The professor is one of six contributors to a mind-bending collection of economic thinking that appeared in The Huffington Post. The basic thrust: the government can keep increasing its spending without worrying about the deficit or the debt. Since the government creates all money, the "federal government neither 'has' nor 'doesn't have' dollars. The government spends by creating new money and taxes by destroying money, which simply involves changing numbers in bank accounts," another contributor, Yeva Nersisyan, wrote. From what we've seen, this line of thinking is manna from heaven for those who don't want to talk about our fiscal problems and want the government to spend a great deal more to spur the economy and create jobs.

There is a small (really small) grain of truth here: governments, or more specifically central banks like the Federal Reserve, can and do deliberately "loosen the money supply" when they think it makes economic sense. In fact, the Fed has done just that at historic levels throughout 2008 and 2009, to goose the economy and keep credit moving. Economists are always ar-

---

[21] Tcherneva is quoted in "The Deficit: Nine Myths We Can't Afford" compiled by Lynn Parramore, The Huffington Post, April 27, 2010, www.huffingtonpost.com/lynn-parramore/the-deficit-nine-myths-we_b_553527.html.

guing over whether and how much the Federal Reserve should be doing this. Obviously, Fed chairman Ben Bernanke thinks he has done the right thing—the economy wasn't growing; unemployment was treacherously high, and there was almost no danger of inflation, so he increased the money supply. But conservative columnist George Will sees inherent risks in this approach. It is "hubris," he writes, "something abundant in Washington, to think inflation can be precisely controlled, like an oven's temperature."[22] So the debate goes on. The Fed does have wiggle room, but most experts say it has to be used judiciously.

Could the Fed really print money in the quantities needed to offset our deficits and rising national debt? The amount of money involved is enormous. The White House is projecting a total of $8.5 trillion in deficits between 2011 and 2020. Just to give you a sense of scope, gross domestic product—the size of the entire U.S. economy—was about $14.2 trillion in 2009.[23] As former U.S. comptroller David Walker points out, "the real fiscal challenge facing the U.S. federal government is driven by the $45 (trillion) to $50 trillion [that we have promised for] Medicare and Social Security)."[24] Relying on the Fed to "print" that much money (actually it buys Treasury bonds with money it prints) is very different from loosening the money supply during an economic downturn. Taking an aspirin or two when you have a headache is one thing. Downing a couple of bottles every day will rip your stomach to shreds.

Why is printing so much money so dangerous? Because it unleashes inflation, which Walker calls "the cruelest tax of all"

---

[22] George F. Will, "Gambling with the Dollar," *Washington Post*, November 12, 2010, www.washingtonpost.com/wp-dyn/content/article/2009/11/11/AR2009111122257.html.

[23] U.S. Bureau of Economic Analysis, Gross Domestic Product: First Quarter 2010 (Advance Estimate), April 30, 2010, www.bea.gov/newsreleases/national/gdp/2010/pdf/gdp1q10_adv.pdf.

[24] Correspondence from David Walker, May 14, 2010.

and one that "tends to harm lower income persons more than the well-off."[25] Prices for all the things you need—housing, gas, food, electricity, etc.—start rising; people stop saving money because they figure it will lose its value sitting in a bank. If inflation gets out of hand (and it can when governments try to cover their debts with massive fiddling with the money supply), it can generate hyperinflation. Officially, hyperinflation is when the monthly rate of inflation is more than 50 percent. Here's a comforting example: At that rate, something that cost $1.00 would cost about $130.00 one year later.[26] Inflation may not be much of a danger now, but a little inflation goes a long way, and risking it spinning out of control is not a prospect anyone should take lightly.

Miracle Cure No. 2. Just Default. When Glenn Reynolds, a University of Tennessee Law School professor who blogs as the "instapundit," asked why the United States can't solve its debt problems by just defaulting, he rubbed a lot of experts the wrong way. But we've heard other people musing along the same lines. What would happen?

Bruce Bartlett, an influential economist who served in the administrations of Ronald Reagan and the first George Bush, says the idea is "simply absurd" and "needs to be nipped in the bud."[27] First and foremost, default means not paying back the people who bought Treasury bonds. Maybe you're saying to yourself that you don't care because we'll just be stiffing some bankers in China and the Cayman Islands, but that's not really the case. Americans buy Treasury bonds, too, and in fact more Americans hold them than for-

---

[25] Letter from David Walker, May 14, 2010.

[26] Michael K. Salemi, "Hyperinflation," Concise Encyclopedia of Economics, www.econlib.org/library/Enc/Hyperinflation.html, accessed May 23, 2010.

[27] Bruce Bartlett, "Another Dumb Right-Wing Idea: Default on the Debt," Capitalgainsandgames.com, February 20, 2010, www.capitalgainsandgames.com/blog/bruce-bartlett/1509/another-dumb-right-wing-idea-default-debt, accessed May 23, 2010.

eigners. According to Bartlett, defaulting would "cause tremendous hardship for millions of Americans because some $800 billion in Treasury securities are owned by private investors, almost $700 billion are owned by mutual funds, more than $500 billion are owned by state and local governments and more than $300 billion are owned by pension funds."[28] And that would probably just be the beginning. Interest rates would likely soar. As we have learned so well in the past few years, meltdowns like this can set off financial panics that can spread globally with terrible and unpredictable results.

There's a somewhat less extreme, but related idea—that we "devalue the dollar" so we can pay back our debts with cheaper money. There is a reasonable debate about whether a weaker or stronger dollar is better for the U.S. economy, but again, we're talking questions of scale. Like "printing more money," devaluing the dollar enough to cover our current and upcoming debt risks unleashing massive inflation—the kind of hyperinflation where your nice dollar cup of coffee costs over a hundred bucks.

Plus, to be perfectly blunt about it, if we default on our debts, why would anyone loan us more money? The Chinese and other lenders who have supported our economy and covered our deficits by buying and holding our Treasury bonds will obviously start doing something else with their money. We can't really believe that they'll continue to be patsies just because it's better for us. In the end, to win back investors' confidence, the United States would have to cut spending and raise taxes—which is exactly what those advocating default wanted to avoid in the first place.

Miracle Cure No. 3: We Can Grow Our Way Out of This. This is one of the most common and popular quick fixes out there, and

---

[28] Bruce Bartlett, "How much does the national debt matter?" MSN.com, March 5, 2010, http://articles.moneycentral.msn.com/Investing/Extra/how-much-does-the-national-debt-matter.aspx, accessed May 23, 2010.

there's more truth in it than in some of the others. Essentially, the argument goes, if the economy grows, the government takes in more tax revenue, because businesses are more profitable and people are earning more money. Plus, if the overall economy is growing faster than the government is piling up debt, then the debt keeps becoming a smaller and less troublesome part of the overall economic pie.

Part of the appeal of this is that it fits in nicely with what everyone wants to do anyway: make the economy grow. There's even some historical evidence: the booming economy of the 1990s was a major factor in balancing the budget in the second Clinton administration, and the post–World War II economic boom was fundamental in getting the national debt down from its all-time high point in just a few years.

So why can't this happen again? Because now, the projections say the national debt is going to grow faster than the economy, not the other way around. Specifically, spending driven by Medicare, Medicaid, and Social Security is going to go up faster than the overall economy will. And because of the double whammy of rising health care costs and an aging population, those are the programs that are going to drive the federal budget. That's the conclusion of the government's own auditors—it's stated flatly in the *Financial Report of the United States Government,* the government's equivalent of a corporate annual report.[29] Independent experts agree. "No reasonably foreseeable rate of economic growth would overcome this structural deficit," concluded the Committee on the Fiscal Future of the United States, a panel set up by the National Research Council and the National Academy of Public Administration.[30] The leaders of President Obama's deficit com-

---

[29] U.S. Department of the Treasury, "Financial Report of the United States Government 2009," www.fms.treas.gov/fr/index.html.

[30] Committee on the Fiscal Future of the United States, "Choosing Our Fiscal Fu-

mission took this as practically a first principle for their work. Co-chairman Alan Simpson was positively pungent about this. "Hell, we could have double [digit] growth for 30 years and never grow our way out of this," the former Wyoming senator snorted.[31]

Don't get us wrong: we need economic growth. We need it to solve our fiscal problems, and we need it for the jobs and prosperity all of us want. But to get the budget under control, we'll need growth plus the spending cuts and revenue increases needed to get ahead of the problem. "We need to weed our government's garden as well as water it," said Gene Steuerle, a fellow at the Urban Institute.[32]

Miracle Cure No. 4. Abolish the Fed. The idea of abolishing the Federal Reserve pops up nearly every time we've been on radio or TV talking about the budget, and although it's clear that people feel strongly about it, we're still trying to figure out exactly why they think it would help resolve the budget problem. Congressman Ron Paul proposed abolishing the Federal Reserve back in 2002 (just after the Internet bubble burst) because he, like others, believes that its "consistent policy of flooding the economy with easy money" is leading to an artificial cycle of economic booms and busts.[33] Paul has impressive company when he questions what the Fed has done over the past few decades with interest rates and the money supply. Quite a few economists and experts blame former Fed chairman Alan Greenspan and his very low interest policies for the housing, mortgage, and banking bubbles that followed his tenure.

---

ture," Summary, January 2010, www.ourfiscalfuture.org/thereport.

[31] Reuters, "Panel says U.S. can't grow its way out of deficits," April 26, 2010, www.reuters.com/article/idUSTRE6301WP20100426.

[32] Eugene Steuerle, Tax Policy Center, "Why Economic Growth Isn't Enough," May 12, 2010, http://taxpolicycenter.org/UploadedPDF/901349-why-economic-growth.pdf.

[33] Ron Paul, U.S. House of Representatives, September 10, 2002, www.house.gov/paul/congrec/congrec2002/cr091002b.htm, accessed May 23, 2010.

That said, most economists don't think you can really abolish the Fed. It's been around since 1913; most other countries have similar institutions, and returning to a system where you have to have gold in the bank to back up U.S. dollars would be a wrenching transition. Being on the gold standard back in the day actually wasn't much fun either. It led to frequent recessions and high unemployment, according to economists who have studied Fed history.[34] Moreover, the decision to try to go back to the gold standard now would be a monumental distraction from solving our budget problems with "who knows what" consequences.

But to us, the real flaw is that this is kind of beside the point. Maybe it would be better to rein the Fed in, or at least watch it more closely,[35] but we still have to decide what to do now about what the country owes and what it has promised. Whether you're using gold, paper, diamonds (like Michael Rennie in *The Day the Earth Stood Still*), or rubber duckies as your currency, you're going to get into trouble if you routinely and continually spend more than you take in.

The idea of the quick fix is always out there. Eat all you want and still lose weight. Make a fortune flipping foreclosed houses. We can listen to these "don't worry, be happy" nostrums and risk everything we have, or we can settle down, hear each other out, make some compromises, and solve our problems. What we can't do, as David Walker puts it, is continue to exempt ourselves "from the fundamental laws of prudent finance."[36]

---

[34] For a good discussion of the controversy over the Fed and the gold standard, take a look at Anthony Mirhaydari, "Should the Fed Be Abolished?" MSN.com, http://articles.moneycentral.msn.com/learn-how-to-invest/should-the-fed-be-abolished.aspx?page=al, accessed May 23, 2010.

[35] More recently, Congressman Ron Paul and others have proposed "auditing" the Federal Reserve. You can even listen to an "Audit the Fed Song" laying out their reasoning if you visit www.ronpaul.com/legislation/audit-the-federal-reserve-hr-1207/.

[36] Correspondence from David Walker, May 14, 2010.

CHAPTER 15

OK, if You're So Smart...

By now, you've got a pretty good idea of what the country's facing. You've probably got some ideas what should be done, too. So let's see what you can do about it. People used to say any American child could grow up to be president. Well, in this chapter, that means you.

David Walker, the former U.S. comptroller general who has pushed for action on the debt problem for years has a succinct recommendation: "When you find yourself in a hole, the first thing is to stop digging."

That's a great quote, and has a lot of truth in it, but it's also slightly misleading. If you're digging a hole in the ground, and you decide you don't want to go any deeper, you just put down the shovel. It's a passive choice, even a restful one, since digging a hole in the ground is hard work. It implies that to stop digging is easy and that the hard part is climbing out of the hole again.

The fact is, when you're talking about the federal budget, *the hole gets deeper when you sit on your hands and do nothing.* Every year the government runs a deficit, Washington has to borrow money, the debt gets bigger, and the hole gets deeper. And running a deficit is the default setting. It's easy. Balancing the budget takes effort. Even trimming the deficit down a little takes effort. Leaning on your shovel makes things worse.

Unfortunately, attacking this problem is a lot more like losing weight (we find that as depressing an analogy as you do). You've got to work at it, eat less and exercise. And just like deficit reduction, there are a lot of people out there pushing fad diets in which you can somehow eat anything you want, watch TV all day, make no sacrifices of any kind, and still lose twenty pounds. In both cases, it's not going to happen.

Think of the worksheet in this chapter as your chance to be both president and gym trainer. In fact, you get to be somewhat more powerful than either the president or your gym trainer, because (a) you don't need to negotiate any of your choices with Congress and (b) whatever you decide actually gets done—there's no going home from the gym and eating an entire pie.

The goal of the exercise is to stop digging the fiscal hole by trying to balance the federal budget in a given year. We've given you a list of programs and revenue sources. You can increase, decrease, or eliminate any item you want, but you are limited to those "discretionary" programs that can vary from year to year. (There are, as we've discussed, a lot of things that could be done with entitlements, but very few of them pay off right away, so they don't affect a one-year budget). A few things are off limits—you can't cut interest payments on the debt, for example. The banks have to get their money.

In the real world, of course, the long-term entitlement problems are the bigger concern, but controlling the year-to-year budget is a good start. Also in the real world, there are political and economic consequences to any of these decisions. We've pointed them out in the worksheet. You can factor them into your decisions, or not, as you please. But you should realize that the real president and Congress are going to be weighing these consequences, whether you do or not.

PROGRAM In millions of dollars Minus indicates revenue	2009 BUDGET	YOUR BUDGET	PROS	CONS	WHO CARES
Agriculture	**2009 Total $22,237**				
Farm income stabilization (aka, crop subsidies)	$17,635		This has kept a lot of family farms in business	Most of this money now goes to big agribusiness, which can take care of itself	The farm lobby. Don't underestimate them
Research and services (including inspections)	$4,602		Research helps keep us the world's breadbasket, and there has to be a watchdog over the nation's food supply	Greater self-regulation might be cheaper, and the food industry knows it has to keep its act clean	The food industry, along with anyone who eats
Community and regional development	**2009 Total $27,650**				
Area and regional development, including rural/Indian programs	$3,221		Promotes economic growth in some of the poorest areas in the country	There's serious question whether these programs are effective as is	People in poor, rural areas
Disaster relief and flood insurance	$16,710		Helps out people suffering from flood, fires, and general "acts of God"	Flood insurance, in particular, may encourage people to rebuild in dangerous areas instead of moving somewhere safer	Disaster victims, anyone living on the coasts, and everyone who wants people to get help in a crisis

PROGRAM	2009 BUDGET	YOUR BUDGET	PROS	CONS	WHO CARES
Community development	$7,719				
Commerce and housing credit (a real grab bag category)	**2009 Total** **$291,535**		This category has really exploded since 2008, when it was a mere $27.8 billion, but that's because the bailouts for Wall Street and the automakers are in here. The good news is that the government is projected to make most of that money back, and this section should return to normal. The White House actually projects a $25 billion profit here in 2010 and spending $22 billion in 2011.		
Mortgage credits	$99,760		Helps low-income folks get homes		Homeowners, plus the building and banking industries
Postal service	–$978		Don't you want your mail?		Everyone who gets mail, plus the postal unions
Deposit insurance	$22,573		Guarantees you don't go broke just because your bank does		Everyone with a bank account
Other "advancement of commerce" including the bailouts for banks and automakers	$170,180		Besides the bailouts, all kinds of useful stuff: economic statistics, patents, small business loans, international trade help, etc.	The bailouts make lots of people practically sputter with rage, since it largely involves saving banks from their own folly.	The business world in general

PROGRAM	2009 BUDGET	YOUR BUDGET	PROS	CONS	WHO CARES
Education, employment and social services	**2009 Total $79,746**				
Elementary, secondary and vocational	$53,206		Helps local schools offer better programs, particularly in special education and to meet "Race to the Top" goals	Schools have always been a local responsibility—federal aid is small compared to the state and local money involved	Parents, teachers
Higher education	−$3,258		Helps millions of people go to college	We should encourage more people to save for college, not to expect government aid	All the middle-class families expecting to send their kids to college
Research and general education aids (Library of Congress, Smithsonian, Public Broadcasting)	$3,456		Some of the best-loved institutions in the country	Public broadcasting, in particular, draws heavily on private funds	Kermit the Frog, who has many supporters, not to mention teachers, book lovers, people who love shows with British accents
Training and employment	$7,652		A key element in helping displaced workers adjust and welfare recipients into jobs	There's mixed evidence on whether job training actually works. Plus there are programs scattered around multiple agencies	The unemployed

PROGRAM	2009 BUDGET	YOUR BUDGET	PROS	CONS	WHO CARES
Social services	$17,044		Federal support for local programs helping children, the elderly, and the disabled	This subsidizes local programs, which may be worthy but could also be funded locally	Children, the aging, and the disabled, plus everyone who cares about them
Other labor services (statistics, law enforcement, etc)	$1,646		We need to know the unemployment rate, for example, and enforce health and safety laws		Economists, workers, unions
General government	2009 Total $22,026		Somebody's got to pay for this stuff. Buried in there are some significant items, like the IRS, White House operations (including anti-drug campaigns and OMB), and of course Congress itself.	There's always something to cut here—lots of people could do with fewer limos. Plus, a simpler tax code could mean we'd spend less on collections.	Enough said
Congress and legislative functions	$3,813				
Executive direction and management	$535				
Central fiscal operations	$10,752				

PROGRAM	2009 BUDGET	YOUR BUDGET	PROS	CONS	WHO CARES
Central personnel management	$102				
Property and records management	$554				
General purpose fiscal assistance	$4,097				
Other general government	$3,174				
Offsetting receipts	−$1,001				
Health	**2009 Total $334,327**				Anyone who ever gets sick, eats, or buys an appliance
Health care services (public health, substance abuse, mental health, disease control)	$300,010		Fights just about every disease you care to name, and you'll be glad of them should pandemic flu strike		
Research and training (National Institutes of Health, clinical training, etc.)	$30,565		Conducts medical research on nearly everything from cancer to cankers		There's a plethora of groups who lobby for research on specific diseases (often at the expense of others)

PROGRAM	2009 BUDGET	YOUR BUDGET	PROS	CONS	WHO CARES
Consumer and occupational health and safety (FDA, OSHA, Consumer Product Safety Commission)	$3,752		Keeps food, workplaces, and household products safe	Can be hidebound and slow to both approve good products and stop bad ones	Consumer groups and business
International Affairs	**2009 Total $37,529**				
Development and humanitarian aid	$22,095		Helps those in the poorest nations on earth	Critics say this money is often wasted or ineffective	Foreigners. And foreign policy experts who say you might need that goodwill down the road
Security assistance (including military aid)	$6,247		Helps our allies defend themselves (and us, by extension)	Often goes to regimes with nasty human rights records	
Conduct of foreign affairs (mostly embassies and diplomatic operations)	$12,152		If you're going to negotiate with people, you need negotiators		
Foreign information and exchange	$1,330		Builds a positive image of the U.S. abroad—a useful thing to have	This hasn't been working so well lately	
Financial programs	−$4,295				

PROGRAM	2009 BUDGET	YOUR BUDGET	PROS	CONS	WHO CARES
Justice system	**2009 Total** $51,549		Law and order is fundamental to any society	You can argue whether lots of these efforts are winnable and cost-effective (like the war on drugs) or whether some federal crimes should be handled by local police	Everybody cares about crime, and a society where no one upholds the law is no society at all
Federal law enforcement (including FBI, DEA, ICE, Homeland Security, ATF, IRS enforcement, Secret Service)	$27,552				
Federal prisons	$7,298				
Criminal justice assistance (Victims benefits, pensions, aid to local agencies)	$4,616				
Federal Courts/ Litigation	$12,083				
Natural Resources and the Environment	**2009 Total** $35,574				

PROGRAM	2009 BUDGET	YOUR BUDGET	PROS	CONS	WHO CARES
Water (Corps of Engineers, Bureau of Reclamation)	$8,063		Keeps rivers and harbors navigable	Critics say many flood-control measures actually make things worse, and nature should take its course	Anyone on the coast, shipping industry
Conservation and land management (Forest Service, Fish and Wildlife, public lands)	$9,813		Preserves vast areas of public lands, especially in the West	Get hits from both sides—business says there isn't enough exploitation of these lands, environmentalists say there's too much	Governors, who'll have to find the money to do this if it's cut
Recreational resources (national parks, landmarks)	$3,550		Staggeringly beautiful, perhaps the greatest tourist attractions in the world	Tourists could be paying more of the freight with higher fees	Vacationers
Pollution control	$8,276		Critical to quality of life and protecting the environment	Too bureaucratic and rulebound for many in business	Anyone who cares about pollution, i.e., almost everyone
Other natural resources	$5,872				
National Defense	**2009 Total $661,049**		Most of this budget comes down to a debate about whether we have too much military or not enough. The U.S. outspends every other country on Earth on defense yet still finds itself overstretched in Iraq and elsewhere. You can increase the budget or curtail the missions, but despite the considerable waste documented here, this is mostly about policy choices		

PROGRAM	2009 BUDGET	YOUR BUDGET	PROS	CONS	WHO CARES
Personnel	$147,348				
Operations/ Maintenance	$259,312				
Atomic energy defense activities	$17,552				
Procurement	$129,218				
Research and development	$79,030				
Family housing	$2,721				
Other	$1,499				
Military con-struction	$17,614				
Defense-related activities	$6,755				
Net interest	**2009 Total $186,902**	$186,902	This is the cost of doing business— the govern-ment needs to borrow money	As we've mentioned, this is going to get out of hand if noth-ing is done	Right now, just the banks. If things don't change, we'll all start car-ing about this
Science, space, and technology	**2009 Total $29,449**		Generally, advances human knowledge and provides untold long-term practi-cal benefits	For many, this is in the "nice-to-have" category, particularly given earth-bound problems	Scientists. Engineers. Trekkies
Space flight and research	$18,397				
General science and basic research	$11,052				

PROGRAM	2009 BUDGET	YOUR BUDGET	PROS	CONS	WHO CARES
Transporta-tion	**2009 Total $84,289**				
Ground (High-ways and rail, including aid to states)	$54,103		Allows states to keep roads, including interstates, in good repair	This is where most pork-barrel spend-ing happens. And roads really should be a state responsibility.	Drivers. Plus, this is a prime congressional "earmark" area. Voters love a new road.
			Trains are environmen-tally friendly and an important option in the Northeast	They're not so important in the rest of the country. And Amtrak should pay for itself like any other business	Business and professional people in the Northeast Cor-ridor—you'll find they're surprisingly loud
Air, includ-ing the FAA, airports, air traffic control, research	$20,799		The country really can't run without reliable air travel	A lot of this goes to small airports that don't get much traffic	Anyone who flies. Plus the airlines, and any commu-nity with an airport, large or small
Water, including marine safety	$9,093		Safe shipping is critical to the economy, not to mention recreational boaters	Shipping lines and boaters could shoulder more of the cost	Boaters, merchant seamen
Other trans-portation	$294				
Veterans' benefits	**2009 Total $95,429**		Those who served our country deserve to be protected and rewarded	You rarely hear any actual opposition to this—it's mostly a ques-tion of whether the system can be more efficient	Veterans, plus anyone who feels strongly about veter-ans. Which adds up to a lot of people

PROGRAM	2009 BUDGET	YOUR BUDGET	PROS	CONS	WHO CARES
Income security for veterans	$45,952				
Education, training, rehabilitation	$3,495				
Hospital/ medical care	$41,882				
Housing	−$578				
Other benefits and services	$4,678				
Medicare	**2009 Total** $430,093	$430,093	Okay, if you've been paying any attention at all during the course of this book, you know that you can't just draw a line through these items. But we're leaving them in to remind you what a large share of the budget they represent		
Social Security	**2009 Total** $682,963	$682,963			
Income Security	**2009 Total** $533,224		This is a grab-bag of cash benefits to individuals, including federal retirees, the disabled, the unemployed, food stamp recipients, free school lunch, low-income housing aid and others. Essentially you're talking about aid to people who for whatever reason can't completely fend for themselves. But obviously people get this aid for very different reasons: a federal retiree and a child getting free school lunches may have very little in common, and the programs work in completely different ways		
General retirement and disability	$8,218				The disabled
Federal employee retirement and disability	$118,119				Retirees, current workers, and their unions

PROGRAM	2009 BUDGET	YOUR BUDGET	PROS	CONS	WHO CARES
Unemployment compensation	$122,537		In the midst of the Great Recession, more people need this than ever, and Congress has extended benefits	Some critics argue extending unemployment keeps people from seeking work	People out of work
Housing assistance	$50,913				The poor, and those who care about them
Food and nutrition assistance	$79,080				See above, and add educators for the school lunch program
Other income security	$154,357				
Energy	2009 Total $4,749		This includes civilian energy projects like the Strategic Petroleum Reserve, energy conservation grants, research and development of alternative energy, and so on. A lot of the costs are offset by fees and profits from agencies like the Tennessee Valley Authority		
Energy supply	$2,045				
Energy conservation	$1,432				
Emergency energy preparedness	$754				
Energy information, policy, regulation	$518				
YOUR TOTAL EXPENSES=					

REVENUE SOURCE	2009 BUDGET	YOUR BUDGET	PROS	CONS	WHO CARES
Individual income taxes	**2009 Total** $915,308		It's a tax that falls heaviest on wealthier people—the more you make, the more you pay	Even so, any changes (up or down) resonate through the whole economy	Everybody
Corporation income taxes	**2009 Total** $138,229		They've got lots of money	Raise these too high and companies may cut jobs or pass the cost on to consumers	You know who
Excise taxes	**2009 Total** $62,483		Besides the taxes below, this category also includes some dedicated trust funds, such as for highway and airport improvements		
Tobacco	$12,841		Besides bringing in money, this will cut smoking	Anybody who's likely to quit smoking because of the cost has already done it. We're down to the hard core now	Smokers, naturally, and tobacco companies
Alcohol	$9,903		See above, just replace "smoking" with "drinking"	How much of a burden should one industry take on?	Drinkers and brewers— remember, there's a lot more of them than smokers
Gasoline	-$10,324		Would encourage conservation, fuel-efficient cars and energy independence	For many Americans, driving is a necessity, not a luxury— there's only so much cutting back they can do	Drivers, the oil industry, the auto industry— that covers just about everyone

REVENUE SOURCE	2009 BUDGET	YOUR BUDGET	PROS	CONS	WHO CARES
Telephone	$1,115				
Social Insurance and Retirement receipts	**2009 Total** $890,917		This includes most of the payroll taxes you pay, including Social Security and Medicare. As you know by now, the government borrows any taxes that aren't needed for those programs to pay for general operations, money the government will need to pay back to Social Security and Medicare when needed		
Old-age, survivors and disability insurance	$654,009				
Hospital insurance	$190,663				
Railroad retirement/ pension fund and social security equivalent account	$4,213				
Unemploy- ment insurance	$37,889				
Other retirement	$4,143				
Other receipts	**2009 Total** $98,649				
Estate and gift taxes	$23,482		Besides the money, elimi- nating this tax means wealthy fami- lies would get their billions tax-free	This can be a particular burden to families that inherit small businesses or farms	People with large estates and their families

REVENUE SOURCE	2009 BUDGET	YOUR BUDGET	PROS	CONS	WHO CARES
Customs duties/fees	$22,453		One of the government's oldest sources of revenue—even predates the income tax		
Federal Reserve earnings	$34,318				
Other misc. receipts: passports, national park entry fees, etc.). You could always add more, like a charge for using the Global Positioning System	$17,805		If you need these services, you should pay for them	Doesn't bring in that much money and might price some people out (do you want to make it harder for poor people to visit a national park?)	Anybody who needs something specific from the government. An enormous range of businesses.

YOUR TOTAL EXPENSES=

YOUR TOTAL REVENUE=

DID YOU BALANCE THE BUDGET?

IF YOU RAISED TAXES ON "X," HOW MUCH WOULD YOU GET?

What happens on the revenue side depends greatly on how you go about it. So it's a vast oversimplification to just write new numbers in here. Still it's a useful exercise. To get you started, here are some rule-of-thumb estimates you can use for how much money could be raised, courtesy of the Congressional Budget Office.

TAX INCREASE	RAISES IN ONE YEAR (2010 ESTIMATE)
Raise individual tax rates for everyone by 1 percentage point:	$19.0 billion
Raise just the top tax rate by 1 percentage point	$3.2 billion
Eliminate the tax deduction for state/local taxes	$11.7 billion

TAX INCREASE	RAISES IN ONE YEAR (2010 ESTIMATE)
Eliminate the child tax credit	$2.9 billion (in 2011)
Increase the cigarette tax by $1 a pack	$10.1 billion
Increase alcohol tax to $16 per proof gallon	$5.7 billion
Increase motor fuel tax by 50 cents per gallon	$43.6 billion
Raise fees to cover all food safety inspections	$884 million
TAX CUT	**CUTS REVENUE IN ONE YEAR (2010 ESTIMATE)**
Eliminating the alternative minimum tax	$10.5 billion
Extending the Bush individual tax cuts	$6.7 billion (or $2.5 trillion by 2019)

★★★★★★★★★★★★★★★★★★★★★★★★★★★★★★★

CHAPTER 16

The
"Where Does the Money Go"
Voter Protection Kit

Half of the American people never read a newspaper. Half
never vote for president. One hopes it is the same half.

—*Gore Vidal*

Unless you've spent the last couple of years on a tropical island dodging smoke monsters and arguing about free will, you know that there's a major election coming up in 2012—a presidential primary and campaign, plus elections for the entire House of Representatives and a third of the Senate. We're not saying that the country's budget problems should be the only issue you consider, but after reading so many pages about how serious this is, we hope you will take a very careful look at what the candidates are saying about taxes and spending, Social Security and Medicare, balancing the budget, and getting a handle on the long-term debt. Still, given the nature of politics and campaigns today, that's sometimes easier said than done. People who are running for office quite naturally try to say things that will please as many voters as possible. They also try to avoid saying things that their opponent can use in attack ads or that wind up on You-Tube, causing them no end of grief. That's why most of them really don't go into too much detail about how they would address the problem of balancing the budget and making sure that the nation doesn't find itself in financial peril when the boomers start leaving the workforce in big numbers.

But the truth is that the people who are elected the next time around—as president, senators, or members of the House—will face hundreds of decisions that will make the country's chances of getting through this in good shape either better or worse. Most of the candidates understand this (and some may even be worrying about it), even though they aren't talking about it much at all.

In this chapter, we've pulled together a few tools to help you feel your way through the political finessing, so you can try to determine whether your candidate will take this problem seriously or not, and if so, what direction he or she will head in to address it. Here's what we have for you.

We start off with our "simultaneous translations" section—what we've labeled as the handy-dandy pocket guide to the political soft sell. The idea here is to help you understand what generally lies behind some oft-heard political rhetoric.

Second, we suggest some steps you can take personally to generate some public energy on this issue. You can act on some of these suggestions in upcoming elections. You can act on the others any old time. Remember, even if the election turns out your way, it's important to keep the pressure on and give your guy or gal the backing he or she will need to get the country moving on this.

Third, we have taken this opportunity to nag just a bit (sorry, we couldn't resist). We've included five signs that you're being a lazy citizen (we've had some moments of laziness ourselves from time to time) and five signs that you're really part of the problems (not you, of course, but maybe someone you know).

Finally, we strongly recommend that you check out the Web site for the book, www.wheredoesthe-moneygo.com. We'll be offering tips on groups, publications, and Web sites that will keep you up to date on all things budgetary, plus we'll be adding our own comments and blogs as the campaigns go forth. Our organization, Public Agenda, works with an array of different organizations devoted to getting more citizens up to speed on the country's long-term budget issues and talking about them in sensible, fair-minded ways. We have some suggestions in the appendix as well.

But first, here are some of the basics in our voter protection kit:

SIMULTANEOUS TRANSLATIONS—A HANDY-DANDY POCKET GUIDE TO THE POLITICAL SOFT SELL

Politicians are people pleasers par excellence. You can't get very far in politics without learning to talk about policies so most people say, "Umm, that sounds pretty good." Selling ideas and getting people to support them (and you, if you're the politician) is the very heart of politics. There's nothing deeply wrong about it as long as it's not deliberately deceitful or misleading.

Putting your best foot forward is essential in business; it's crucial in romance, and it's utterly indispensable in political life. In recent elections, the news media and the pundits have often gotten themselves into snickering fits over candidates who can't come up with a "vision that resonates with America today" or who repeatedly "get off message." Voters don't generally reward these candidates, either, so getting the words right is often the difference between political success and failure.

Getting the words right is also often the result of a fair bit of work and not a little amount of money. Politicians gearing up for elections typically hire consultants and conduct focus groups to test different ways of saying things. Once candidates have refined their "message," they and their "surrogates" (their supporters and staff) often speak from "talking points"—those phrases you hear over and over again—campaign stop after campaign stop, interview after interview, speech after speech, until everyone is "sick of it."

Using talking points is common in campaigns and in between elections as well. Sometimes the news media have a little fun with this by showing clips of people all over Capitol Hill using the very same words to describe some hot potato political issue. The perpetrators are either "scripted," or "good at staying on message" depending on your point of view. Personally, we think a little more spontaneity and a little less packaging would be nice, but we'll leave that fight for another day.

Concerns about excessive government spending are hardly new. *Credit:* Spending Uncle Sam's Money *by T. Dart Walker (1869– 1914), U.S. Senate Art and History Collection*

Spending Uncle Sam's Money (1899)

SUCH A NICE SLOGAN . . .

The problem for the issue we're talking about right now—the country's looming budget mess—is when voters respond to nice-sounding words and don't bother checking up on what these nice-sounding words actually mean. As we've cautioned before, and we'll caution again, you simply have to read past the headlines. You can't give someone your vote or back their plan just because you like the slogan. Politicians may sell their policies like they were products, but they're not. If you don't like what Congress and the president have done with the federal budget, you can't take it back to the store and exchange it. You have to live with it until the next election comes around. So before you buy into anything, you need to find out what's really being proposed and take the time to decide whether you think it's fair, workable, practical, ethical, reasonable—whether it's something you can live with.

Here's some of the prevailing political soft sell from both Democrats and Republicans, the left and the right. All these ideas and phrases sound utterly wonderful, but if you're smart, you'll approach them with caution. Make sure that you really buy into what they represent. These will seem pretty old hat to you if you're a bit of a policy wonk yourself, but, frankly, we're surprised at the number of Americans who take these lovely little phrases at face value.

"We've got to lick this budget problem by eliminating waste, fraud, and abuse in government." You would have to be a crazy person (or a beneficiary perhaps) not to want waste, fraud, and abuse hacked out of government. There's plenty of it in there. The problem here is that all too often, this phrase allows politicians to pretend that we don't have to do anything else to solve the country's money mess—nothing that will *upset* anyone. We won't have to cut any popular programs. We won't have to raise any taxes. Just clean up that nasty old waste, fraud, and abuse. If you've read every page of this book up to now, you know it's just not that simple. If you've been skimming (it's OK; we've been known to skim ourselves), go back to chapter 5 to get a more realistic view.

"A growing economy—that's the way to fix the budget problem." It's hard to find anyone who doesn't want the economy to grow, especially after the high rates of joblessness and financial turmoil the country has endured lately. But in today's political life, politicians and elected officials who repeatedly call for "growth" are generally saying that the budget and the long-term issues with Social Security and Medicare should take a backseat to their ideas for spurring economic growth. Actually, forget the backseat. Some of them want to hide the country's budget problems in the trunk where no one will see them, maybe even conceal them under the spare tire. For conservatives, spurring growth typically revolves around tax cuts. For liberals, it often means having the federal government spend more to create jobs or to stimulate the economy. Don't get us wrong. We need to get the economy growing, and some of the specific ideas may be worth a serious look. The trouble is when someone claims that the country's budget problems don't really matter or suggests that economic growth will make it all go away. The government's own auditors and budget experts say growth alone just won't do it. Given

A Falling Off of Bosses (1881)

And concerns about influence and corruption are not new either. *Credit: Unidentified, after Thomas Nast* Harper's Weekly *wood engraving*

where we are now, when candidates propose another tax cut or higher spending, they need to offer a top-notch case for how it's going to help and not put us even deeper into the hole.

"It's time to invest in the middle class. That's the first priority." Fewer than one American out of ten considers himself either lower or upper class, so recommending proposals to benefit the middle class is bound to be popular.[1] At the moment, phrases like this are often an indicator that the speaker wants to put more government money into education and child care—also very popular. The dilemma is that upping spending on education and child care will obviously cost money; the U.S. government is already in debt, and we have even bigger expenses coming up with the boomer retirements. To our way of thinking, politicians who propose these kinds of "middle-class investments" are honor bound to talk about how they will pay for them and what they plan to do to address the country's longer-term budget problems. And if you're a voter who basically supports this kind of government spending, you're honor bound to think about how to cover the costs as well.

"It's time for people to take responsibility for their futures and make their own choices." Most Americans believe whole-heartedly in taking responsibility for your own future, and we all like to be able to make choices. In today's politics, however, this kind of slogan often means that candidates support the idea of private accounts in Social Security and medical savings accounts or vouchers perhaps as a way to reform Medicare. Sometimes candidates who support these approaches will talk about having "an ownership society." Like responsibility and choice, ownership is a fine thing. But as the whole country learned during the mortgage crisis, there's no advantage to

---

[1] According to a May 2006 *USA TODAY*/Gallup survey, 42 percent of Americans say they are middle class, 31 percent working class, 19 percent upper middle class, 6 percent lower class, and 1 percent don't know.

"owning" something you can't afford, or that isn't worth what you paid for it. Owning a home is often considered a major step forward in becoming a solid part of the middle class. Nearly all of us can remember the first car we ever owned.[2] There are some interesting and responsible ideas for Social Security and Medicare reform that emphasize choice and ownership and gradual change of the current system, with an eye to how they will affect the budget. We cover them briefly in chapter 9. We also encourage you to find out more about how ideas like this would work at the Web sites of groups like Heritage and Cato (which support private accounts) and the American Association of Retired Persons, or AARP (which opposes them). The main point here is whether your candidate has done his or her homework and has a well-thought-out proposal that includes a careful transition from what we have now to something different. You'll occasionally hear people say that the country should never have started Social Security and Medicare or that they're Ponzi schemes the way they operate now. But the vast majority of people see Social Security and Medicare as advances, and millions of middle-class and lower-income Americans have paid payroll taxes for years believing they could count on these programs in their old age. It's a fair debate as to whether these programs need fundamental reform or more modest changes. But it is unconscionable to suggest that we have no obligation to people who followed the rules when they were working and will need these programs to avoid poverty in their old age. Does your candidate have an honorable, responsible plan, or it is just bluster?

"We have to keep our promises to America's seniors." We're all taught not to break promises, especially to people we love and value, and it would be hard to find anyone—left, right, or center—who really wants to leave a lot of older Americans in poverty and without adequate health care when they are too old

[2] A 1975 Plymouth Duster and a beautiful green VW Beetle, in case you were wondering.

and frail to work. The problem with that little phrase, "keep our promises," is that it sometimes means that the speaker considers any change whatsoever to Social Security or Medicare as verboten. There's an important and genuine difference between treating these programs (or any other government program or any tax cut, for that matter) as sacrosanct, and developing policies that honor the society's promise to ensure that old age is not a time of fear and want. So when you listen to a politician talk about "keeping our promises," find out what he or she really means. And if he considers Social Security and Medicare untouchable, it's time to ask him how he plans to pay the bill.

TAKING MATTERS INTO YOUR OWN HANDS

By now, we hope you're concerned enough to want to do something personally about the country's budget problems. A good Wisconsin man we once knew used to talk about being "mad enough to make a rabbit fight a bear." Maybe that's how you're feeling about now. And on this issue, a few hopping mad rabbits might not be a bad thing.

You could run for office yourself of course, and if you think you've got the determination and tough skin it takes to become a political candidate, here's to you. John Adams and Thomas Jefferson didn't envision Congress as a body of full-time, lifelong politicians with their own political action committees and permanent campaign advisers, so maybe it is time to think about bringing some "less-professional" types to Washington. You could be one of them.

MAKE YOUR CHECK OUT TO . . .

You can also give money out of your own pocket to pay down the debt. The Treasury Department accepts donations to pay the debt at its Web site, www.treasurydirect.gov/govt/reports/ pd/gift/gift.htm. You can give money and specify that it only be used to pay down the debt. In fact, the Treasury received close to $3 million in contributions to pay down the debt in 2009. As they so deftly put it, "gifts to reduce debt held by the public may be inter vivos gifts or testamentary bequests." We guess that means they'll take the money whether you're dead or alive.

Whether you're tempted to donate or not, the treasury-direct.gov Web site is worth a visit. It has daily "to-the-penny" reports on how much money the country owes, and consequently it's one of the few places you'll ever see the nation's trillions of dollars in debt completely written out. You can also find out how much the country owed every year since 1791. The lowest point seems to be $33,733 in 1835 (that was under President Andrew Jackson, just in case that slipped your mind). The highest, of course, is right now.

But if you're not planning on running for office and can't quite bring yourself to put money into the government's till given its track record on using your hard-earned dollars to date, there are still important things you can do—you personally.

Get thee to those "meet the candidate" sessions. Ask questions about the budget and the debt and the aging of the boomers. Yes, we said this before, but it is so, so important. We have some pivotal elections ahead. In nearly every community, there are campaign events and campaign offices where you can go and talk to people about this budget issue, show your concern, ask questions, and (we hope) give this issue a push up on the political agenda. It's not necessarily easy to talk one on one to the presidential candidates or to senators and their challengers in big states. But you can almost certainly talk to candidates for the House. In nearly every district in the country, the incumbents and the challengers spend a couple of months going around the district meeting and talking with potential voters. *This is your chance!* A lot of the events aren't crowded at all; in fact, most candidates have to hire someone to run around town beforehand to dust up participants. Otherwise their boss will end up sitting there talking to five or six people, which can make a candidate very grumpy. Call the candidates' headquarters and/or visit their Web sites to find out when they'll be at a location near you. Ask them about their position on the budget and the debt and how to address the problems facing Social Security and Medicare because of the retiring boomers. And don't let them brag about how they're going to cut taxes or spend more on kids or whatever their shtick is without asking them (politely of course) what their idea would mean for the deficit and the debt.

And one final thought on this. You may think that we're suggesting that you hound the candidates "on the other side" of whichever side you're on, but we're not. The best thing you can do is to make sure that candidates you support and are likely to vote for know that you care about this issue. Politicians are much more concerned about what their supporters think than what their opponents think. And make sure they know that you'll be checking on how they handle it once they're in office.

Talk about this issue to people you know. It's vital to talk to people who will be in Congress and other areas of government since they'll be casting votes and making decisions that either move the country toward solutions or make the situation worse. But don't stop with the politicians. You can help build a movement of people concerned about this issue just by talking to the people you know.

When we first started writing about this topic in 2007, we had the chance to observe focus groups of typical Americans talking about the country's budget problems. The focus group moderator would generally start out by asking the dozen or so participants to name the most important issues facing the country. In those days hardly anyone mentioned the country's routine deficit spending or rising debt. But when just one person brought the problem up, it really made an impact. That's because a lot of us know in our heart of hearts that it just can't be a good idea for the government to routinely spend more than it takes in. And most of us can quickly see how the country's budget problems affect nearly everything we care about.

Just talking to people you know about this issue may seem trivial, but don't underestimate how much influence you can have—especially if you can help people get beyond grousing about Washington and the government (after a short warm-up of course; we all need to vent a little), and get them talking about the choices we have to make. Talking with family, friends, and neighbors is the way a lot of us learn about issues and sort through our views on them. And if you're a boomer parent with kids who will be (or should be) voting soon, you owe them this. They'll be the ones starting careers, trying to raise families, buying their first home, struggling to make ends meet if and when the really bad economic scenarios come into play. You wouldn't send them out into the world without helping them understand the health and safety risks they need to avoid. Make sure they understand this risk as well.

Share information on this issue with your friends. Come on now, we know you're sending those Jay Leno and David Letterman jokes to your friends, or maybe it's been recipes. And what about all those photos of the kids or the cat that you're posting on Facebook? We also know that word of mouth about movies, books, TV shows, restaurants, products, and issues spread around cyberspace by people who know each other can be very powerful. Communications and advertising professionals call this viral marketing. (Being able to come up with a new name for "word of mouth" that looks good on a PowerPoint slide is why they get the big bucks and the corner office.) Now, we're not suggesting that you drive your loved ones crazy with a daily blitz on the state of the country's finances. Nor are we suggesting you spam people. But passing along a good article or op-ed on this issue every now and then seems entirely appropriate given the stakes. We've included a list of Web sites that have good information on this issue on a regular basis (see the appendix). Make a habit of visiting them every once in a while, and when you see something interesting and important, pass it along.

Contact journalists who cover the issue—or who should have covered this issue but didn't. A lot of reporters, editors, and news producers think that most Americans don't want to hear about the choices the country faces, or that we'll be bored if they include any of the details that make this issue so difficult to solve. If you've come this far in this book, you know that this issue is anything but boring. It's a threat to our country and our way of life, and we need good journalists to give it the attention and explanation it warrants. And you don't need to be shy or feel like this is not your place. The truth is that good journalists who report on serious public policy and political issues often wonder whether they're having an impact, whether people are actually reading or listening. Some journalists we've talked with even say that they appreciate hearing from readers, viewers, or listeners about their stories, provided the feedback is reasonable and polite, of course. No one wants to hear from someone who is swearing, screaming, or frothing at the mouth.

Some journalists even obligingly include e-mail addresses in their columns and shows, so that's your invitation. Contact reporters, editors, producers, and webmasters to suggest more coverage on this issue and the options for solving it. Contact them when they cover proposals for new spending or for tax cuts and suggest that the next time they do a story like this, they include information about how the idea would affect the budget and the debt. Just as important—maybe even more so— take a moment to compliment good coverage when you see it. Like anyone else, journalists like to know that someone appreciates the work they do. And then they can show the higher-ups that someone does indeed care about this issue.

Become a maven. In his influential book *The Tipping Point*, Malcolm Gladwell describes the impact that individuals who care a lot about an issue have on society's ability to make progress. "Mavens" don't have to have PhDs in the subject at hand; they don't have to hold elected office or appear regularly on CNN or Fox. They don't have to be wealthy or powerful. They do have to care about an issue and be willing to put in some work to try to promote change.

If you care about what you've been reading, and you're ready to roll up your sleeves, there is quite a bit of help out there. One way to start down the road to mavenhood is to organize a meeting among people you know or with an organization you're familiar with to talk about this issue and trade ideas about how to address it. A number of nonpartisan organizations have materials, moderator training, and other kinds of help for you to do just that. Visit the book Web site—www.wheredoesthemoneygo.com. We'll be spotlighting and listing their upcoming events and online activities. Or take the plunge and organize your own discussion—maybe get people together to talk about the ideas we cover in chapter 9 or let people try their hand at our "OK, If You're So Smart" worksheet. We'll be keeping an up-to-date version ready online if you and your friends and family are willing to get out your calculators and have at it.

FIVE SIGNS YOU'RE BEING A LAZY CITIZEN

In *Where Does the Money Go?* we've been fairly tough on the nation's leaders. There are some fine and honorable individuals in government these days (we'll even go out on a limb and say that there are actually a fair number of them), but as a group, our leaders have let us down.

But we, meaning the public at large, haven't asked very much of them, have we? There's no reason to feel either smug or victimized. Not enough of us pay attention to politics, much less vote or become active. A lot of us just are not doing as good a job as we need to do when it comes to being responsible citizens.

A lot of this is about attitude. In our view, too many people these days can't tell the difference between good government and good customer service. You can get good customer service at the drive-through window at McDonald's: you pull up, talk to the squawk box, and pull out with your supersize helpings of high-fructose corn syrup–related products.

Government isn't that simple. Oh sure, it's fair to expect the government to process your passport renewal or building permit application promptly, maybe even as promptly as McDonald's gets out hamburgers. The difference is that we're not expected to take an active role in how McDonald's is managed. The company tries to respond to what customers want, but it's not holding elections every couple years to decide whether the bacon stays on the Egg McMuffin. The federal government, in its way, is waiting for that kind of signal.

We know, we know. Life is hectic these days; there's not enough time to do everything we should be doing to earn those good "doobee" awards. But some of us have gotten a little too lazy, a little too complacent in the citizenship department. Could that be you? We've listed five signs to look out for, and if any of these sound a little familiar, we hope you'll think about putting in some extra effort. We really, really need you back.

1. You're not registered to vote (or you've let your registration lapse). Politics is not a spectator sport. You can't just watch the political debate from the sidelines and boo when things don't go your way. And yes, we know, sometimes the choices among the candidates can be pretty uninspiring. But this low-voter-turnout thing has allowed very small groups (special interests, lobbyists, big political donors) to have far too much say in what the country does. We've got to get in there and fight the good fight. So if you're not registered, turn on your computer and go to www.vote411.org this very moment. Follow the directions there, and get it done. And then, please, please inform yourself about the candidates and cast your vote. In the lottery of life, being born in the United States is a big, big win. Nearly every person in this country is safer, warmer, and better fed and has more opportunities than billions of people around the globe. There's just no excuse for not fulfilling this small obligation of citizenship.

And, by the way, that includes not being deterred by long lines, broken voting machines, or other Election Day hassles. People are willing to stand in line so they can have an iPad before anyone else does. They will bring blankets and a picnic cooler and spend the whole night waiting in line to get play-off tickets if their hometown team is a contender. But they won't sacrifice a half hour to go vote for their choice for president? The League of Women Voters' VOTE411 site gives you the basic information you need to make sure you're not turned away from the polls. Once you decide who you're going to vote for, don't let anything keep you out of that booth.

2. You vote only in presidential elections. The presidential election is the big kahuna, no doubt about that. But on this budget issue, no president can fix the problem by himself—or herself. And if we happen to get a president next time around who's not paying attention to this issue, you're going to want people in Congress to stop him or her from doing even more financial damage. So your senators and representatives are essential players in resolving this mess. In most states, there are multiple opportunities to go somewhere and actually speak to these people directly. Do it. Find out about them and their stands. Talk to them about the budget. We're not sure whether it's a good thing or a bad thing, but most senators and representatives are essentially running for office all the time. Take advantage of this. Give them a piece of your mind (politely, of course), and give them your support at the ballot box when they deserve it.

3. If they agree with you on X, they've got your vote. Many Americans have an issue they really care about. Abortion and immigration are two that come to mind. Naturally, we all look for candidates who agree with us in our "most important" area. That's entirely legitimate, and we would never suggest that you support candidates who represent the "wrong" view in an area you're genuinely passionate about. But in most cases—and especially in the primaries—there are several candidates whose views generally fall on your side of the issue. You really need to investigate how these people look at the other important issues the country faces. Just because they're good on X, that doesn't mean they're good on everything else. And—we're just asking, of course—you might want to support some candidates who are good on your issue, even if they're not especially eloquent or dramatic about it, because they have some important things to say in other areas. The country has a lot of very important decisions coming up in the next several years. We need people in political office who can operate effectively on a number of fronts.

4. You never listen to candidates' debates. Sure, you can get some idea of what candidates and elected officials stand for by watching or reading the news. And if you want to find out how truly wonderful they all are—every last one of them—you can watch their ads, go to their Web sites, and read their campaign literature. But if you want to find out what they think and why, and how it differs from what the other candidates think and why, your best bet is one of the debates. There are more and more debates taking place, and based on what we've seen recently, the journalists who moderate them and try to move things along (it's usually reporters, anchors, and the like) are doing a better job of focusing on important issues. So while you don't have to watch all the debates in their entirety (that probably is for political junkies), you should watch at least one. And don't just look for the gaffes (most politicians do say something relatively stupid at one point or another, as do most of the rest of us). Use this opportunity to compare and contrast. Think about who has the best ideas and is most likely to follow through on them.

5. You just read the headlines. OK, at least you're glancing at the news, which is definitely commendable. But particularly on this budget issue, that's not enough. You really need to read at least a few paragraphs to find out what's really happening. The headline screams "Big Tax Hikes Proposed," and it turns out to be a proposal so modest that you won't even notice that your taxes have changed come April 15. The headline screams "Candidate Backs Social Security Cuts," and it turns out that he or she is really talking about changes that affect only high-income recipients. You can make up your own mind about whether the proposal is really something you can live with, but do it based on the facts—not on a headline someone wrote to get your attention.

FIVE SIGNS YOU'RE PART OF THE PROBLEM

When it comes to being good citizens, there's another group of Americans who are not just lazy—they've checked out entirely. The news? It bores them. Politics? They can't be bothered. Elections? "Come on, man. I'm just not into that stuff." Most of us know someone who falls into this category—those people are not exactly few and far between. We would be amazed if any of those so-called citizens actually read this book, but if you're feeling a little out of sorts about people who take the country for granted while they enjoy its benefits, you could show them this list. Maybe it will at least induce a smidgen of guilt.

1. You can name every woman who claims to have had sex with Tiger Woods, but you don't recognize the name of the vice president or the Speaker of the House. We're prepared to let you slide on the names of the secretary of agriculture and the surgeon general. We're even willing to give you a pass if the names of the vice president and the Speaker are on the tip of your tongue, but you just can't quite come up with them right now. But the fact that the E! network does not hire Joan and Melissa Rivers to do red-carpet fashion snark at the State of the Union address is no excuse for not knowing who the nation's leaders are.

2. You're getting all your news from comedians. How can you even understand the jokes without knowing what actually happened? This seems strange to us, but apparently late-night TV is as close to the news as some people get these days. Sorry, folks, it's just not enough. And as much as we love Jon Stewart, and as intelligent and thought-provoking as his interviews are, you still need to keep up with the *real* news. It's so easy now, with all the online sources available. Really, there's just no excuse.

3. You watch every single game in the NCAA tournament, but you don't have time to keep up with politics. OK, do you sense a theme here? We're talking about people who'd rather be amused than informed. There you are watching sixty-five teams fight it out during March Madness (and who knows how many baseball games in the summer and football games in the fall), and you say you don't have time to watch the news or participate in an election. Sorry, this just doesn't cut it with us. We like sports. Sports are a fine thing. But if you can make time to be a fan, you can make time to keep up with what's happening in the world and in our country. You can find the time to fulfill the most minimal role of a citizen.

4. You're just focused on your family. Politics doesn't matter to you. Most people who say things like this have one or more lovable little creatures at home, and they absolutely should be the focus of your attention the lion's share of the time. But if you really care about their future, you better start paying attention to politics as well. Right now, this very year, elected officials are making decisions that will determine what kind of economy and government the next generation will have. You can make kids zip up their jackets and wear bike helmets, but they're still heading off into a world where crushing financial obligations are going to make their lives much, much harder than necessary. If you stick with that "politics doesn't matter line," you're really not doing those little kids any favors.

5. The news is depressing. You'd rather not know. All right, you've got us there. The news often is depressing. It can also be frustrating, even infuriating. Sometimes it's even scary. But just because you're not paying attention doesn't mean it's not happening. In this day and age, the ignorance-is-bliss approach is selfish, stupid, and dangerous. If enough of us run off to some "I'd rather not know" la-la land, it could eventually bring us all down.

CHAPTER 17

The Last Word:
Six Realities We Need
to Accept to Solve
This Problem

I want you to get up right now, sit up, go to your windows,
open them and stick your head out and yell—"I'm as mad as
hell and I'm not going to take this anymore!" Things have got
to change. But first, you've gotta get mad!

—*Howard Beale (Peter Finch) in Paddy Chayefsky's
screenplay of* Network, *1976*

A couple of hundred pages ago, we started off with "The
Six Points You Need to Know to Understand the Federal Budget Debate." Our goal was to explain why this issue
is so important and help you start thinking about the direction you want the country to take to solve the problem.

Along the way, we expect we've occasionally aggravated
readers who are genuine budget experts by "oversimplifying" the issue. Yes, we admit it—this is a once-over-lightly
treatment. At the same time, we've probably perplexed quite

a few readers who aren't budget pros at one point or another. We were occasionally baffled ourselves while we were writing this, so there's no reason to expect that other people won't be as well. Some of the details are extremely complex and confusing. Still and all, if you just stop multitasking for an hour or so, if you just concentrate on what we've laid out here, we're pretty sure you can get a handle on this—enough of a handle to help out yourself and your country.

The U.S. Senate in Session (1874)

The United States has a representative government, but it is our responsibility to vote and vote wisely. *Credit:* The United States Senate in Session *by unknown artist,* Harper's Weekly *wood engraving, U.S. Senate, Art and History Collection, and 108th Congress by U.S. Senate Photo Studio*

If you haven't gotten all the numbers down pat yet, don't worry. The numbers change all the time anyway—it's the big picture you need to keep an eye on. If you haven't pinned down your own list of best tax and spending policies yet, don't worry about that, either. Frankly, we're not so sure that any of us should have a list like that right now—especially not one that's carved in stone like the Ten

Commandments. To get started, though, you might want to check into the ideas and proposal contained in some of the following:

★ Chris Edwards over at the Cato Institute has rather bravely published a list of very precise cuts that would whittle the budget down to size (look for *Downsizing the Federal Government,* available at www.downsizing-government.com). You may not like all of them (if you're typical, you probably won't like all of them), but we give the Catos credit for putting some specifics on the table.

★ On the other side of the debate, the Center for American Progress, a progressive think tank, has come up with its "Path to Balance," which you can find at www.american-progress.org/issues/economy/budget.

★ The American Association of Retired Persons (AARP), which is about as committed to Social Security as any organization out there, offers a list of different ideas for reforming Social Security and calculates how much each would help in stabilizing trust funds. Raising taxes on higher income workers could cover 39 percent of the shortfall; moving the retirement age to 70 by 2040 would cover a whopping 61 percent according to AARP's research. (The full list is at http://assets.aarp.org/rgcenter/econ/i3_reform.pdf.)

★ The nonpartisan Committee on the Fiscal Future of the United States offered four different paths to solving the budget problem, ranging from a big-government, high-tax plan to a small-government, low-tax plan, and a couple options in between, at www.ourfiscalfuture.org.

★ President Obama invited leaders from across the political spectrum to participate in a "summit" to discuss different solutions for the country's budget problems. You can download the report on the deliberations at the White

House Web site at www.whitehouse.gov/assets/blog/
Fiscal_Responsibility_Summit_Report.pdf.

We've added some tools of our own—our own little
budget worksheet (chapter 15) and a "greatest hits" list of
alternative ways to tackle the Social Security and Medicare
issue (chapter 9).

JUST DON'T GET TOO ATTACHED

Be forewarned, though. Even if you carefully work your
way through every single one of these tools (and others),
you may still feel uncertain about exactly what the country
should do. And that's just fine from our point of view. It's
even preferable as far as we're concerned. If we've all made
up our minds—if we've all got our lists of deal breakers—
the country will end up spending the next couple of decades fighting it out. If enough of us remain open-minded
and flexible, if enough of us are still prepared to listen and
adapt, the country will be in a better position to find the
compromises to work our way out of this fix.

So from our point of view, a little indecision is an entirely good thing, but there are some things that really
shouldn't be up in the air. We close the book with another
set of six ideas—in this case "Six Realities We Need to Accept to Solve This Problem."

Reality No. 1: We have to start now. There really is no time
to lose. Every year we wait just bulks up the debt and limits
our options. Postponing discussions about what to do about
the problems facing Social Security and Medicare won't
make them go away. No matter which kinds of solutions we
choose, they will be easier financially and politically if we
start now.

Reality No. 2: We have a short-term problem and a long-term problem—we need to address them both. For the past couple of years, most of our political leaders and commentators have been acting like we have an either-or choice: fight the recession or fix the budget. Spend more on stimulus and extend the Bush tax cuts, or tighten our belts before the national debt gets out of hand. But this is a false choice. There's absolutely no reason we can't do two things at once—unless, of course, our political culture is so partisan and gridlocked that it effectively can't walk and chew gum at the same time. Given what's happened to the U.S. economy, the government may need to keep priming the pump, and we may need to make some investments now to strengthen our ability to compete internationally in the future. Doing that means it won't be possible to balance the budget next year—or even for the next several years. But we can start making concrete decisions about how we'll start bringing the budget into balance when the crisis is over, and we can certainly start making government more efficient and wringing out some of the waste. We can also make some choices and start phasing in changes to address the longer-term problem of how to pay for Medicare and Social Security while keeping the national debt under control. To our way of thinking, we simply have to get going on both fronts—they're interrelated and intertwined. If we don't, we could end up with the worst of both worlds: a sluggish economy now, and a budget crisis later.

Reality No. 3: We need to address waste, fraud, and abuse, and then we need to move on. While we were writing this book, we were often angry at the way people in Washington misuse the public's money. Check out the news almost any day of the week, and you'll find examples of government waste and inefficiency, of decisions being made for the few and not for Americans at large. Routine cost overruns on government contracts, unconscionable waste on reconstruction projects in Iraq, bills written by lobbyists—we could go on, but others will do it for us. It's more than time to go after the waste and carelessness that characterizes way too much of what Washington does. But once we put reforms into place, we have to move on. We have to let go of the pipe dream that all we need to do to get the budget back on track is to strip the waste out of the system. No organization, no business, no household ever operates with pure efficiency—we do have human beings involved here, after all. What's more, even slashing everything that could conceivably be considered wasteful or problematic just won't solve the overarching problem. We have some tough decisions to make. We need to face up to them.

Reality No. 4. We need to demand candor from politicians and be willing to accept it when they offer it. It's a cop-out to get mad about what Congress and the administration do when we repeatedly reward their worst behavior. We need to stop voting for candidates who promise new programs or tax cuts without specifying how they will pay for them. We have to stop letting candidates slide by with vague answers about "balancing the budget and cutting the deficit in X years." That's just not enough. We need to demand that candidates and elected officials start talking frankly and realistically about taxes and spending. If we don't do our part as citizens and voters, we will leave the next generation with a horrendous mess not of their making.

Reality No. 5: We need to think about what we can live with— not what we personally want. Every one of us has ideas about what government should spend more on, what it should cut, who should pay more taxes, and who should pay less. Chances are we're just not going to get our way. We simply have to be prepared to compromise and make adjustments in our plans and our thinking. We can and should have a good full-out national discussion over the major pieces—tax policy, how to balance the budget, how to change Social Security and Medicare. Let's have some good old-fashioned arguments about a whole range of ideas. But we can't take our ball and go home if the political winds don't blow our way. Not doing anything about this problem is by far the worst solution of all.

Reality No. 6: Being angry isn't enough. We started this chapter with the well-known scene from the movie *Network*, where Howard Beale says he's mad as hell, and he's not going to take it anymore. How could we resist? That's exactly the way many of us feel when we first start to wrap our minds around how irresponsible our leaders have been with the country's finances. They've made terrible decisions about the budget for years now, and they've put the country's future in jeopardy. And talk about an equal opportunity indictment—Democrats, Republicans, liberals, conservatives, politicians from the North, South, East, and West have all done their part in getting us where we are today—some $14 trillion in debt just when massive numbers of Americans are entering old age and beginning to rely on the government programs they've been counting on for years. It is one hell of a mess. The American public has every right to be angry, but fuming and screaming and sulking by itself won't change anything. In *The Iliad* (or, if you prefer, the Brad Pitt movie *Troy*), Achilles sulked in his tent while his best friend died and the Athenians nearly lost the war. Things didn't start to turn around until he got up and put his armor on (although it was clever Odysseus who really saved the day). Luckily, no swords or breast-plates will be needed here. To solve our budget problems, we need to simmer down, get some basic facts under our belts, and look at our options honestly. And then, we've got to be willing to listen to each and compromise (see Reality No. 5).

We're convinced the budget problem can be solved. Americans have faced challenges like this before, and we were able to address them. After World War II, for example, the country's debt was higher than the country's entire gross domestic product, and yet the country recovered and eventually prospered.

Today's problems are different. Despite some tough times recently, the country is still wealthy and productive. The answers are not easy, but they are not horrifying, either. No one is talking about throwing older people out of hospitals when they are ill or leaving younger ones to fend for themselves when their time comes to retire. Many elected officials are willing to take this on if we support them. And we sense that much of the American public is ready to think about this problem seriously as well. But addressing this problem—making better decisions in the thousands of questions and turning points that will come up—means creating a different political discourse from the one that prevails now.

As we've done the research for this book, we've run across a lot of talk about agendas: What does the budget debate mean for the progressive agenda? What does it mean for the conservative agenda? What often gets lost in this argument is that addressing our budget problems is about preserving the nation's ability to make those choices. When a fiscal crisis hits, your options for making the world a better place narrow down very quickly. Paying off your debts becomes the agenda, whether you like it or not. Ask the Greeks (the modern ones, not the ancients). Ask the Argentines. Getting the budget on the right track now is how you preserve your options for the future.

If there's one hope we have for this book, it's that our readers will begin to look at every single discussion about spending and taxes, about Social Security and Medicare, with a different and more critical eye. We all need a little refrain in our heads: What can we afford? Where will we get the money? What does this mean for the future? Are we being fair to those who come after us? We believe that if the American people start asking themselves these questions, the country will soon be on a more responsible path.

Places to Go, People to Meet

We'll be updating and adding to this collection of Web sites and publications regularly at our book site, www.wheredoesthemoneygo.com. We'll also be keeping an updated version of the "OK, If You're So Smart" worksheet online, and we'll be blogging and publishing more on this issue ourselves. We hope you'll visit.

1. THE SWEET SPOTS FOR INFO

Here are some of the Web's best places to find out more.

Office of Management and Budget (www.whitehouse.gov/omb/budget)
This is where you will find the president's annual budget request and rationale for spending the country's money in the coming year. Not surprisingly, the OMB puts the best foot forward on the president's plans, but this is the place to go

if you want the details of both the current budget and what's in the works. For example, there are "fact sheets" for every department—the Department of Education, Department of Justice, and so on—describing performance goals for each and detailing how the president's budget is being allocated. There are also fact sheets for each state so you can see how much money your state got for public schools, highway construction, children's health insurance, etc.

The site also houses major administration publications focusing on budget issues such as the report on the February 2009 summit convened by the White House to "solicit ideas and discuss solutions to our long-term fiscal imbalance with a broad array of national leaders—from both political parties, from in and out of government, and from Washington, D.C. and the country as a whole." Even though it's part of the government, the Office of Management and Budget has several Web resources that ought to be useful for budding reformers.

The **OMB Earmark Database** is the best way of trying to track down earmarks—the little pork-barrel projects quietly tucked away in the budget. Unfortunately, the database has some serious limitations. For example, the site can't tell you who sponsored the earmark (very critical) or even the ultimate beneficiary of the funding (even more critical). The site is at http://earmarks.omb.gov.

OMB also has several other sites providing information on government finances. **Recovery.gov,** with the tagline "Track the Money," is designed to lay out stimulus spending across the country and provide a way to report waste and fraud in the programs.

Congressional Budget Office (www.cbo.gov)

The CBO is an independent agency set up to give Congress reliable budget estimates. It's nonpartisan and highly respected, but we're not going to kid you. A lot of CBO reports are a pretty rough read for—well, probably for anyone who's not a budget analyst. When we were using the site, we noticed that the most accessible material from the CBO is generally found in testimony presented before Congress. You might want to have a glass of water handy, because they are really, really dry. Nonetheless, the CBO is the place to go for all sorts of detailed projections on what would happen if the Congress cuts spending and/or raises taxes in dozens of different ways. The CBO's "Budget Options" series are the place to look.

Government Accountability Office (www.gao.gov)

Formerly known as the General Accounting Office, this is the federal government's auditor. This agency is about as independent as federal bureaus get—its boss, the comptroller general, is appointed to a fifteen-year term, and GAO auditors review the operations of every government agency and issue often-stinging reports on how the government could function better. The GAO also issues an annual audit of the country's finances, the **Financial Report of the United States Government**. The 2009 audit is at www.gao.gov/financial/fy2009financialreport.html, and you can watch the GAO Web site for annual updates. The GAO also produces a "citizen's guide" to accompany the audit which is authoritative, succinct, and well worth reading (the 2009 guide is at www.gao.gov/financial/fy2009/09guide.pdf). You can also keep current on GAO reports and analyses through its Twitter feed and YouTube channel.

The Debt to the Penny (www.treasurydirect.gov/NP/BPDLogin? application=np)

The government's Treasury direct site includes a daily report on what the country owes down to the penny, along with historical information about the debt and more specialized information for financial types on buying and selling governments bonds. And just in case you're motivated, here's where you can make your voluntary contribution to help pay off the debt.

Monthly Treasury Statement (www.fms.treas.gov/mts)

This site lists the government's income and expenses for the last month, the last year, and the year before that. It's a little more headache-inducing (you can download the monthly statement in Excel, which should give you a little warning), but it is chock-full of specifics on just where the country's money comes from and where it's spent, and not just in the major categories.

Fedspending.org and USAspending.gov

These are both searchable databases of federal grants and contracts. **Fedspending.org** is the original, run by the group OMBWatch, while **USAspending.gov** is run by OMB itself. Both sites allow you to search by department, contractor, state or congressional district, and whether the contract involved competitive bidding or not. It's a great resource for looking at the generally less-examined question of who the federal government pays to do its work.

Stimulus.org

Set up by the Committee for a Responsible Federal Budget, Stimulus.org sets out how the economic stimulus and Wall Street bailout money is being spent much more clearly than anything the government has put out there. You can break out the spending by the type of action, the target group (consumers, banks, housing, manufacturing, etc.) or by agency. The site also offers regular updates and background briefings on what the various packages do and how much they cost.

2. GUIDES TO THE ISSUE—LET THEM EXPLAIN IT ALL TO YOU

The Fiscal Wake-Up Tour Online (www.concordcoalition.org/
fiscal-wake-tour-online)
The Fiscal Wake-Up Tour is a series of panel discussions on
the budget and the debt held in communities nationwide
over the past several years. The "tour" features some highly
respected experts with a range of backgrounds and points
of view, including former comptroller general David Walker,
Stuart Butler of the Heritage Foundation, Isabel Sawhill of
Brookings, and Bob Bixby of The Concord Coalition. If you
can catch the real thing locally, we certainly encourage you
to attend, but if you can't, this online video version is an
excellent preview.

The Federal Budget in Pictures; Budget Chartbook (www
.heritage.org/budgetchartbook/)
This "budget in pictures" collection features almost four
dozen graphs covering everything from federal spending and revenue to the growth in Social Security, Medicare, and Medicaid. The Heritage Foundation, one of the
best-known conservative think tanks, regularly revises
and updates this series of charts describing the major
trends in the federal budget. It's a good place to start for
an overview of the problem. Available online at www
.heritage.org/research/features/BudgetChartBook/.

The $9 Trillion Debt: Breaking the Habit of Deficit Spending
(www.nifi.org)
Written by Keith Melville in 2007 for the National Issues
Forums, this article is currently being updated.

i.o.u.s.a. If you prefer video—or someone you know does—this 2008 film by Patrick Creadon is a rousing introduction to the country's budget crisis. It's a fast-paced documentary featuring interviews with mega-hitters like Alan Greenspan and Warren Buffett. It also follows members of the "Fiscal Wake-Up Tour" as they travel from city to city trying to bring this issue to public attention. The DVD is available from Amazon, and you can view an abbreviated version of the documentary at the Web site of the Peter G. Peterson Foundation (http://www.youtube.com/watch?v=O_TjBN-jc9Bo) and on YouTube as well.

3. GROUPS WORKING ON THE ISSUE

Committee for a Responsible Federal Budget (www.crfb.org) This is a nonprofit, nonpartisan group that is "committed to educating the public about issues that have significant fiscal policy impact." It is led by Maya MacGuineas, a respected budget expert, and it's board is a who's who of former heads of Congressional budget committees, the CBO, OMB, and the Federal Reserve. The Web site features a simulator that gives visitors a chance to try their hand at getting the country's debt to 60 percent of GDP by 2018. It also includes blogs and news releases responding to ongoing developments related to the budget and a set of charts you can download and share.

America Speaks
This nonprofit organization works to give citizens an opportunity to discuss important national problems, and, in its words, give the public "a greater voice on the most important policy issues that impact their lives." With a $4.2 million dollar grant from three major foundations—The

Peter G. Peterson Foundation, the MacArthur Foundation, and the Kellogg Foundation—the group organized a "national town meeting" in June 2010 where participants nationwide could talk about a range of policy options "framed by a diverse, bipartisan group of experts." The group is now working to bring the insights of citizens to national leaders including the President and his National Commission on Fiscal Responsibility and Reform and Congress. The Web site—http://usabudgetdiscussion.org/—has tools for citizens who want to become more active on the issue.

Concord Coalition (www.concordcoalition.org)

Concord was founded during the early 1990s as an organization "advocating fiscal responsibility while ensuring Social Security, Medicare, and Medicaid are secure for all generations." The Concord folks are "budget hawks"—they want action on this issue—so they do have a point of view, but the group is widely respected for its bipartisanship and strong command of the facts. The Web site features blogs and issues briefs on what's happening in Congress and the administration related to the budget and the debt. The site also lists upcoming speaking events and panel discussions that Concord organizes nationwide. The Concord Coalition is a sponsor of the Fiscal Wake-Up Tour, a series of town hall meetings about this problem occurring around the country, in partnership with the Brookings Institution, the Heritage Foundation, the Committee for Economic Development, and the Committee for a Responsible Budget.

Our Fiscal Future (www.ourfiscalfuture.org)

This nonpartisan initiative to get the federal budget on a sustainable path grew out of the Committee on the Fiscal Future of the United States, a nonpartisan commission organized by the National Research Council and the National

Academy of Public Administration. The committee report itself offered four different paths to put the budget on a sound footing, ranging from a big-government, high-tax option to a small-government, low-tax option. The Our Fiscal Future initiative is designed to build public support for political action, led by NAPA and our organization, Public Agenda. This is a great place for people who care about the issue to find out more and get organized, no matter what their political views.

4. POINTS OF VIEW

In *Where Does the Money Go?* we haven't taken positions on the various solutions for addressing the country's financial problems, but there are plenty of think tanks and advocacy groups that have. We hope, by now, that you'll find yourself curious about what they have to say. Here are some of the most important that have done significant work in this area.

American Association of Retired Persons
With over 35 million members, AARP is generally considered the country's most influential organization representing older Americans. In the "Issues and Elections" section of the AARP Web site (www.aarp.org), you can read the organization's position papers on Social Security and Medicare, among other related issues.

American Enterprise Institute
One of the country's leading conservative research organizations, its Web site (www.aei.org) is a gateway to AEI's substantial library of reports and publications, many of which address budget and tax issues and Social Security and Medicare. AEI is home to a number of respected budget experts, such as Kevin Hassett, R. Glenn Hubbard, and

Daniel Shaviro, along with Mark B. McClellan, former head of the FDA.

Brookings Institution

Brookings (www.brookings.edu) has long been one of Washington's dominant think tanks, home to a banner list of scholars. Just a small sampling of Brookings publications on this theme includes *Saving Social Security: A Balanced Approach,* by Peter A. Diamond and Peter R. Orszag (Brookings Institution Press, 2005), *Social Security and Medicare: Individual vs. Collective Risk and Responsibility,* edited by Sheila Burke, Eric Kingson, and Uwe Reinhardt (Brookings Institution Press, copublished with the National Academy of Social Insurance, 2000), and the *Restoring Fiscal Sanity* series of publications mentioned on page 312. The 2007 edition of *Restoring Fiscal Sanity,* edited by Alice M. Rivlin and Joseph R. Antos (Brookings Institution Press, 2006), focuses on health care costs.

Cato Institute

Even if you come from the liberal side of the aisle, you have to admire the libertarian Cato Institute for being willing to get specific. Cato's *Project on Social Security Choice* (www. socialsecurity.org/catoplan) and its *Downsizing the Federal Government* project—www.downsizinggovernment.org/—provide some of the most detailed information available about private accounts, Social Security, and potential cuts throughout the federal budget.

Center for American Progress

Headed up by former Clinton chief of staff John Podesta, Center for American Progress says that it is working to create a "long-term, progressive vision for America." If you're wondering about the liberal/progressive stance on ideas like reforming Social Security, balancing the budget, and managing the country's long-term budget problems, this is the place to go. In 2009, the group sponsored conference entitled "Developing a Progressive Approach to the National Deficit," which featured experts such as Alan Blinder, Paul Krugman, Robert Reischauer, and Laura Tyson discussing a wide range of options—the video is available on the Web site. The site also contains frequent analyses of specific budget areas including defense spending, tax policy, and discretionary spending (www.americanprogress.org).

Center on Budget and Policy Priorities

The center is one of the few nongovernmental research organizations focusing specifically on budgetary policy at both the state and federal level. It's generally categorized as a liberal organization, but like Cato, the Center on Budget and Policy Priorities doesn't shy away from specifics. The organization provided detailed analyses criticizing President Bush's plans for private accounts in Social Security, and it has current analyses assessing the benefits of the stimulus spending and the government's efforts to create jobs during and following the recession of 2008 and 2009. The blog by CBPP head Robert Greenstein is a powerful voice for progressive views on ongoing budget issues (www. cbpp.org).

Center for Economic and Policy Research

Led by economists Dean Baker and Mark Weisbrot, this center is dedicated to "promote democratic debate on the most important economic and social issues that affect people's lives," and comes at the issues from a progressive perspective. Overall, they're sharply critical of "deficit hawks" and Baker also writes the "Beat the Press" blog on economics coverage in the media (www.cepr.net).

Club for Growth

The Club for Growth (www.clubforgrowth.org) believes "prosperity and opportunity come through economic freedom." The club recommends candidates who support its policy goals—extending the Bush tax cuts, personal accounts in Social Security, repealing the estate tax, and others—and sponsors a Club for Growth PAC to provide campaign funds. The site has fresh commentary on current debates, including articles and op-eds from its economic policy council.

Heritage Foundation

For more than thirty years, the Heritage Foundation has been an influential and respected conservative source of research to "formulate and promote conservative public policies based on the principles of free enterprise, limited government, individual freedom, traditional American values, and a strong national defense." The Heritage Web site (www.heritage.org) offers scores of research reports, issue backgrounders, and commentaries on the issues introduced here.

OMB Watch

OMB Watch (www.ombwatch.org) describes its goal as increasing "government transparency and accountability; to ensure sound, equitable regulatory and budgetary processes and policies; and to protect and promote active citizen participation in our democracy." OMB Watch contains plenty of information about budget developments on the Hill and the status of various budget-related debates. The perspective is liberal, it's fair to say, and the group has voiced some reservations about the president's budget commission and whether too many of its members are "fiscal hawks" who will urge Congress to "act immediately by attacking 'entitlements,' including Medicare, Medicaid, and Social Security." The group's blog, "The Fine Print," covers many issues related to government performance on the environment, health, and safety, in addition to budget issues.

5. GOOD READS

Comeback America: Turning the Country Around and Restoring Fiscal Responsibility, by former U.S. comptroller general David Walker (Random House, 2009). In its review, Booklist called *Comeback America* an "excellent book" that explains the country's long-term budget challenges in a clear and compelling way. Walker, former president of the Peter G. Peterson Foundation, has been sounding the alarm on this issue for years, and some of his strongest criticism is for elected officials who continue to overpromise when the country is already deeply in debt.

The Coming Generational Storm: What You Need to Know about America's Economic Future, by Laurence J. Kotlikoff and Scott Burns (MIT Press, 2005). The authors lay out the policy challenges posed by the sheer size of the baby boom. By 2030, the authors point out, walkers will outnumber strollers and Social Security and Medicare will be treading water or worse. Kotlikoff and Burns discuss a number of policy solutions and include what they term a "life jacket"—advice for individuals to see them through the tough times ahead.

Do Deficits Matter? (University of Chicago Press, 1997) and ***Taxes, Spending, and the U.S. Government's March toward Bankruptcy*** (Cambridge University Press, 2007), by Daniel Shaviro. A professor of law and taxation at New York University, Shaviro has written extensively about budgetary issues with his main focus on the long-term impact of today's spending patterns. Shaviro's blog, Start Making Sense (danshaviro.blogspot.com), also frequently touches on taxation, budget, and entitlement issues.

Running on Empty: How the Democratic and Republican Parties Are Bankrupting Our Future and What Americans Can Do About It, by Pete G. Peterson (Picador, 2005). A former secretary of commerce, cofounder of the Blackstone Group, and board member of Public Agenda, Peterson is a longtime critic of routine deficits and unrealistic government promises. *Running on Empty* is actually the latest of a series of Peterson books on the topic. In *Running on Empty,* Peterson charges that the country's current leadership has "presided over the biggest, most reckless deterioration of America's finances in history."

Forgive Us Our Debts, by Andrew L. Yarrow (Yale University Press, 2008). Yarrow (a former colleague at Public Agenda) covers the history of the debt in the United States, the mechanics of federal financing, and the possible consequences, both for individuals and society at large, of not addressing the problem. The book, currently being updated, also describes reforms that would help, in Yarrow's words, "to get us out of the woods."

6. BEFORE YOU VOTE

Project Vote Smart provides biographical information, voting records, interest group ratings, and campaign contact information for candidates for national and state offices. Vote Smart has a good track record for nonpartisanship and providing specific, helpful information for voters. Definitely worth a visit at www.votesmart.org.

Open Secrets works to give a direct, detailed answer to any voter's request to "show me the money." This is the Webby Award–winning site of the nonprofit, nonpartisan Center for Responsive Politics, a group that focuses on money and politics. Enter the name of your member of Congress, and you'll find out how much money he or she raised in the last election and how much came from business, labor, PACs, and so on. This is definitely the place to go if you want to know who is paying the way for the candidates you're considering. It's at www.opensecrets.org.

Maplight.org tries to go Open Secrets one better (in fact they use Open Secrets' data) by tying campaign contributions to legislation. You can search for bills, find out which lobbying groups and organizations favored or opposed the legislation, then see how the contributions match up with the way legislators voted. They're funded by the Sunlight Foundation, the Wallace Alexander Gerbode Foundation, and the Arkay Foundation.

FactCheck.org specializes in helping voters sort out the truth in campaign ads, campaign speeches, and other election sloganeering. You can sign up for a regular news feed, which might be a good idea during the campaign season when the going gets rough, and the truth begins to suffer as a result. Fact Check operates out of the Annenberg Public Policy Center at the University of Pennsylvania. We consider it a must-visit every campaign season.

We're almost to the end of the book now, so it's OK to admit something: You're not sure who your member of Congress is. Not to worry; many people aren't. But this is easily fixed. A number of sites offer zip code searches to help you find out who represents your town in Washington, but the official congressional sites, **www.house.gov** and **www. senate.gov,** will do just fine. If you want to find out ways of lobbying your representative—petitions you can sign, addresses you can write to—you can try **Congress.org**, a private site that offers a lot of that information. And to track bills in Congress, search voting records, and get basic information about how the legislative branch works, you can't beat the Library of Congress's Thomas site, named for Thomas Jefferson, who surely would approve of empowering people via the Internet, if he was still around. You can find the site at **Thomas.loc.gov.**

Remember that old line about how 90 percent of success in life consists of showing up? It's certainly true on Election Day (unless you live in vote-by-mail Oregon, in which case 90 percent of success consists of having a postage stamp). But for the rest of us, if you're going to make a difference, you've got to register and then show up at your polling place on Election Day. If you've got basic questions about how to register, where your polling place is, and what to do if someone challenges your right to vote, the **vote411. org** Web site run by the **League of Women Voters** has the answers.

★★★★★★★★★★★★★★★★★★★★★★★★★★★

ACKNOWLEDGMENTS

There are many, many people who advised and aided us while we were working on *Where Does the Money Go?* Ruth Wooden at Public Agenda sparked the idea of us writing a book, and Deborah Wadsworth from our board helped us transform a vague notion into a reality. In this case, it is absolutely true that we would not have completed this book without them. All of our Public Agenda colleagues have been enthusiastic, encouraging, and helpful. We would especially like to thank Francie Grace, Allison Rizzolo, Sanura Weathers, and David White for their work in promoting and fine-tuning the book.

Jenny Choi and Nancy Cunningham were our indispensable fact checkers. We have benefited from the intelligence, professionalism, and good humor of Jud Laghi and Larry Kirshbaum at LJK Management, and Matthew Inman and Teresa Brady at HarperCollins. Working with them has been a wonderful experience. We would also like to thank James Capretta, Keith Melville, Alice Rivlin, and Andrew Yarrow, who read drafts of the first edition book and gave us enormously helpful advice and counsel. We're also very grateful to Jill Danzig for her expertise and support in helping promote the first edition.

Daniel Yankelovich's resounding belief in the good sense of the American public lies behind every word we have written, and for his insight and inspiration, we thank him.

Our families and friends have been remarkable—tolerant when we were distracted and encouraging when we were tired. We especially want to thank Susan Wolfe Bittle and Josu Gallastegui for their unfailing love, support, and patience—not to mention their willingness to read yet another draft without rolling their eyes.

Books by
SCOTT BITTLE &
JEAN JOHNSON

Who Turned Out the Lights?
Your Guided Tour to the Energy Crisis

ISBN 978-0-06-171564-8 (paperback)

Using pop culture references to help define the fundamental concepts behind the energy crisis, Scott Bittle and Jean Johnson explain this complex topic in a way that any reader can understand—without resorting to the usual left vs. right politics.

Included are nonpartisan solutions to some of the country's most threatening energy problems, refreshingly new ideas on the agenda, and complete answers to common questions, including ways for readers to stay informed.

"An invaluable read for anyone interested in our energy past, present, and future."
—Ron Pernick and Clint Wilder, authors of *The Clean Tech Revolution*

Scott Bittle & Jean Johnson
AUTHORS OF *WHERE DOES THE MONEY GO?*

Who Turned Out the Lights?
YOUR GUIDED TOUR TO THE ENERGY CRISIS

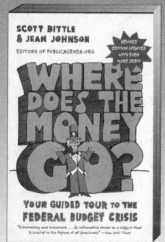

SCOTT BITTLE & JEAN JOHNSON
EDITORS OF PUBLICAGENDA.ORG

REVISED EDITION UPDATED WITH EVEN MORE DEBT!

WHERE DOES THE MONEY GO?

YOUR GUIDED TOUR TO THE FEDERAL BUDGET CRISIS

"Entertaining and irreverent.... An informative primer on a subject that is crucial to the future of all Americans." —*New York Times*

Where Does the Money Go? Revised and Updated
Your Guided Tour to the Federal Budget Crisis

ISBN 978-0-06-202347-6 (paperback)

Updated to reflect the financial crisis of 2008–09 and the sweeping legislation passed by the Obama administration in its first year, this irreverent and candid guide to the federal budget crisis explains in plain English exactly what the Fat Cats in Washington are arguing about.

Scott Bittle and Jean Johnson explore why elected leaders on each side of the fence have so far failed to effectively address crucial financial issues and explain what you can do to protect YOUR future.